D0891877

Courts and Kids

*Pursuing Educational Equity
through the State Courts*

MICHAEL A. REBELL

THE UNIVERSITY OF CHICAGO PRESS   CHICAGO AND LONDON

MICHAEL A. REBELL is executive director of the Campaign for Education Equity; professor of law and educational practice at Teachers College, Columbia University; and adjunct professor of law at Columbia Law School. He is the author or coauthor of many books, including *Moving Every Child Ahead: From NCLB Hype to Meaningful Educational Opportunity.*

The University of Chicago Press, Chicago 60637
The University of Chicago Press, Ltd., London
© 2009 by The University of Chicago
All rights reserved. Published 2009
Printed in the United States of America
18 17 16 15 14 13 12 11 10 09   1 2 3 4 5

ISBN-13: 978-0-226-70619-1
ISBN-10: 0-226-70619-2

Library of Congress Cataloging-in-Publication Data

Rebell, Michael A.
  Courts and kids : pursuing educational equity through the state courts / Michael Rebell.
    p. cm.
  Includes index.
  ISBN-13: 978-0-226-70619-1 (cloth : alk. paper)
  ISBN-10: 0-226-70619-2 (cloth : alk. paper)
    1. Educational equalization—United States.   2. Educational law and legislation—
United States.   3. Discrimination in education—Law and legislation—United States.
I. Title.
  LC213.2.R427 2009
  379.2′60973—dc22

                                                            2009015673

♾ The paper used in this publication meets the minimum requirements of the American National Standard for Information Sciences—Permanence of Paper for Printed Library Materials, ANSI Z39.48-1992.

Contents

Acknowledgments

This book expands a paper I presented at the third annual symposium of the Campaign for Educational Equity at Teachers College, Columbia University, entitled "Equal Educational Opportunity: What Now?" which was held in November 2007. The symposium focused on the implications of the U.S. Supreme Court's decision in *Parents Involved in Community Schools v. Seattle School District*[1] and especially on the enhanced significance of the state courts' role in education adequacy litigation, given the federal courts' retrenchment from active involvement in school desegregation cases, a pattern that culminated in the *Seattle* decision. The symposium was made possible by the generous support of the Laurie M. Tisch Foundation and JP Morgan Chase.

Many colleagues provided insightful comments on the draft paper and the manuscript for the book. I am especially grateful to Jessica Wolff for both her substantive suggestions and her patient editing assistance. Professors Jeffrey Henig, Neil Komesar, James Ryan, and Peter Schuck offered many helpful suggestions for improving this work, and Eric Hanushek challenged my thinking on a number of points. I thank Alfred Rosenblatt, whom I first encountered as a Court of Appeals judge involved in the court's decision in *CFE v. State of New York*,[2] for being willing, after his retirement from the court, to discuss my concepts of the role of the courts and to provide wise counsel on how these ideas relate to judicial perceptions. Deborah T. Poritz, former chief justice of the New Jersey Supreme Court, also added immensely to my understanding of judges' perspectives through her careful reading of the manuscript for this book and her candid comments about it. Needless to say, although I benefited from the suggestions of these scholars and judges, the positions espoused in this book, and any errors in the text, are my own.

The research assistance of Vinay Harpalani and Adam Waite was exceptional, and the feedback that they and many of the other students in my classes at Columbia Law School and Teachers College offered continually challenged me to reconsider many of my proposals. Without Jessica Garcia's technical support, I could never have produced a readable version of this manuscript.

I owe many thanks to Molly Hunter, Anna Douthat, Claudia Mendez, and other members of staff at the Campaign for Educational Equity and the National Access Network for their support and assistance. I am also grateful to Susan Fuhrman, president of Teachers College, for her counsel on many policy issues and her support of the symposium and of the Campaign's research and policy activities. Elizabeth Branch Dyson, my editor at the University of Chicago Press, who encouraged me to expand this work into book form, was a constant source of inspiration, useful suggestions, and good cheer throughout the writing process. Completion of the editing process was also aided immensely by the exceptional copyediting skills of Sharon Brinkman.

Preface

This short book culminates a professional lifetime of thinking about the role that the courts should play in promoting institutional reform. The views I express stem from my involvement as a litigator in a number of major institutional reform litigations, as well as years of deliberation and analysis as a teacher and a scholar. This combination of activism and reflection has produced a book that may baffle people who expect books to be either scholarship, that is, objective weighing of the evidence without prior commitment to a particular conclusion, or advocacy, that is, selective arrangement of facts and arguments to achieve a fixed set of goals. This book is, in fact, a combination of scholarship and advocacy, and my premise is that the tension between the two can be a creative one, less a case of oil and water that cannot mix than a sweet-and-sour delicacy that entices the taste buds.

I first became fascinated by the role of the courts in promoting social reform as a law student during the heyday of the Warren Court. I marveled then at the prospect of principled judges reshaping wayward social institutions in keeping with constitutional values. Being a child of the '60s, after graduation, I sought to participate in this process by helping to litigate education reform cases, especially in the areas of desegregation and school decentralization.

I soon learned, however, that not all judges acted in principled ways and not all judicial remedies resulted in positive social reform. I realized that reshaping complex institutions is itself a highly complex task and that successful litigation in education law cases—which I define as actually improving students' opportunities and outcomes rather than merely obtaining a favorable court decree—requires a "thick" theory of how positive change can be advanced through the courts. That realization led me to return to academia and to build a professional career that has combined part-time teaching and scholarly writing with a substantial litigation practice focused on education reform. After litigating a major case, I have always found it important to reflect, through my teaching and writing, on what was accomplished through a particular lawsuit and what was not. Armed with insights that I obtained from active engagement with my students and academic colleagues, I would then design my next institutional reform litigation with those perspectives in mind.

For example, in 1979, I initiated a major lawsuit in New York City on behalf of a class of thousands of students with disabilities that resulted in a significant ruling from the federal district court and an ongoing remedial process.[1] After over a decade of working on implementing the remedy in this case, I became frustrated with the limited progress we had made in instituting reforms that would make a real difference in children's lives. Judicial oversight had to some degree degenerated into "bean counting," crediting numbers of cases that were being processed within the regulatory timelines rather than focusing on the quality of the instruction the students were receiving in the classroom. I was also concerned about the formalities of class action representation, which allowed attorneys like me to continue to speak on behalf of thousands of putative clients I had never met without fully knowing their views or how they were being affected by our actions. I decided, therefore, to organize a major symposium at Yale Law School where I was then teaching to explore the question of how client views might better be understood and how the remedial process in an institutional reform case like this might be rendered more effective.

The symposium was a multiday event involving judges, lawyers, law professors, elementary and high school teachers and administrators, parents, and students. We analyzed the role of the courts in a variety of settings and reached the overall conclusion that the way to improve the efficacy of judicial remedies was to include not only lawyers, advocates, and government officials in the development of the details of the remedy but also the school board members, administrators, and teachers who would have to implement them and the parents, students, and general public who would need to understand and support them.

I coauthored a law review article that elaborated on this theme and recommended that judges and attorneys in future institutional reform cases incorporate public engagement techniques in their remedial decrees.[2] At this same time, in my litigation practice, I was asked to initiate a constitutional challenge to New York State's education finance system—a litigation that became the Campaign for Fiscal Equity (CFE) case, which is discussed in some detail in this book. At the outset, I told the CFE board of directors that if we should prevail in obtaining a favorable ruling from the court (which at the time we considered a real long shot), we needed to implement the kind of public engagement remedial approach that I had outlined in the article. The board agreed to adopt this approach, and, as I discuss in chapter 6 of this book, an emphasis on public engagement, initiated years before a final decision was rendered by the court, became one of the hallmarks of the CFE litigation—and, I believe, one of the major reasons for its eventual largely positive outcome.

The CFE example illustrates how I have attempted to combine legal advocacy and serious scholarly inquiry throughout my career. In regard to both litigation and scholarship, my goal has been to understand as profoundly as possible how the law can be used to help bring about positive social change. I take scholarship seriously, and I use it to guide my litigation strategy; likewise, I take litigation seriously, and I use it to inform my scholarly writing. I believe that it is possible to have a fixed advocacy goal and to develop the means to achieve it through an objective weighing of the relevant evidence and of the arguments that both supporters and opponents of that goal have articulated.

I think it important to disclose my personal perspective to readers up front. Clearly, I have an advocate's point of view: I agree with our national policy that all children are entitled to "fair, equal and substantial educational opportunities,"[3] and I think that the courts have an important and a necessary role to play in implementing this vision.[4] At the same time, I recognize that the courts—as well as presidents, governors, legislatures, and school officials—have been endeavoring for the past half century without adequate success to achieve these ends and that thoughtful critical perspectives are needed to improve our understanding of how this crucial goal might be attained. I leave it to my readers to reach their own conclusions about whether I have realized the productive synthesis of committed advocacy and objective scholarship that I have sought to achieve in writing this book.

New York, April 2009

Introduction

In 2004, forums and commemorations around the country marked the fiftieth anniversary of *Brown v. Board of Education*,[1] the United States Supreme Court's landmark ruling outlawing school segregation. Most commentators expressed concern that the vision of equal educational opportunity that the United States Supreme Court had articulated in *Brown* had not yet been achieved, but many also articulated "a sense of hope" about the possibility of its realization in the future.[2] Three years later, however, the Supreme Court, with newly appointed Chief Justice John Roberts at its helm, substantially thwarted this hope with its ruling in *Parents Involved in Community Schools v. Seattle School District*.[3]

The *Seattle* case drastically constrained the ability of local school districts to implement *voluntary* school desegregation plans. It invalidated racial integration plans adopted by the school boards in Seattle and in Louisville with strong community support that resembled the plans that many school districts—including Louisville itself—had implemented when operating under direct court orders in years past.[4] In supporting the position of the relatively few white parents whose children were denied their first choice school assignments under these plans,[5] the Court has now essentially turned the doctrine of equal educational opportunity on its head by using its own historic ruling in *Brown*—which was clearly intended to advance educational opportunities for African American students—as a precedent for limiting these very same opportunities.

Seattle, in fact, culminates a series of Supreme Court decisions over the past few decades that have reversed the strong stance the federal courts took in the 1960s to eliminate school desegregation and provide equal educational opportunity for all children. The federal courts' withdrawal from the desegregation fray highlights the significance of the extraordinary series of rulings by state courts that have upheld challenges to inequitable state systems for financing public education and that mushroomed over this same time period.

The federal courts' retreat began with the U.S. Supreme Court's ruling in 1973 that the Fourteenth Amendment did not prohibit de facto segregation[6] and its subsequent ruling in 1974 that extensive patterns of urban segregation could not be remedied by metropolitan area solutions without a showing of intentional segregation by the suburban school districts.[7] This was followed in the 1990s by a series of cases that encouraged federal district courts to terminate desegregation decrees if the "vestiges" of desegregation had been ameliorated "to the extent practicable"[8] — even if racial integration had not been achieved and black children in these districts still were performing at shockingly low levels of academic achievement.[9]

This shift in Supreme Court jurisprudence[10] has resulted in a clear trend of rising resegregation throughout the country. Indeed, Justice Stephen Breyer, dissenting in *Seattle,* noted that, in 2000, over 70 percent of all black and Latino students attended predominantly minority schools, a higher percentage than thirty years earlier. Furthermore, between 1980 and 2003, the percentage of white students in schools attended by the average black student fell from 45 to 29 percent.[11]

At almost precisely the same time as the federal courts began to retreat from active promotion of school desegregation, the state courts began to consider the surprising series of cases that have promoted equal educational opportunity by invalidating dozens of inequitable state education finance systems. Since 1973, such cases have, in fact, been filed in forty-five of the fifty states. The state courts took on the responsibility for reviewing the massive inequities in public education financing throughout the United States after the U.S. Supreme Court ruled in *San Antonio Independent School District v. Rodriguez*[12] that education is not a fundamental interest under the federal constitution. Overall, plaintiffs have prevailed in 60 percent of these state court litigations, and, in the more recent subset of "education adequacy" cases decided since 1989, plaintiffs have won twenty of twenty-nine (69 percent) of the final liability decisions.[13]

These cases have taken a pragmatic approach to equal educational opportunity. As a 2007 *New York Times* article reported,

> Nationwide, minority parents in struggling school districts have skirted the debate over racial integration and pushed instead for more money for their children's schools in lawsuits demanding that states give poor districts more resources . . . As a practical matter, lawyers say, fiscal-equity cases . . . are increasingly important as other tools to address racial inequities are cut off.[14]

Even if movement toward racial balance in the schools has now been stalled, the prospect of ensuring adequate resources for all students can continue to fuel progress toward meaningful educational opportunity for low-income and minority students.[15]

The repercussions from the *Seattle* decision may also, however, have negative implications for continuing progress toward equal educational opportunity through the state court education finance decisions. On its face, *Seattle* does not speak to the specific issues taken up in these cases, but implicit in the Supreme Court's increasingly constrained approach to equal educational opportunity is a disparagement of judicial efforts to remedy the inequities that continue to plague the nation's public schools. Justice Clarence Thomas's concurring opinion in *Seattle* was quite explicit on this point. He said that "this Court does not sit to . . . solve the problems of troubled inner city schooling . . . We are not social engineers."[16]

Similar skepticism regarding the propriety of judicial efforts to implement *Brown*'s vision of equal educational opportunity, and of the courts' ability to do so, have also increasingly been advanced by critics of the education funding decisions of the state courts. Familiar refrains that "courts are usurping the power of the legislature"[17] have been accompanied by more nuanced arguments that courts cannot deal with the complex policy issues involved in contemporary education reform and that "the reach of the courts . . . will hit a frustrating 'wall' quickly as such litigation seeks squarely to address student achievement through standards—and assessments—based lawsuits."[18]

Such attacks on the state courts' efforts to remedy constitutional violations by state education finance systems constitute a second dimension in the current legal assault on *Brown*'s legacy. Although *Brown* is best known for outlawing racial segregation in the schools, the landmark decision also inspired a broad range of judicial involvements in promoting institutional reform that is now deeply rooted in both federal and state jurisprudence. The Supreme Court's second ruling, *Brown II*,[19] was issued a year after the initial constitutional holding: it authorized the federal district courts to oversee the implementation of school desegregation by local school districts. In doing so, it initiated a "new model of public law litigation,"[20] in accordance with which both federal and state courts have for the past half century issued broad remedial decrees that go beyond the traditional judicial role of resolving private disputes between individuals and substantially affect the implementation of public policy.

Accordingly, over the past fifty years, the federal courts have promoted institutional reform in the schools not only in regard to desegregation but also in areas like bilingual education, gender equity, and special education. They have also fostered reforms in other social welfare areas, including the deinstitutionalization of services for the developmentally disabled and the improvement of prison conditions. State courts similarly have taken on such "new model" responsibilities both in regard to fiscal equity and educational adequacy and also in such sectors as land-use regulation and gay rights. The strong stance of the federal courts on school desegregation in the 1960s fueled the civil rights movement, just as the strong stance of the state courts in the past two decades has led to a national wave of state education finance reform throughout the United States.

The new model of public law litigation has become such an established part of the legal landscape that conservatives as well as liberals now routinely look to the courts to remedy legislative or executive actions of which they disapprove. Indeed, if "judicial activism" is defined in terms of declaring legislative acts unconstitutional, the conservative Rehnquist Court was the most activist in American history. Until 1991, the United States Supreme Court struck down an average of about one congressional statute every two years. From 1994 to 2004, the Court struck down sixty-four congressional provisions, or about six per year. This invalidated legislation has involved civil rights, social security, church and state, campaign finance, and a host of other major social policy issues.[21] The Roberts Court appears to be continuing or even accelerating this trend. During its first term, in addition to the dramatic *Seattle* decision, which strongly undermined local community control of schools, the Court overruled key parts of the McCain-Feingold campaign finance law, rejected the longstanding interpretation of pay discrimination laws by the federal Equal Employment Opportunity Commission, and invalidated state laws regarding late-term abortions.[22]

Ironically, it is in the realm of equal educational opportunity law, where judicial involvement in public policy implementation first began, that the new judicial role is most on the defensive. Not only have the federal courts almost fully abdicated their responsibility to promote school desegregation, but the highly successful state court efforts to promote fiscal equity and educational opportunity are now the prime targets of a resurgent movement to curb what critics call "a perversion of the judicial process [that] has only managed to divert attention from the serious task of school reform . . ,"[23]

The simple reality is, however, that, as Professor Chemerinsky bluntly put it, "without judicial action, equal educational opportunity will never exist."[24] Only with court involvement has our nation made significant inroads into our intractable educational inequities. This is not to say that the courts alone have in the past or can in the future ensure educational equity. The greatest progress toward school desegregation was achieved in the late 1960s when Congress's enactment of Title VI of the 1964 Civil Rights Act,[25] which authorized the termination of funding to school districts that failed to desegregate their schools, was combined with active enforcement efforts by the federal Office for Civil Rights and by assiduous efforts of federal courts throughout the South to implement *Brown*. Similarly, fiscal equity and education adequacy reforms have proved most effective in states like Kentucky, Vermont, and Massachusetts, where the legislative and executive branches decided early to cooperate with their state courts in developing effective remedies to cure constitutional inequities in school finance.

In recent years, the prime educational goal of the federal government and of virtually all of the states has been to eliminate achievement gaps and to provide all students with a meaningful opportunity to achieve proficiency in challenging academic standards.[26] There is broad consensus among business leaders, government officials, and educators that achieving both excellence and equity in this manner is critical to the nation's future. The stakes involved in this endeavor are extremely high, both for the individuals involved and for the nation as a whole. Whereas thirty years ago, a high school dropout earned about 64 percent of the amount earned by a diploma recipient, in 2004 he or she would earn only 37 percent of the graduate's amount.[27] Inadequate education also dramatically raises crime rates and health costs, denies the nation substantial tax revenues, and raises serious questions about the civic competence of the next generation to function productively in a complex democratic society.[28] The stark fact is that over the next fifty years, the students from minority groups who are now disproportionately represented among dropouts and low-achieving students will constitute a majority of the nation's public school students. If they are not capable citizens and productive workers, the continued vitality of our democratic culture and America's ability to compete effectively in the global marketplace will be seriously jeopardized.[29]

The premise of this book is that our national educational goals, which, in essence, call for the full implementation of *Brown*'s vision of equal educational opportunity, cannot be achieved without the concerted efforts of all three branches of the government. Much of the recent progress toward attaining these goals has resulted from the active involvement of the state courts, working together with state legislatures and state governors, in the remedial stages of educational equity litigations. Substantially greater progress could be achieved if the value of the courts' principled perspectives and of their sustained oversight capabilities were fully understood and if judicial efforts, especially at the remedial stages of litigations, were properly coordinated with appropriate policy initiatives of the legislative and executive branches.

Utilizing a comparative institutional approach, I will propose a conceptual framework and a practical model for advancing educational equity through an active colloquy between the state courts and the other two branches of state government. Chapter 1 will review the history of the judicial activism debate and will demonstrate that, despite continuing critical commentary in the popular press and partisan political rhetoric, the legitimacy of the courts' new role and their capacity to effectuate it has, in fact, become an integral aspect of the functioning of modern government that has been widely accepted by courts, Congress, state legislatures, and the public at large. Chapter 2 will examine the state courts' involvement in the education finance and "sound basic education" litigations over the past thirty years and will focus particularly on the extraordinary pattern of plaintiff victories in those cases since 1989 and their significance.

The discussion in chapter 3 addresses how we should define and assess the extent to which courts have been successful in these litigations. Courts, in their remedies, need to convey the ultimate meaning of compliance. They need to make clear that compliance is not just a matter of doing better or of adding more money but of achieving a concrete end—a sound basic education—that has specific input and outcome characteristics. Asserting that success must mean the promotion of equal educational opportunity that provides all students a sound basic education on a sustained basis, I postulate that constitutional compliance means developing and implementing (1) challenging academic and performance standards, (2) adequate funding, and (3) effective programs and accountability mechanisms, all of which should culminate in (4) substantially improved student performance.

Chapter 4 contends that to achieve success, in the broad terms set forth in the previous paragraph, requires an effective ongoing dialogue among the three branches of government. It introduces the concept of comparative institutional analysis and suggests that this analytic perspective provides a basis for developing a model of a functional separation of powers in which the judicial, legislative, and executive branches working together can deal effectively with difficult social policy issues like providing meaningful educational opportunity for all children. A specific approach for doing so is proposed and described in detail in chapter 5. This "successful-remedies model" calls for courts to outline in general, principled terms the expectation that the legislative and executive branches will develop challenging standards, fair and adequate funding systems, and effective programs and accountability measures, but it leaves to the political branches the responsibility for formulating these policies, so long as they are well conceived and well implemented and promote student progress.

Since significant compliance cannot be achieved overnight, in most cases courts would need to maintain nominal jurisdiction over a multi-year period; however, actual interventions should be rare if expectations regarding the importance of ultimate outcomes and the limits of judicial intervention procedures are clearly spelled out in advance. Adoption of the proposed comparative institutional model as a framework for judicial remedies will allow the state courts, working effectively with the legislative and executive branches, to achieve lasting success in state education finance litigations.

The concluding chapter confronts the political realities involved in implementing this model. Although some undoubtedly will view my call for long-term judicial oversight to ensure constitutional compliance as unwarranted judicial activism, I argue that (1) the proposed successful-remedies model involves less actual judicial involvement than meets the eye; (2) the comparative institutional approach upon which the model is built is consistent with empirical evidence that effective social reform requires a cooperative, functional division of labor among the three branches of government; and (3) the productive colloquy among the three branches that is at the core of this model has worked well at times in the past and can function even better in the future if courts and educational advocates take specific actions to foster a supportive political culture by, among other things, engaging the public in this endeavor to the maximum extent possible.[30]

CHAPTER ONE

Educational Policy Making and the Courts

The early days of judicial enforcement of desegregation decrees occasioned a wide-ranging academic debate on judicial activism. The courts' forays into policy making in areas that traditionally had been considered to be in the legislative or executive domain were repeatedly attacked as violating traditional separation of powers precepts.[1] Defenders of the courts' new role argued that the judges were merely adapting traditional concepts of judicial review and their obligation to enforce constitutional rights to the needs of a complex administrative state.[2] They argued that "[n]o branch could correctly claim to be the representative of the people. Representation was to be by each of them, according to the functions they performed."[3] Probably the most influential academic analysis of these issues was that of Harvard law professor Abram Chayes who related the growth of judicial involvement in the reform of public institutions since *Brown* to the broader expansion of governmental activities in the welfare state era.[4]

The courts' institutional capacity to carry out these broad new remedial tasks successfully was also widely questioned. Critics claimed that courts were incapable of obtaining sufficient social science data and that judges were generally unable to understand and digest the data that were obtained.[5] They also contended that judges lacked coherent guidelines for resolving policy conflicts and that, therefore, they would fail to undertake a comprehensive policy review or to consider the overall implications and consequences of their orders.[6] Defenders of this new judicial role retorted that the courts' lack of established organizational mechanisms was a virtue, not a vice, because it permitted a flexible response that could be tailored to the needs of the particular situation.[7] They emphasized that the courts had always delved into complex social and economic facts[8] and that processes of judicial appointment or election assured that judges were "likely to have some experience of the political process and acquaintance with a fairly broad range of policy problems."[9]

In the 1980s, my colleague Arthur R. Block and I undertook two major empirical studies to test the validity of the competing arguments in the judicial activism debate in actual instances of educational policy making by courts, legislatures, and a major administrative agency, the Office of Civil Rights in the U.S. Department of Health, Education and Welfare (OCR).[10] In regard to the separation of powers issues, we concluded that judicial deliberations tended to be based on general constitutional principles rather than on policy considerations directed toward immediate consequences, although in many circumstances the distinctions between "principle" and "policy" were difficult to draw. Significantly, however, judges tended to approach the issues in a distinctly different way: their decisions tended to reflect a "rational-analytic" decision-making mode (defined in terms of judgments reached and supported by fact and analysis in the light of explicit standards of judgment), in contrast to the mutual adjustment processes (defined in terms of the reconciliation of positions of competing interest groups through political bargaining) that tend to predominate in legislative decision making.

One of the other major conclusions of our comparative empirical studies was that the evidentiary records accumulated in the court cases were more complete and had more influence on the actual decision-making process than did the factual data obtained through legislative hearings. The latter tended to be window-dressing occasions that were organized to justify political decisions that had already been made.[11] Fact gathering through the administrative process proved to be more comprehensive and more sophisticated than that of either the courts or the legislatures, at least in this massive OCR special investigation context, but questions arose concerning the objectivity of the agency's use of the data since the OCR tended to adopt a "prosecutorial" stance in its approach to the evidence.[12]

In regard to remedies, our studies concluded that judicial remedial involvement in school district affairs was both less intrusive and more competent than was generally assumed, largely because school districts and a variety of experts generally participated in the formulation of reform decrees, with the courts serving as catalysts and mediators. OCR proved effective in administering remedial agreements that called for immediate, statistically measurable implementation, but in regard to the major New York City faculty desegregation agreement that required phased-in implementation over a number of years, the agency's staying power and its ability to respond flexibly to changed circumstances was markedly less effective than that of the courts.[13]

In the years since our study was completed, the courts' role in social science fact-finding and in overseeing remedial processes has become more extensive and more established. The U.S. Supreme Court substantially expanded the authority of federal judges to determine the admissibility of scientific evidence when it ruled in 1992 in *Daubert v. Merrell Dow Pharmaceuticals, Inc.*[14] that judges must determine whether expert evidence proffered by a party is "scientifically valid."[15] Essentially, federal judges now are being asked to assess expert evidence and "to make informed discriminations between good and bad science."[16] Academic researchers have also begun to look to the courts as a source for effective resolution of major social science issues because the courts' discovery processes are sometimes more comprehensive than the data-gathering techniques available to professionals in the field. Clive Belfield and Henry M. Levin, two leading educational researchers, recently found that

> . . . courts can navigate well through (disputed) social science arguments regarding educational outcomes, educational inputs (the education production function), and the deployment of teacher inputs. Moreover, rulings themselves can offer useful guidance to researchers on what fields of inquiry are important for resolving key public policy concerns, on what empirical evidence and which methodologies are deemed most valid, as well as indicate new areas for academic interest.[17]

They concluded that "[b]oth in terms of resources and access to documents, data, and personnel, the Court's investigation far exceeded that typically made by researchers."[18]

The public also has come to look to the courts for an assessment and resolution of highly controversial issues involving sensitive questions of science and public policy. For example, the volatile issue of whether in-

telligent design is a valid scientific theory that should be taught to high
school biology students has apparently been resolved by the recent decision of a federal district court judge in Dover, Pennsylvania.[19] The
judge's declaration that "after a six week trial that spanned twenty-one
days and included countless hours of detailed expert witness prepara-
tions, the Court is confident that no other tribunal in the United States is
in a better position than are we to traipse into this controversial area"[20]
was widely accepted. A national commentator noted,

> In this case [the courtroom] proved to be an ideal forum . . . The trial also
> allowed the lawyers to act as proxies for the rest of us, and ask of scien-
> tists questions that we'd probably be too embarrassed to ask ourselves. In a
> courtroom, you must lay an intellectual foundation in order to earn a line of
> questioning—and so the lawyers stripped matters neatly back to the first prin-
> ciples of science.[21]

And one of the Dover school board members remarked,

> This is a judge making a ruling on a case where both sides got to present their
> side, fully. This should bring some closure at least for our community. I'm
> sure there are many other communities throughout the United States that
> will be waiting for this verdict with great interest.[22]

Although a few legal scholars still analyze philosophical issues
of judicial review, particularly from a comparative international law
perspective,[23] academic discussion of the legitimacy of the courts' enhanced role has been muted in recent years. Chayes's contention that the
courts' expanded role is a fundamental judicial reaction to deep-rooted
social and political trends seems to be borne out by the fact that the activist stance initiated during the Warren Court era has, as discussed above,
persisted to a large extent through the Burger, Rehnquist, and Roberts
years and that conservatives no less than liberals now tend to look to the
courts routinely to remedy legislative or executive actions of which they
disapprove.[24] As Malcolm Feeley and Edward Rubin have noted,

> [Judges] are part of the modern administrative state. . . . And they fulfill their
> role within that context. Under certain circumstances that role involves pub-
> lic policy makings; as our state has become increasingly administrative and
> managerial, judicial policy-making has become both more necessary for

judges to produce effects and more legitimate as a general model of governmental action.[25]

Vehement criticism of particular instances of active judicial involvement in the social policy sphere does still resound in political debates and in the popular press. The irony here is that while these pundits persist in arguing that the courts' new role is usurping legislative powers, Congress and the state legislatures themselves are continually asking the courts to take on more of these policy-making activities by passing regulatory statutes that directly or implicitly call for expanded judicial review. A prime example is the Individuals with Disabilities in Education Act in which Congress set forth a detailed set of substantive and procedural rights and explicitly established a new area of court jurisdiction for individual suits, regardless of the amount in controversy.[26] Even critics of judicial involvement in social policy making have recognized this trend toward creating new statutory rights that explicitly or implicitly expand the enforcement responsibilities of the courts. Thus, Ross Sandler and David Schoenbrod decry the fact that

> By extrapolating [the *Brown* precedent] to a whole host of newly minted rights, [Congress has] created a new governmental lineup in which one set of officials at the federal level largely escapes accountability for the costs of the laws they pass and another out of officials at the state and local levels lacks the power to balance the costs of implementing the federal statutory rights against other competing priorities.[27]

As Mark Tushnet notes, these authors' criticism of the activism of the courts is misguided since, as they themselves acknowledge, the political branches, through clear democratic processes, authorized and required them to enforce the affirmative rights at issue.[28] Under these circumstances, as Chayes aptly put it, we should "concentrate not on turning the clock back (or off), but on improving the performance of public law litigation."[29]

Concerns about the courts' capacity to engage in sophisticated fact gathering and remedial processes have also been muted by empirical investigations of what courts actually do in these cases. One of the shortcomings of the judicial activism debate was its focus on the limitations of the judicial branch, while it ignored the comparable institutional shortcomings of the legislative and the executive branches. For example,

Donald Horowitz, one of the foremost critics of the courts' new role, cat-
alogued a bevy of examples of alleged judicial incompetence, ranging
from receiving information in a skewed and halting fashion to failing to
understand the social context and potential unintended consequences
of the cases before them.[30] As Neil Komesar has forcefully pointed out,
however, Horowitz's critique, like that of many of his current disciples,
was unreasonably one-sided:

> Horowitz's study can do no more than force us to accept the reality of judi-
> cial imperfection. By its own terms it is not comparative, and that is far more
> damning than Horowitz supposes. All societal decision makers are highly
> imperfect. Were Horowitz to turn his critical eye to administrative agencies
> or legislatures he would no doubt find problems with expertise, access to in-
> formation, characterization of issues, and follow-up. Careful studies would
> undoubtedly reveal important instances of awkwardness, error and deleteri-
> ous effect.[31]

The implications of Komesar's comparative institutional approach
are profound, and his insights provide a fruitful basis for constructing
a conceptual framework for effective judicial involvement in promoting
equal educational opportunity. I will return to this issue in chapter 4.
First, however, we need to consider the problems and possibilities raised
by judicial involvement in sound basic education litigations by discussing
in more detail the state courts' experiences to date with these cases.

CHAPTER TWO

The State Courts' Active New Role

A s the Supreme Court's insistence on effective remedies in federal desegregation cases began to flag in the 1970s, civil rights advocates initiated new legal challenges in state courts to the systems that most states had used to finance public education. As noted in the introduction, constitutional challenges to the inequitable and inadequate funding of public education have been litigated in the state courts of forty-five of the fifty states since 1973, and, in recent years, plaintiffs have won almost 70 percent of them. Many of these suits resulted from a growing awareness among civil rights lawyers that substantial resources would be needed to overcome the accumulated vestiges of school segregation and that most minority students still attended school in poor urban or rural school districts that were substantially underfunded in comparison with schools in affluent, largely white suburban districts.[1] The root cause of this inequity was that state education finance systems historically have been based largely on local property taxes, a pattern that inherently disadvantages students who attend school in districts with low property wealth.

Parents of students in one such Texas school district brought a legal challenge, *Rodriguez v. San Antonio Independent School District*,[2] that reached the U.S. Supreme Court in 1973. The *Rodriguez* plaintiffs lived in Edgewood, a district in the San Antonio metropolitan area, whose students were approximately 90 percent Mexican American and 6 percent African American. The district's property values were so low that even though its residents taxed themselves at a substantially higher rate than did the residents of the neighboring largely Anglo district, they were able to provide their schools with only about half the funds on a per-student basis that were available to their more affluent neighbors. The Supreme Court agreed that Texas's school finance system was inequitable, but, nevertheless, it denied the plaintiffs' claim, primarily because it held that education is not a "fundamental interest" under the federal Constitution.[3] Governmental actions that do not involve fundamental interests are generally upheld by the federal courts if the authorities have any rational explanation for their actions. In this case, the Supreme Court said that the tradition of local control of education was sufficient justification for the continuation of state education finance systems, even if they resulted in gross inequities.

The Supreme Court's ruling in *Rodriguez* precluded the possibility of obtaining fiscal equity relief from the federal courts. Surprisingly, the state courts, which historically had not been innovators in constitutional civil rights issues, picked up the baton. Shortly after the U.S. Supreme Court issued its decision in *Rodriguez,* the California Supreme Court held that even if education is not a fundamental right under the federal Constitution, it clearly was so under the California constitution.[4] Soon thereafter, courts in states like New Jersey, Connecticut, and West Virginia also declared their state education finance systems unconstitutional.[5]

Difficulties in actually achieving equal educational opportunity in the initial fiscal equity cases, however, seem to have made other courts less inclined to uphold these claims. In some states, equity decisions resulted in more state aid flowing to low-wealth districts, but the main beneficiaries were tax payers whose property tax bills were cut or capped while little if any extra money was allocated to the schools. In Connecticut, for example, following plaintiffs' victory in *Horton v. Meskill,*[6] state school aid increased dramatically from $409 million to $743.1 million between 1979 and 1984, but by the time the new aid formula was fully phased in, districts with low per-pupil expenditure levels were still spending about as little as before, relative to other districts.[7] In other situations, courts deferred to the legislature to devise a remedy for the inequities and then found themselves embroiled in prolonged litigations to compel the legislature to act or to improve inadequate remedies. Thus, in New Jersey, three years after the court's initial liability finding in 1973, the New Jersey Supreme Court had been involved in no less than five follow-up compliance litigations.[8]

Courts in other equity cases directed the state legislatures to remedy the inequities simply by ordering legislatures to eliminate disparities in educational expenditures. Thus, in the second round of the *Serrano* litigation in California, the trial judge held that wealth-related disparities among school districts (apart from categorical special needs programs) must be reduced to "insignificant differences," which he defined as "amounts considerably less than $100 per pupil."[9] Unfortunately, this equalization mandate, combined with a constitutional cap on increases in local property taxes, known as Proposition 13, which had been adopted by California's voters at the time, resulted in a dramatic leveling down of educational expenditures. Whereas California had ranked fifth in the nation in per-pupil spending in 1964–65, by 1994–95 it had fallen to forty-second.[10]

Despite an initial flurry of proplaintiff decisions in the mid-1970s, a decade later, the pendulum had decisively swung the other way. Plaintiffs won only two decisions in the early 1980s, and, as of 1988, fifteen years after *Rodriguez,* fifteen of the state supreme courts had denied any relief to the plaintiffs, compared with the seven states in which plaintiffs had prevailed.[11] Since 1989, however, there has been a dramatic reversal in the outcomes of state court litigations: plaintiffs have prevailed in the vast majority (twenty of twenty-nine) of final liability or motion to dismiss decisions of the states' highest courts since that time.[12] What is the explanation for the newfound willingness of state courts—which have historically been reluctant to innovate in areas of constitutional adjudication—to uphold challenges to state education finance systems?

This dramatic turnaround in judicial outcomes is directly related to a shift in legal strategy by plaintiff attorneys. At the end of the 1980s, civil rights lawyers changed their focus from equal protection claims based on disparities in the level of educational funding among school districts to claims based on opportunities for a basic level of education guaranteed by the specific provisions in the state constitutions. Interestingly and significantly, at least seven of the recent proplaintiff decisions, those in Arizona, Idaho, Maryland, Montana, New York, North Carolina, and Ohio, were written by the same courts that had ruled in favor of defendants only a few years earlier.[13]

The education clauses of almost all of the state constitutions contain language that requires the state to provide students with some substantive level of basic education. The specific language used to convey this concept includes calls for establishing an "adequate" education,[14] a "sound basic education,"[15] a "thorough and efficient" education,"[16] or a "basic system of free quality public elementary and secondary schools."[17] Most of these provisions were incorporated into the state constitutions as part of the common school movement of the mid-nineteenth century, which created statewide systems for public education and attempted to inculcate democratic values by bringing together under one roof students from all classes and all ethnic backgrounds.[18] Some of them, especially in the New England states, date back to eighteenth-century revolutionary ideals of creating a new republican citizenry that would "cherish the interests of literature and science"[19]—an archaic phrase that the Massachusetts Supreme Judicial Court has now interpreted as requiring the provision of "an adequate education."[20]

Although the state constitutions use different language to connote this concept of a substantive basic education, there is broad consensus among the courts that have applied these concepts as to its core meaning.[21] Virtually all of the courts that have defined their constitutional language have agreed that a basic education that meets contemporary needs is one that ensures that a student is equipped to function capably as a citizen and to compete effectively in the global labor market. For example, the Vermont Supreme Court declared that the state's right to education clause "guarantees political and civil rights" and preparation "to live in today's global marketplace."[22]

In these cases, courts focus on the substance of the education students are actually receiving in the classroom rather than on the more abstract consideration of comparative amounts of school district funding that were at issue in the equity cases. The evidence in the education clause cases graphically exposes the flagrant lack of educational opportunity that the educational systems in most of the states continue to impose on millions of poor and minority students more than fifty years after the Supreme Court's decision in *Brown,* and the judges have responded accordingly. For example, one poor rural Arkansas school district had a single uncertified mathematics teacher to cover all high school mathematics courses. The teacher was paid $10,000 a year as a substitute teacher, which he supplemented with $5,000 annually for school bus driving.[23] Many high schools in California's low-income and minority communities do not offer the curriculum students must take just to *apply* to the state's public universities.[24] Passing an examination in a laboratory science course is required for high school graduation in New York State, but thirty-one New York City high schools had no science labs.[25] In South Carolina, annual teacher turnover rates exceed 20 percent in eight poor, rural, mostly minority school districts, and in those districts graduation rates fall between 33 and 57 percent.[26]

In addition to the persuasive power of the evidence of distressing educational inadequacy that has been revealed in the record of these cases, another major reason for plaintiffs' victories was the emergence of the standards-based education reform movement at about the same time. These reforms responded to a series of major commission reports in the 1980s that had warned of a "rising tide of mediocrity"[27] in American education—a phenomenon that was said to be undermining the nation's ability to compete in the global economy. Comparative international assessments revealed poor performance by American students, especially in science and mathematics,[28] and United States Department of Education assessments indicated that few American students "show the capacity for complex reasoning and problem solving."[29]

In 1989, President George H.W. Bush convened a National Education Summit, which was attended by all fifty governors, business leaders, and educators. The result of the summit was a major effort by the federal government to articulate specific national academic goals.[30] Continued focus on the need for comprehensive, effective reforms geared to specific goals led to enactment of the federal Goals 2000 Act[31] and more recently the No Child Left Behind Act (NCLB).[32] Because education remains primarily a state and local responsibility in the United States, NCLB and the applicable federal regulations call for the development of standards at the state rather than the national level, and the state standards-based reform movement has, in recent years, become the primary arena for these reform initiatives.

Standards-based reform is built around substantive content standards in English, mathematics, social studies, and other major subject areas. These content standards are usually set at sufficiently high cognitive levels to meet the competitive standards of the global economy, and they are premised on the assumption that virtually all students can meet these high expectations if given sufficient opportunities and resources. Once the content standards have been established, every other aspect of the education system—including teacher training, teacher certification, curriculum frameworks, textbooks and other instructional materials, and student assessments—should be made to conform with these standards. The aim is to create a coherent system of standards, resources, and assessments that will result in significant improvements in achievement for all students.[33]

With the advent of standards-based reform, the concept of educational opportunity gained substantive content. The message underlying the reforms was that most state education systems—and certainly school districts that primarily served poor and minority students—probably fell below, rather than above, the new level of expectations. Standards-based reform also put into focus the fundamental goals and purposes of our system of public education. It reinforced the courts' orientation to probe the intent of the eighteenth- and nineteenth-century drafters of the provisions in the state constitutional clauses that established public education systems and to evaluate the contemporary significance of these provisions. In addition, the new state standards provided the courts with practical tools for developing judicially manageable approaches for dealing with complex educational issues and implementing effective remedies. They provided judges with workable criteria for crafting practical remedies in these litigations.

The new emphasis in these cases on a basic substantive level of educational opportunity has additional inherent appeal. This approach does not threaten the concept of local control of education, the main rationale for most of the decisions in prior equity rulings in favor of the defendants. The education clause cases do not undermine the prerogative of local communities to set their own tax rates "because locals would remain free to augment their programs above th[e] state-mandated minimum."[34] To the extent that an emphasis on statewide standards is inconsistent with local control, those centralizing tendencies were already created by the regulatory framework of the standards-based reform movement.

The new constitutional approach also tends to invoke less political resistance at the remedial stage because rather than raising fears of leveling down educational opportunities currently available to affluent students, it gives the promise of leveling up academic expectations for all other students. Although standards-based reforms would most dramatically improve the performance of the lowest achieving students, the reforms are comprehensive and intended to provide benefits to almost all students. Instead of threatening to shift money from rich districts to poor districts, therefore, the emphasis on providing all students a basic, substantive level of educational opportunity offers the possibility of enriching opportunity for all.[35]

Most of the literature in this field (including my own previous writings) uses the term "education adequacy" to describe these cases that draw on the education clauses of state constitutions. At this stage in the history of this litigation, however, "adequacy" has become a misleading label for the level of substantive educational opportunity that the courts have described in these cases, and the terminology used to describe these judicial decisions should be updated. "Adequacy" connotes a minimal level of education, but the courts in these cases clearly have in mind a concept that emphasizes the educational skills that students need to function as citizens and productive workers in the twenty-first century, and this concept is far more than minimal. As one commentator put it (and many others have concurred), it is clear that "the concept of an adequate education emerging from state courts invalidating school finance systems goes well beyond a basic or minimum educational program that was considered the acceptable standard two decades ago."[36] On the other hand, the literal connotations of language found in some state constitutions like "thorough and efficient" and "high quality" seem to exceed the level of educational opportunity the courts have in mind. The term "sound basic education" used by the courts in New York, North Carolina, South Carolina, and Wisconsin appears to describe most accurately the midrange level of quality educational training in substantive skills that virtually all of the courts have agreed is necessary for students to function productively in the twenty-first century.

Furthermore, as James Ryan points out, the hard distinction between equity and adequacy cases in the literature is somewhat misleading. Many adequacy cases have an equity dimension, and disparities in resource availability constitute a major element of the proof that is actually offered at many of these trials.[37] Ryan proposes use of the term "comparability" for describing and categorizing these cases, but that expression has its own limitations. It overemphasizes the equity dimension and ignores the courts' emphasis on identifying a basic substantive level of core resource inputs and particular substantive skills as outcomes of a meaningful educational opportunity.[38]

I think the term "sound basic education" is the best phrase available for the concept that often is described as "educational adequacy." Sound basic education connotes that students need a core, fundamental level of education in order to succeed in the contemporary world and that to be sound this basic level of education must allow them to function competently as citizens and to compete effectively in the modern economy. Al-

though the term, therefore, signifies a quality basic education, it does not
imply full equality at any cost. "Sound basic education," therefore, cap-
tures the combination of basic resource inputs that are reasonably related to substantive outcomes that are defined in terms of fundamental
citizenship and employment skills upon which courts have tended to focus in these cases. Accordingly, that is the term I will use in this book.

Overall, the sound basic education approach to defining and ensuring educational opportunity has broad and forceful appeal. This approach draws from and affirms the nation's common school traditions,
advances equal educational opportunity, and promises to meet the nation's civic and economic challenges for the twenty-first century. It also
helps courts to surmount the remedial stumbling blocks they faced in the
equity cases by providing judges with judicially manageable standards
for crafting practical remedies. Plaintiffs' 70-percent victory rate in these
cases reflects this potent appeal.

When judges have examined whether students today are, in fact, receiving the educational opportunities they need to prepare them to function productively as citizens and workers in the twenty-first century, it
is striking that the current level of resources that the states are providing has been found deficient in terms of this common sense requirement
virtually 100 percent of the time. Almost all of the defendant victories
at the liability stage of sound basic education litigations since 1989 that
were noted earlier in this chapter occurred only where the state's highest courts ruled that the sound basic education issue was not "justiciable," meaning that they did not consider it proper for the courts to even
consider these questions consistent with separation of powers precepts.
Thus, they dismissed these cases at the outset, before any trial was held
and any evidence of inadequacy could even be considered.[39] Whenever
judges of the highest state courts have actually examined the details of
the "savage inequalities"[40] that continue to be imposed on most low-
income and minority students in the United States, they have virtually
unanimously held that these conditions deny students the opportunity to
be educated at the basic levels that are needed to function well in contemporary society.

In other words, the seven states that have held for defendants at the
basic liability stage in sound basic education cases—Alabama, Florida,
Illinois, Nebraska, Oklahoma, Pennsylvania, and Rhode Island—have
done so not because they determined that the current state system was,
in fact, providing students a sound basic education. Rather, they avoided

confronting the evidence and answering that critical question by holding that there were "no judicially manageable standards" that would not "present a substantial risk of judicial intrusion into the powers and responsibilities assigned to the legislature . . . "[41] or that the court was "unable to judicially define what constitutes an 'adequate' education or what funds are 'adequate' to support such a program."[42] In issuing these summary rulings and refusing to even look at the evidence, these courts ignore the data, the expert testimony, and the history of state and national standards-based reforms that the overwhelming majority of their sister courts have found can, in fact, provide them with judicially manageable standards.

In most cases when defendants raise these justiciability arguments, the courts reject them out of hand as being both overstated and inconsistent with the courts' core constitutional responsibilities. As the Arkansas Supreme Court put it, "This court's refusal to review school funding under our state constitution would be a complete abrogation of our judicial responsibility and would work a severe disservice to the people of this state. We refuse to close our eyes or turn a deaf ear to claims of a dereliction of duty in the field of education."[43] Similarly, the Idaho Supreme Court stated, "[W]e decline to accept the respondents' argument that the other branches of government be allowed to interpret the constitution for us. That would be an abject abdication of our role in the American system of government."[44]

The concept of "justiciability," upon which the seven state courts relied in dismissing plaintiffs' claims, was based on a federal doctrine that the U.S. Supreme Court articulated in 1962 in *Baker v. Carr*,[45] a major decision that held that the complex issue of legislative reapportionment *was* justiciable. In *Baker,* the Court set forth six specific guidelines for determining when an action taken by the executive and/or legislative branch constitutes an unreviewable, nonjusticiable "political question":

Prominent on the surface of any case held to involve a political question is found a textually demonstrable constitutional commitment of the issue to a coordinate political department; or a lack of judicially discoverable and manageable standards for resolving it; or the impossibility of deciding without an initial policy determination of a kind clearly for nonjudicial discretion; or the impossibility of a court's undertaking independent resolution without expressing lack of the respect due coordinate branches of government; or an unusual need for unquestioning adherence to a political decision already made;

or the potentiality of embarrassment from multifarious pronouncements by various departments on one question.[46]

A number of commentators have questioned the analytical validity of this justiciability doctrine. Martin Redish argued that the doctrine is not normatively defensible because

> Once we make the initial assumption that judicial review plays a legitimate role in a constitutional democracy, we must abandon the political question doctrine, in all of its manifestations. The doctrine inherently implies that one or both of the political branches may continue conduct that could conceivably be found unconstitutional, without any examination or supervision by the judicial branch. The moral cost of such a result, both to society in general and to the Supreme Court in particular, far outweighs whatever benefits are thought to derive from the judicial abdication of the review function.
>
> This does not mean that the Court, in reaching its constitutional decisions, should not, in certain cases, take into account the comparative expertise that the political branches may have in deciding whether certain actions are essential, or the institutional limitations on the judiciary's power to supervise day-to-day operations of the government, particularly when emergency actions may be required. But in each case, if the Court is to perform the essential function of protector against a lawless government, the Court must draw the final constitutional calculus.[47]

The Supreme Court itself has invoked the doctrine sparingly, generally in contexts involving national security[48] or internal procedures of the other branches.[49] Even within these categories, however, the Court has also determined that some controversies are justiciable.[50] Indeed, in *Baker,* the very case in which the Court articulated the six-fold justiciability test, the Court held that the issue of legislative reapportionment was justiciable, and the federal courts over the past four decades have become extensively involved in scores of reapportionment cases; in doing so, they have wrestled with a host of knotty political and policy issues involving application of the "one-person, one-vote" standard that the Court established in this area.[51]

Whatever the continued vitality of the justiciability/political question doctrine in the federal courts, however, there is no justifiable basis for applying it in state court sound basic education cases. In contrast to the negative restraints of the federal constitution, the structure of most state

constitutions, especially in key areas of state responsibility like education, incorporate "positive rights" that require affirmative governmental
action—and implicitly call for judicial review if the other branches fail to
take that action. The implications of such positive rights in state constitutions have been explained as follows by Professor Helen Hershkoff:

> When the state constitution mandates a specific purpose and thus authorizes
> the government to carry out the stated goal, the legislature and the governor
> have a duty to achieve, or at least to help promote, the constitutional man-
> date. . . . [A] positive constitutional right imposes an affirmative obligation on
> the state to realize and advance the objects and purposes for which . . . pow-
> ers have been granted . . . Judicial review in such a regime must serve to in-
> sure that the government is doing its job and moving policy closer to the con-
> stitutionally prescribed end.[52]

Most state courts clearly agree, and this is why they emphatically reject defendants' attempts to apply federal political question precedents
to sound basic education cases. As the Montana Supreme Court recently
put it, "As the final guardian and protector of the right to education, it is
incumbent upon the court to assure that the system enacted by the Legislature enforces, protects and fulfills the right [to education]."[53]

The few state courts that have invoked the political question doctrine to deny plaintiffs in sound basic education cases their day in court
have offered feeble justifications for doing so.[54] Illinois is a prime case
in point. Like most other states, Illinois construed the political question
doctrine narrowly after *Baker,* and, for the thirty-four years between the
time *Baker* was decided and 1996, the year when it first considered a
sound basic education claim, the Illinois court had never declared *any*
matter a nonjusticiable political question.

In fact, in 1981, in a case in which it reviewed the governor's obligation to convene the state senate in order to elect a president of the senate, the Illinois Supreme Court firmly articulated in classic terms the
reasons that courts must oversee legislative compliance with constitutional norms:

> It is the duty of the judiciary to construe the Constitution and determine
> whether its provisions have been disregarded by the actions of any of the
> branches of government. [citations] While this court cannot exercise legis-
> lative powers . . . the judiciary has always had the right and duty to review

legislative acts in light of the Constitution. As the court said in *Donovan v. Holzman* (1956), 8 Ill.2d 87, 93, 132 N.E.2d 501, "[t]he mere fact that political rights and questions are involved does not create immunity from judicial review."[55]

Inexplicably, however, in 1996, when it was called upon to decide a major sound basic education case, the Illinois Supreme Court did not refer to these clear precedents. Instead, despite the very strong affirmative language of article 10, section 1, of the Illinois constitution, which requires the legislature to "provide for an efficient system of *high quality* public institutions and services," the Illinois Supreme Court simply asserted that the question of whether the educational institutions and services in Illinois are "high quality" is outside the sphere of the judicial function.[56] The court pointed to two of the specific *Baker* criteria, a lack of judicially discoverable and manageable standards and the impossibility of deciding the question without an initial policy determination of a kind clearly for nonjudicial discretion. It noted, however, that most of the other state courts that had considered educational adequacy had established "judicial standards of educational quality reflecting varying degrees of specificity and deference to the other branches of government."[57]

The argument that there is of a lack of "judicially manageable standards" is particularly inapt in this area. The Texas Supreme Court spelled out in detail precisely how manageable the applicable standards are in this area:

[We do not] agree with the State defendants that the constitutional standards of adequacy, efficiency, and suitability are judicially unmanageable. These standards import a wide spectrum of considerations and are admittedly imprecise, but they are not without content. At one extreme, no one would dispute that a public education system limited to teaching first-grade reading would be inadequate, or that a system without resources to accomplish its purposes would be inefficient and unsuitable. At the other, few would insist that merely to be adequate, public education must teach all students multiple languages or nuclear biophysics, or that to be efficient, available resources must be unlimited. In between, there is much else on which reasonable minds should come together, and much over which they may differ. The judiciary is well-accustomed to applying substantive standards the crux of which is reasonableness . . . [in applying concepts of] due process of law, equal protection, and many other constitutional standards.[58]

The other state courts that have invoked *Baker*'s political question criteria in declaring a sound basic education case nonjusticiable have similarly failed to set forth any plausible reasoning for failing to carry out their constitutional obligation to review the legislature's implementation of affirmative constitutional rights in education. For example, even though it had stated in a prior case involving teachers' collective bargaining rights that "the people in whom the power of government is finally reposed have the right to have their constitutional rights enforced,"[59] the Florida Supreme Court, in *Coalition for Adequacy v. Chiles,*[60] a 1996 sound basic education case, invoked the political question doctrine to deny plaintiffs relief, citing *Baker* but no Florida state cases. Similarly, the Alabama Supreme Court, which recently reevaluated the *Baker* standards and refused to apply the political question doctrine to claims of overcrowding and poor prison conditions,[61] nevertheless, took the extraordinary step of reopening on its own motion its prior sound basic education ruling and retroactively declared education adequacy nonjusticiable.[62]

Education, an area that is designated for special positive attention in most state constitutions, is receiving less, not more, constitutional protection from these state courts. This occurs even though, as most of the courts in their sister states have repeatedly acknowledged, available standards for crafting judicial remedies are more readily available in this area than in many others. Is there an explanation for this doctrinal inconsistency?

The Nebraska Supreme Court was actually quite explicit in providing one. In *Nebraska Coalition for Educational Equity and Adequacy v. Heineman,*[63] it discussed at some length the difficulties that courts in Arkansas, Kansas, Alabama, Texas, and New Jersey have had with crafting remedies in sound basic education cases and also in dealing with numerous appeals and controversies regarding their implementation. After tracing this pattern of remedial complexity, the court bluntly concluded, "The landscape is littered with courts that have been bogged down in the legal quicksand of continuous litigation and challenges to their states' school funding systems. Unlike those courts, we refuse to wade into that Stygian swamp."[64]

At the heart of the concern of the Nebraska Supreme Court, and apparently of the other six state courts that have denied relief to plaintiffs on justiciability grounds, was "the volume of litigation and the extent of judicial oversight [that] provide a chilling example of the thickets that can entrap a court that takes on" an adequacy litigation.[65] These courts have not determined that schoolchildren in their states are receiving a sound basic education, and there is no reason to believe that they would differ with their colleagues in many other states who have determined that their legislatures have been derelict in carrying their educational responsibilities in relation to the sobering challenges of the twenty-first century. They have simply decided, without even hearing any evidence, that even if millions of children are being denied these critical rights, the courts are not capable of doing anything to substantially improve the situation.[66]

This skepticism about what courts have accomplished and can accomplish at the remedial stage of sound basic education litigations is unwarranted. Although all of the five states highlighted in the Nebraska opinion have experienced delays and difficulties at the remedy stage, the bottom line, as will be discussed in more detail in the next chapter, is that in four of the five states (Arkansas, Kansas, New Jersey, and Texas) substantial progress has ultimately been achieved in terms of effective reforms of the state's education finance system and/or improved student achievement. Little real reform has resulted from the Alabama litigation; however, there, as noted above, the state supreme court suddenly reversed course and vacated its prior orders and judgments in the case before the legislature had taken any action to implement the outstanding orders and judgments.

The Nebraska remedial overview also omitted any mention of states like Kentucky, Massachusetts, and Vermont where major reforms were quickly and effectively implemented within months of the court's ruling. The court's intervention in Kentucky has resulted in dramatic reductions in spending disparities among school districts,[67] the redesign and reform of the entire education system, and an increase in that state's student achievement scores.[68] In Massachusetts, enactment of the Education Reform Act of 1993 in response to that state's adequacy litigation has also sharply reduced the funding gaps between rich and poor school districts,[69] and the percentage of students achieving proficiency on state tests has risen dramatically.[70] Similarly, in Vermont, within months of the court's decision the legislature enacted a dramatic set of sweeping education finance reforms that have led to noticeable improvements in student outcomes.[71] In Arizona, despite some initial compliance complications, guidelines issued by the court were effectively followed within a few years of the court's initial constitutional ruling. As a result of the litigation in Arizona, facilities standards have been aligned with the state's learning standards, and all school buildings are being brought up to the new code.[72]

Despite these and many other examples of rapid reform and impressive progress after a judicial ruling, it is nevertheless true that the courts' extraordinary record of support for students' rights at the liability stage in sound basic education cases has not been matched by a similar consistent record of success in ensuring that students actually receive the benefits of these constitutional guarantees at the remedy stage. One of the major reasons for delay and resistance to constitutional mandates in these cases is that the "the literature on law and courts is replete with analysis of rights, but considerably more limited when it comes to examining the nature of remedies"[73]; simply put, there is an "absence of a legitimate legal discourse"[74] that supports and guides appropriate judicial intervention. As discussed in the previous chapter, the charges of inappropriate judicial activism, which originated with political opposition to the desegregation decrees of the federal courts in the 1960s and 1970s, have substantially less applicability to the contemporary sound basic education decisions of the state courts. Nevertheless, they have undermined public and political support for judicial involvement at the remedy stage and have also affected many judges' understandings of their proper remedial roles.

We can, however, learn from the state courts' experiences, both positive and negative, at the remedial stage and develop an appropriate and effective approach to judicial involvement that can vindicate children's rights without submerging the courts in a "Stygian swamp." I will describe such a remedial path in detail in the chapters that follow. Before embarking down that road, however, we need to define more precisely the end that is being sought. What is a positive outcome for this type of litigation? How ultimately should we define "success" at the remedy stage of a sound basic education case? These are the questions that I will seek to answer in the next chapter.

CHAPTER THREE

Defining Success in Sound Basic Education Litigations

Plaintiffs' extraordinary winning record at the liability stage of the sound basic education cases is both an indication of the depth of the continuing denial of educational opportunities to most low-income and minority students more than fifty years after *Brown v. Board of Education* and a reflection of the continuing vigor of America's egalitarian tradition that still strongly seeks to overcome these inequities. A key question, however, is, on balance, what have these judicial interventions accomplished? Have the many court orders issued by state courts throughout the country resulted in lasting reforms that are providing children the opportunity for a quality basic education? Or have they, as some critics have claimed, "not significantly altered the patterns of low student achievement observed over the last several decades?"[1] To answer this question, it is important first to define what "success" means in this context.

As discussed in the previous chapter, plaintiffs' victories in many states have resulted in rapid or eventual legislative action that has reduced inequities in funding, increased overall educational expenditures, and in some cases led to improvement in student achievement. In some states, the mere filing of a complaint has led to significant reforms,[2] and, in others, a satisfactory settlement was reached before the case went to trial.[3] Even when court rulings deny relief to the plaintiffs, sometimes the very fact that there has been litigation puts the issue of school finance reform at the top of the legislative agenda, in some cases prompting significant legislative changes.[4]

In other instances, however, strong resistance from the governor and/ or the legislature has delayed or impeded mandated reforms. In Kansas, for example, the legislature defied the state supreme court's deadline for a substantial funding increase on several occasions, threatened to revoke the court's jurisdiction over education finance issues in the future, and backed down in the final confrontation only after the court had threatened to close down all schools in the state by prohibiting the continued operation of an unconstitutional education finance system.[5] In New Jersey, parity in funding between rich and poor districts and a dramatic improvement in student test scores in poor urban districts has been achieved but only after almost two dozen follow-up court orders had been issued since 1973.[6] In West Virginia, the legislature virtually ignored the courts' extensive orders throughout the 1980s but then implemented some more limited reforms after another follow-up litigation was initiated in the mid 1990s.[7] In Ohio, the legislature had partially responded to a series of court orders by, among other things, reducing funding inequities and improving school facilities following a declaration of unconstitutionality. However, the legislature's failure to implement judicial orders effectively and the judges' unwillingness to confront the legislature led the state supreme court to retreat from the fray and terminate the cases before an appropriate remedy had been fully effectuated.[8]

Should these litigations be considered successful, unsuccessful, or, perhaps, partially successful? The literature that has addressed this question to date has tended to focus on the fiscal equity aspect of challenges to state education finance systems but not on the educational adequacy dimensions. The two most common measures of success researchers have employed have been the extent to which disparities in the levels of spending among school districts in a state have been ameliorated and the extent to which overall spending on education has increased. On both of these measures, the cases have generally been rated as being successful. Virtually all of these studies have concluded that the litigations have resulted in a narrowing of interdistrict expenditure disparities and an increase in educational spending.[9]

Analyses of expenditure patterns in specific states also confirm the general conclusion that litigation does result in a reduction in spending disparities and an increase in educational expenditures.[10] For example, in Kentucky, where the key case was decided almost two decades ago, the courts' intervention has resulted in "stunning" improvements in interdistrict equity and in educational expenditures:

> In 1985–86, just before the suit was filed, Kentucky spent $3,759 per child, forty-eighth among the states and shamefully below the national average ($5,679). A decade later, with its $600 million annual tax increase, it was spending $5,906, thirtieth in the nation, and still below the national average ($6,546) but with a far narrower gap. Measured in constant dollars, American school spending had increased 15 percent during that decade, Kentucky's by 57 percent . . . And the huge spending gaps between the richest and the poorest districts were closed—indeed . . . on average, the poorer districts now spend slightly more than the richest.[11]

Similarly, in Texas, the overall level of funding increased over 30 percent during the course of the *Edgewood* litigation, and the students in the bottom half of the wealth scale enjoyed state aid increases of $1.9 billion, while those in the top half gained only $491 million;[12] in New Jersey, as a result of the *Abbott* litigation, the lowest wealth districts now actually outspend the affluent districts by $900 per pupil.[13]

One important question that tends not to be answered in these fiscal equity success studies is how long these funding gains last. Although the cases are apparently quite successful in increasing educational expenditures and reducing interdistrict disparities in the initial years after a court decree, there may be substantial backsliding in later years after the court has relinquished jurisdiction. For example, in Kansas, the *Montoy* litigation was initiated in 1999 because the legislature had substantially modified the reforms in school funding that the Kansas courts had upheld five years earlier, and funding inequities and inadequacies once again undermined students' rights to a "suitable education."[14]

The largely positive evidence that litigation appears to reduce spending disparities and raise educational expenditures indicates that from an equity perspective, the cases have been quite successful, at least for an initial time period after the court has intervened. These findings are also relevant to an assessment of the larger question of whether these cases succeed in providing students a sound basic education. Since it would seem axiomatic that adequate funding that is necessary to provide qualified teachers, up-to-date textbooks, and adequate facilities is a prerequisite for affording children a sound education, then the additional funding that has resulted from these cases should lead to increased opportunity and to improvements in student achievement.

Somewhat surprisingly, however, over the past forty years, there has been extensive discussion in the academic literature, in the popular press and by the courts, as whether "money matters" in education. One of the reasons the United States Supreme Court cited for declining to become involved with fiscal equity reform in the *Rodriguez* case thirty-five years ago was that "the scholars and educational experts are divided . . . [over] the extent to which there is a demonstrable correlation between educational expenditures and the quality of education."[15]

The academic discussion of this issue was triggered by the famous Coleman report that was issued in 1966. The study, undertaken for the U.S. Department of Health, Education, and Welfare by a team of researchers led by James S. Coleman, a respected sociologist, concluded that the largest determinants of student achievement are not school resources but the "educational backgrounds and aspirations of other students in the school."[16] In the years since the release of the Coleman report, however, a vast literature has pinpointed significant methodological flaws in its analysis. Extensive empirical investigations, more advanced regression analyses, and other techniques indicate that the report's conclusions were overstated.[17] In any event, the proper conclusion to be drawn from Coleman's work is not that we should invest less in students' educations; on the contrary, Coleman himself concluded that society needs to make much greater investments in creating the kind of "social capital" that makes up for the deficiencies engendered by poverty and that "children and youth need to succeed in schools and as adults."[18]

In recent years, the main voice challenging the assumption that spending more money will improve educational outcomes has been that of Eric Hanushek, an economist at Stanford University's Hoover Institution. Hanushek has argued that "key resources—ones that are the subject of much policy attention—are not consistently or systematically related to improved student performance."[19] Hanushek's position is largely based on analyses he has undertaken of thirty-eight primary studies of the relationship between teacher/student ratios, teacher education, teacher experience, teacher salary, facilities, and other such inputs, measuring outcomes mostly in terms of standardized test scores but also in some instances including "dropout rates, college continuation, student attitudes, or performance after school."[20] Hanushek's approach has been criticized for not adequately accounting for across-district variations in the costs of educational services (such as teacher salaries) and the proportion of students with special needs who require additional, more costly services;[21] other critics have challenged the subjectivity of the "vote-counting" approach Hanushek used to determine which aspects of each study would be counted in the overall analysis.[22]

The courts have also grappled extensively with the question of whether money matters in education. In most of the equity and sound basic education cases, this question was a central legal issue, and extensive expert testimony addressed the technical economic and social science aspects of the issue at trial. For example, in the recent Kansas litigation, more than half a dozen experts on both sides of the issue presented detailed testimony on whether money matters. The court concluded that it was "persuaded by the evidence that there is a causal connection between the poor performance of the vulnerable and/or protected categories of Kansas students and the low funding provided by their schools."[23] Overall, the issue of whether money matters in education was directly considered by the state courts in thirty of these cases. In twenty-nine of them, the courts determined explicitly or implicitly that funding affects educational opportunity and achievement.[24]

There is something almost surreal about all of this scholarly and judicial attention to whether money matters. Certainly, no parent, teacher, or school administrator in any low-wealth school district in the United States—or, for that matter, in any affluent community—genuinely believes that money does not matter in education. If money did not matter, wealthy parents would not send their children to private schools with annual tuitions that now often exceed $25,000, nor would they move to wealthy suburbs that spend in excess of $20,000 per pupil to educate their students well. As a state court judge in rural North Carolina bluntly put it after hearing extensive evidence on the subject, "Only a fool would find that money does not matter in education."[25]

In the end, all of the elaborate analyses and technical discussions in the academic literature and in the legal decisions come down to a basic consensus that, of course, money matters—if it is spent well. Hanushek himself recently acknowledged that "money spent wisely, logically, and with accountability would be very useful indeed."[26] The critical question, then, in assessing the success of the judicial interventions in the sound basic education cases is whether the extra funds are being spent well and are being used in ways that actually provide students the sound basic education guaranteed by their state constitutions.

The most obvious gauge of whether the increased expenditures have been spent well would be improved scores on student achievement tests and other measures of increased student learning. The available data indicate some dramatic improvements in student test scores in a number of states in which remedies from a major sound basic education case have been in place for a decade or more. For example, Massachusetts was first in the nation in both reading and math on the 2007 National Assessment of Education Progress (NAEP) tests.[27] Between 2000 and 2007, the failure rate of tenth graders taking the highly challenging Massachusetts Comprehensive Assessment System exams for the first time has dropped dramatically from 47 to 13 percent.[28] New Jersey has also seen dramatic improvements in student achievement on state assessments: from 1999 to 2005, mean scale scores rose nineteen points in fourth grade mathematics. The greatest increases occurred in the *Abbott* districts, which were the focus of the judicial remedies; the achievement gaps between the *Abbott* districts and the rest of the state were almost cut in half.[29] In addition, Kentucky's free and reduced lunch students outscored students from similar backgrounds nationally by seven points in fourth grade reading and by five points in eighth grade reading on the 2007 NAEP tests.[30]

However, although test score measures obviously are relevant, they cannot, at least at the present time, serve as the sole or even the major indicator of the success or failure of a judicial intervention. As the New York Court of Appeals noted, although performance levels on various examinations obviously "are helpful, [they] should also be used cautiously as there are a myriad of factors which have a causal bearing on test results."[31] Changes in testing methodology and student demographics over time often make it difficult to compare test scores that are collected for different years.[32] In addition, many of the existing state tests are not well aligned with the state standards and/or are not properly validated in accordance with professional psychometric requirements.[33]

An additional problem is that because of the federal No Child Left Behind Act's exclusive focus on reading and math assessments, in many cases, performance measures tend to be limited to test scores in these areas, rather than including the full range of subjects that are covered by most state standards and that are needed to prepare students to function

productively as citizens and in the workplace. Referring to a recent compliance follow-up decision of the Texas Supreme Court, James Ryan illustrates the problems that can result from narrow focus:

> The court recognized that there were still funding disparities and that fund-
> ing might not be sufficient to meet all curricular demands. It recognized that
> there were still wide gaps in performance; that dropout rates were high; that
> relatively few students were prepared to enter college and that there was a
> shortage of highly qualified teachers. But none of this ultimately mattered be-
> cause "the undisputed evidence is that standardized test scores have steadily
> improved over time, even while tests and curriculum have been made more
> difficult."[34]

Test scores can also be manipulated. For example, spectacular increases in passing rates, from 52 percent in 1994 to 72 percent in 1998 on
all three of the Texas Assessment of Academic Skills exams, a predecessor to one of the tests relied on by the Texas Supreme Court in the case
discussed by Ryan, were later attributed to factors other than improved
learning: large numbers of students dropped out of school before taking
the tenth grade exam and a substantially larger number of students were
classified as "special education," so that their exam results were not included in the proficiency calculation.[35]

Graduation rates, which are often used as an indicator of student
achievement, have also been unreliable since there is no agreed-upon
standard for measuring this rate. For example, some states include only
students who graduate high school after four years, while others include
students who take as long as seven years to graduate, and some include
those who receive alternative diplomas or general equivalency diplomas,
while others do not.[36] Data collection difficulties, especially in regard to
the number of students who drop out, can result in dramatic overestima-
tion of graduation rates.[37]

When using student achievement measures to gauge the success of
sound basic education cases, consideration must also be given to the time
period assessed. This issue has two dimensions. The first is that data will
be relevant for judging success only after a sufficient period of time has
passed to allow the reforms to take effect and for them to have an impact
on students' behaviors and outcomes. Although it may be reasonable
now to examine student achievement results from cases decided in the
late 1980s or early 1990s, like Kentucky, Massachusetts, and New Jersey,

it is unreasonable to expect to see dramatic improvements in states in which cases were decided very recently. Accordingly, during the critical initial stages of the implementation of reforms, student test scores can provide little, if any, guidance for judging the value of the reforms or the manner in which they are being implemented.

Second, for the constitutional right to a sound basic education to be satisfied, outcome measures that are indicative of success must be maintained over time. A constitutional guarantee is a permanent right: students must be provided with appropriate educational opportunities not just for a particular point in time but throughout their educational experience. Examples abound of schools achieving large but short-term test score gains that can be attributed to teaching to the test, changes in school population, or outright cheating.[38] For example, on New York City's fourth grade reading exams in 2005, 83 percent of the fourth graders at P.S. 33 in the Bronx scored at or above proficiency, although only 35.8 percent of the fourth graders the year before had reached this level. The next year, the fourth graders' pass rate was 47.5 percent, and the previous year's fourth graders who were now in fifth grade had a pass rate of only 41.1 percent.[39] A key issue in assessing success in sound basic education cases, then, is whether reforms, even if they lead to increased funding for underperforming schools and higher test scores and other outcome indicators, remain in place over a long period of time.

In short, then, success in sound basic education cases cannot be measured solely by initial progress in reducing funding inequities, increasing spending on education, or raising test scores. All of these outcome indicators are important, but they are also limited in their scope and in their accuracy. Undoubtedly advances in psychometric techniques and their implementation can improve the scope and the accuracy of these measurements.[40] But ultimately the measure of success for constitutional purposes—and indeed for all purposes—must be whether the state has succeeded in establishing and maintaining an educational system that provides meaningful educational opportunities to all students and graduates students who have the knowledge and skills needed to function as capable citizens and productive workers. And in the end, whether the state has provided its students with such a sound basic education is a judgment question that must be based not only on the available, but inherently limited, indicators of student outcomes but also on an assessment of the appropriateness and effective use of the standards, resources, and other inputs into the system and whether the systems in place are likely to prepare students to function productively in a modern, diverse society.

Can judgments of this type fairly and efficiently be made? Where can the range of information that is needed to inform such broad-based assessments be obtained? The state courts throughout the country that have been considering sound basic education cases over the past thirty-five years have, in effect, been asking and trying to answer these critical questions. A recent decision of the Superior Court of Alaska summarized well the types of systemic reforms that the experience of the sound basic education cases has shown to be needed to ensure sustained constitutional compliance:

> First, there must be rational educational standards that set out what it is that children should be expected to learn. These standards should meet or exceed a constitutional floor of an adequate knowledge base for children. Second, there must be an adequate method of assessing whether children are actually learning what is set out in the standards. Third, there must be adequate funding so as to accord to schools the ability to provide instruction in the standards. And fourth . . . there must be adequate accountability and oversight by the State over those school districts so as to insure that the districts are fulfilling the State's constitutional responsibility to [provide an adequate education] as set forth in [the state's] constitution.[41]

If these are indeed the critical steps that a state must take to ensure that a constitutionally acceptable educational opportunity is provided to all children, and I believe that they are, then the question for present purposes is what responsibilities courts should assume in sound basic education litigations to ensure that each of these steps are actually being taken.

Although many courts have promoted effective action in one or more of these areas, few courts have taken responsibility for ensuring that all of the elements of a successful remedy are well developed and fully implemented. Moreover, even if appropriate standards and assessment systems are adopted and equitable funding and effective accountability mechanisms are put into place, critical issues remain as to whether these reforms will be sustained and how long judicial oversight should remain in place to ensure continued compliance.

Therefore, in order to measure judicial success in sound basic education litigations, it is important to think in terms of a comprehensive range of inputs and outcomes and their long-term implementation and not merely to look to a snapshot of funding increases or test score improvements at a particular point in time. Only such a comprehensive assessment can verify that the litigation has resulted in a system that can, on a sustained basis, ensure that all students will be provided a meaningful opportunity to receive a sound basic education.

In practical terms, a constitutionally adequate and "successful" educational system, therefore, should be measured by the presence of the following elements.

1. Challenging standards: The development of challenging academic content and performance standards that meet constitutional requirements.
2. Adequate funding: The adoption of a state education finance system that provides sufficient funding to all schools to allow them to provide all of their students with a meaningful opportunity to meet the state standards.
3. Effective educational programs and accountability systems: The development of effective educational programs designed to prepare students to meet state standards and of accountability mechanisms designed to ensure that these programs are properly implemented and funded on a sustainable long-term basis.
4. Improved student performance: Sufficient improvements in performance on validated assessments of academic proficiency and on other indicators such as graduation rates to demonstrate as accurately as possible that all students are receiving the opportunity for a sound basic education on a sustained basis.

If this broad range of sustained activity constitutes the full measure of success in a sound basic education case, to what extent can a court actually oversee such a complex and comprehensive array of tasks? The recent history of the remedial process in Arkansas is instructive in this regard. Initially, the Arkansas Supreme Court ruled out taking on such extensive responsibilities, but as events unfolded, it saw the necessity to do so and developed mechanisms for comprehensively reviewing the state's actions in each of these areas. After holding that the state's educational finance system was denying students their constitutional right to a "general, suitable and efficient education," the Arkansas Supreme Court in 2002 explicitly rejected the idea of retaining jurisdiction to oversee the remedial process. The court stated at that time that "[i]t is not this court's intention to monitor or superintend the public schools of this state."[42] Two years later, however, in response to allegations that the legislature had not complied with its order, the court appointed two special masters and gave them an extensive mandate to examine all aspects of the implementation of a constitutionally acceptable education system.

The court's directive to the masters specifically directed them to review, among other things, (1) the steps taken to assure that a "substantially equal educational opportunity has been made available to all students"; (2) the testing measures put in place to evaluate the performance and ranking of Arkansas students; (3) the cost study the legislature had commissioned and whether a fair funding formula was in place to ensure that "the school children of this state are afforded an adequate education," and (4) whether accountability measures had been implemented to evaluate and monitor how the money was actually being spent in local school districts.[43]

The masters held extensive hearings and issued a detailed report covering each of these areas. While this matter was under review, the legislature met and enacted legislation that dealt appropriately with all of the issues. The court, therefore, once again terminated its jurisdiction of the case and explicitly stated that "it is not this court's constitutional role to monitor the General Assembly on an ongoing basis over an extended period of time until the educational programs have all been completely implemented or until the dictates of *Lake View III* have been totally realized."[44]

A year later, however, the court again became concerned that the state was failing to comply with its own remedial legislation. Consequently, it reappointed the special masters to determine whether the general assembly had engaged in any "backtracking."[45] After analyzing the masters' findings, the court concluded that the general assembly had, indeed, failed to comply with its legislative commitments to improve the education system, and it ordered the general assembly to do so.[46] The next year, the court reappointed the masters to review the legislature's compliance actions, and after they issued a report that found that the general assembly had brought the system into compliance with the constitutional adequacy requirements, the court again accepted their conclusions.[47]

The Arkansas court's experience indicates that implementation of the recommended remedial system for developing and sustaining a constitutionally acceptable system of education, although complex, is both appropriate and feasible. As the Arkansas court itself emphasized in its latest order, in sound basic education cases, there is a need for "constant vigilance to ensure the constitutional goal is met . . . constitutional compliance in the field of education is an ongoing task requiring constant study, review and adjustment."[48] The court's actions—in directing the masters to review legislative and executive actions for developing and implementing challenging standards, adequate funding, and effective accountability and assessment systems—demonstrates both the importance of judicial oversight and the fact that courts can ensure that the other branches carry out their respective functions effectively in each of the remedial areas that are necessary for a successful result.

The Arkansas Supreme Court was firm in its resolve to carry out its constitutional responsibilities:

> We will not waver in our commitment to the goal of an adequate and substantially equal education for all Arkansas students . . . Make no mistake, this court will exercise the power and authority of the judiciary *at any time* to assure that the students of our State will not fall short of the goal set forth by this court. We will assure its attainment.[49]

Was there a better way for the court to have effectuated this resolve and ensured effective compliance with constitutional requirements? Could another approach have ensured compliance without terminating jurisdiction, then reinstating judicial oversight, and three separate times appointing special masters to hold hearings and write four major reports, and issuing six compliance rulings over a multiyear period? Utilizing the important perspectives of comparative institutional analysis that are discussed in the next chapter, in chapter 5 I will propose a principled mechanism that will allow courts to ensure effective implementation of constitutional guarantees of a sound basic education—in a manner that is consistent with requirements for both separation of powers and judicial economy.

CHAPTER FOUR

Crafting Effective Remedie
Comparative Institutional P

A ttaining success in a sound basic education
cess is judged against the comprehensive de
previous chapter—clearly is a formidable task. Bu
sic education for all children is an affirmative man
stitutions, and this egalitarian imperative has als
nation's paramount educational policy through the
Act (NCLB) and as the explicit educational polic
states in the form of a major commitment to stand

The stakes involved in this endeavor are extr
based reform was initiated by the president, fift
ing corporate CEOs at the 1989 National Educa
of their concern at the time for the country's ab
global marketplace. Since that time, America's c
dramatically worsened. While the United States
the highest percentage of students who gradu
among advanced industrialized nations, by 2005,
first.[1] Between 1995 and 2005, the United States
fourteenth in college graduation rates,[2] and in 20
for science assessments among fifteen-year-old
fifth for math assessments.[4] These standings do
lack of progress by Americans but from the acce
the nations with whom we are now competing.[5]

it is unreasonable to expect to see dramatic improvements in states in which cases were decided very recently. Accordingly, during the critical initial stages of the implementation of reforms, student test scores can provide little, if any, guidance for judging the value of the reforms or the manner in which they are being implemented.

Second, for the constitutional right to a sound basic education to be satisfied, outcome measures that are indicative of success must be maintained over time. A constitutional guarantee is a permanent right: students must be provided with appropriate educational opportunities not just for a particular point in time but throughout their educational experience. Examples abound of schools achieving large but short-term test score gains that can be attributed to teaching to the test, changes in school population, or outright cheating.[38] For example, on New York City's fourth grade reading exams in 2005, 83 percent of the fourth graders at P.S. 33 in the Bronx scored at or above proficiency, although only 35.8 percent of the fourth graders the year before had reached this level. The next year, the fourth graders' pass rate was 47.5 percent, and the previous year's fourth graders who were now in fifth grade had a pass rate of only 41.1 percent.[39] A key issue in assessing success in sound basic education cases, then, is whether reforms, even if they lead to increased funding for underperforming schools and higher test scores and other outcome indicators, remain in place over a long period of time.

In short, then, success in sound basic education cases cannot be measured solely by initial progress in reducing funding inequities, increasing spending on education, or raising test scores. All of these outcome indicators are important, but they are also limited in their scope and in their accuracy. Undoubtedly advances in psychometric techniques and their implementation can improve the scope and the accuracy of these measurements.[40] But ultimately the measure of success for constitutional purposes—and indeed for all purposes—must be whether the state has succeeded in establishing and maintaining an educational system that provides meaningful educational opportunities to all students and graduates students who have the knowledge and skills needed to function as capable citizens and productive workers. And in the end, whether the state has provided its students with such a sound basic education is a judgment question that must be based not only on the available, but inherently limited, indicators of student outcomes but also on an assessment of the appropriateness and effective use of the standards, resources, and other inputs into the system and whether the systems in place are likely to prepare students to function productively in a modern, diverse society.

Can judgments of this type fairly and efficiently be made? Where can the range of information that is needed to inform such broad-based assessments be obtained? The state courts throughout the country that have been considering sound basic education cases over the past thirty-five years have, in effect, been asking and trying to answer these critical questions. A recent decision of the Superior Court of Alaska summarized well the types of systemic reforms that the experience of the sound basic education cases has shown to be needed to ensure sustained constitutional compliance:

> First, there must be rational educational standards that set out what it is that children should be expected to learn. These standards should meet or exceed a constitutional floor of an adequate knowledge base for children. Second, there must be an adequate method of assessing whether children are actually learning what is set out in the standards. Third, there must be adequate funding so as to accord to schools the ability to provide instruction in the standards. And fourth . . . there must be adequate accountability and oversight by the State over those school districts so as to insure that the districts are fulfilling the State's constitutional responsibility to [provide an adequate education] as set forth in [the state's] constitution.[41]

If these are indeed the critical steps that a state must take to ensure that a constitutionally acceptable educational opportunity is provided to all children, and I believe that they are, then the question for present purposes is what responsibilities courts should assume in sound basic education litigations to ensure that each of these steps are actually being taken.

Although many courts have promoted effective action in one or more of these areas, few courts have taken responsibility for ensuring that all of the elements of a successful remedy are well developed and fully implemented. Moreover, even if appropriate standards and assessment systems are adopted and equitable funding and effective accountability mechanisms are put into place, critical issues remain as to whether these reforms will be sustained and how long judicial oversight should remain in place to ensure continued compliance.

Therefore, in order to measure judicial success in sound basic education litigations, it is important to think in terms of a comprehensive range of inputs and outcomes and their long-term implementation and not merely to look to a snapshot of funding increases or test score improvements at a particular point in time. Only such a comprehensive assessment can verify that the litigation has resulted in a system that can, on a sustained basis, ensure that all students will be provided a meaningful opportunity to receive a sound basic education.

In practical terms, a constitutionally adequate and "successful" educational system, therefore, should be measured by the presence of the following elements.

1. Challenging standards: The development of challenging academic content and performance standards that meet constitutional requirements.
2. Adequate funding: The adoption of a state education finance system that provides sufficient funding to all schools to allow them to provide all of their students with a meaningful opportunity to meet the state standards.
3. Effective educational programs and accountability systems: The development of effective educational programs designed to prepare students to meet state standards and of accountability mechanisms designed to ensure that these programs are properly implemented and funded on a sustainable long-term basis.
4. Improved student performance: Sufficient improvements in performance on validated assessments of academic proficiency and on other indicators such as graduation rates to demonstrate as accurately as possible that all students are receiving the opportunity for a sound basic education on a sustained basis.

If this broad range of sustained activity constitutes the full measure of success in a sound basic education case, to what extent can a court actually oversee such a complex and comprehensive array of tasks? The recent history of the remedial process in Arkansas is instructive in this regard. Initially, the Arkansas Supreme Court ruled out taking on such extensive responsibilities, but as events unfolded, it saw the necessity to do so and developed mechanisms for comprehensively reviewing the state's actions in each of these areas. After holding that the state's educational finance system was denying students their constitutional right to a "general, suitable and efficient education," the Arkansas Supreme Court in 2002 explicitly rejected the idea of retaining jurisdiction to oversee the remedial process. The court stated at that time that "[i]t is not this court's intention to monitor or superintend the public schools of this state."[42] Two years later, however, in response to allegations that the

legislature had not complied with its order, the court appointed two special masters and gave them an extensive mandate to examine all aspects
of the implementation of a constitutionally acceptable education system.

The court's directive to the masters specifically directed them to review, among other things, (1) the steps taken to assure that a "substantially equal educational opportunity has been made available to all students"; (2) the testing measures put in place to evaluate the performance
and ranking of Arkansas students; (3) the cost study the legislature had
commissioned and whether a fair funding formula was in place to ensure
that "the school children of this state are afforded an adequate education," and (4) whether accountability measures had been implemented
to evaluate and monitor how the money was actually being spent in local
school districts.[43]

The masters held extensive hearings and issued a detailed report covering each of these areas. While this matter was under review, the legislature met and enacted legislation that dealt appropriately with all of
the issues. The court, therefore, once again terminated its jurisdiction
of the case and explicitly stated that "it is not this court's constitutional
role to monitor the General Assembly on an ongoing basis over an extended period of time until the educational programs have all been completely implemented or until the dictates of *Lake View III* have been totally realized."[44]

A year later, however, the court again became concerned that the
state was failing to comply with its own remedial legislation. Consequently, it reappointed the special masters to determine whether the
general assembly had engaged in any "backtracking."[45] After analyzing the masters' findings, the court concluded that the general assembly had, indeed, failed to comply with its legislative commitments to improve the education system, and it ordered the general assembly to do
so.[46] The next year, the court reappointed the masters to review the legislature's compliance actions, and after they issued a report that found
that the general assembly had brought the system into compliance with
the constitutional adequacy requirements, the court again accepted their
conclusions.[47]

The Arkansas court's experience indicates that implementation of
the recommended remedial system for developing and sustaining a constitutionally acceptable system of education, although complex, is both
appropriate and feasible. As the Arkansas court itself emphasized in
its latest order, in sound basic education cases, there is a need for "con-

stant vigilance to ensure the constitutional goal is met . . . constitutional compliance in the field of education is an ongoing task requiring constant study, review and adjustment."[48] The court's actions—in directing the masters to review legislative and executive actions for developing and implementing challenging standards, adequate funding, and effective accountability and assessment systems—demonstrates both the importance of judicial oversight and the fact that courts can ensure that the other branches carry out their respective functions effectively in each of the remedial areas that are necessary for a successful result.

The Arkansas Supreme Court was firm in its resolve to carry out its constitutional responsibilities:

> We will not waver in our commitment to the goal of an adequate and substantially equal education for all Arkansas students . . . Make no mistake, this court will exercise the power and authority of the judiciary *at any time* to assure that the students of our State will not fall short of the goal set forth by this court. We will assure its attainment.[49]

Was there a better way for the court to have effectuated this resolve and ensured effective compliance with constitutional requirements? Could another approach have ensured compliance without terminating jurisdiction, then reinstating judicial oversight, and three separate times appointing special masters to hold hearings and write four major reports, and issuing six compliance rulings over a multiyear period? Utilizing the important perspectives of comparative institutional analysis that are discussed in the next chapter, in chapter 5 I will propose a principled mechanism that will allow courts to ensure effective implementation of constitutional guarantees of a sound basic education—in a manner that is consistent with requirements for both separation of powers and judicial economy.

Crafting Effective Remedies: Comparative Institutional Perspectives

A ttaining success in a sound basic education case—especially if success is judged against the comprehensive definition set forth in the previous chapter—clearly is a formidable task. But ensuring a sound basic education for all children is an affirmative mandate of most state constitutions, and this egalitarian imperative has also been adopted as the nation's paramount educational policy through the No Child Left Behind Act (NCLB) and as the explicit educational policy of virtually all of the states in the form of a major commitment to standards-based reform.

The stakes involved in this endeavor are extremely high. Standards-based reform was initiated by the president, fifty governors, and leading corporate CEOs at the 1989 National Educational Summit because of their concern at the time for the country's ability to compete in the global marketplace. Since that time, America's competitive situation has dramatically worsened. While the United States had, well into the 1960s, the highest percentage of students who graduated from high school among advanced industrialized nations, by 2005, it had fallen to twenty-first.[1] Between 1995 and 2005, the United States also fell from second to fourteenth in college graduation rates,[2] and in 2005 it ranked twenty-first for science assessments among fifteen-year-old students,[3] and twenty-fifth for math assessments.[4] These standings do not result from a total lack of progress by Americans but from the accelerating performance of the nations with whom we are now competing.[5]

The policy statement of the 1996 National Education Summit, endorsed by the president and the governors and corporate CEOs who were present, specifically described the type of cognitive skills students need to compete successfully in the contemporary job market:

> In addition to basic skills, all individuals must be able to think their way through the workday, analyzing problems, proposing solutions, communicating, working collaboratively and managing resources such as time and materials . . . Today's economy demands that all high school graduates, whether they are continuing their education or are moving directly into the workforce, have higher levels of skills and knowledge.[6]

To achieve this level of skill, "Almost two-thirds of today's workforce needs advanced reading, writing, mathematical and critical thinking skills, compared to only 15 percent of workers just twenty years ago."[7]

The stakes are also high for the future of America's democratic political system. Americans have become increasingly cynical and apathetic about participating in politics and policy making The number of citizens voting in presidential elections for the past few decades has barely exceeded 60 percent of eligible voters, and in nonpresidential election years on average only about 40 percent of eligible voters go to the polls.[8]

According to Robert Putnam, voter apathy is symptomatic of a more pervasive and deep-rooted cynicism about civic participation:

> During the last third of the twentieth century formal membership in organizations in general has edged downward by perhaps 10–20 percent. More important, active involvement in clubs and other voluntary associations has collapsed at an astonishing rate, more than halving most indexes of participation within barely a few decades . . . most Americans no longer spend much time in community organizations—we've stopped doing committee work, stopped serving as officers and stopped going to meetings . . . [9]

Education has been shown to increase voter participation,[10] participation in volunteer organizations, and personal tolerance of different viewpoints.[11] One study examined the relationship between education and participation in political primaries in different states and found that a one-year increase in median education level is associated with more than a 13 percent jump in primary turnout.[12] People with a college education participated in the 2004 presidential election at three times the rate of high school dropouts.[13]

John Adams pointed out early in our history that

> a memorable change must be made in the system of education and knowledge must become so general as to raise the lower ranks of society nearer to the higher. The education of a nation instead of being confined to a few schools and universities for the instruction of the few, must become the national care and expense for the formation of the many.[14]

Tocqueville also recognized almost 150 years ago that "in the United States the instruction of the people powerfully contributes to the support of the democratic republic . . . "[15] The critical link between broad-based quality education and the maintenance of a viable democracy also strongly motivated the drafters of the state constitution clauses that underpin the contemporary sound basic education movement. For example, the South Dakota constitution explicitly states, "*The stability of a republican form of government depending on the morality and intelligence of the people,* it shall be the duty of the Legislature to establish and maintain a general and uniform system of public schools."[16] The drafters of the education clause in Indiana's constitution dramatically expressed in quantifiable terms why a constitutional guarantee of a sound basic education was necessary:

> Sir, we have forty thousand voters in our State, who cannot read the ballots which they use . . . Yes sir, and thirty thousand mothers who are rearing our successors and destitute of the very first elements of education. We have, sir, according to the latest census . . . seventy-three thousand two hundred and ninety-nine persons over the age of twenty years, who cannot read and write.
>
> If the present Constitution be correct in asserting that "knowledge and learning generally diffused through a community, (is) essential to the preservation of a free government," what have we a right to expect from the state and condition of learning among us?[17]

The contemporary educational challenge for maintaining a viable democratic system is much greater. The link between democracy and an educated electorate recognized by Adams, Tocqueville, and the drafters of the education clauses in the eighteenth and nineteenth centuries was articulated during an era in which the scope of public discussion was limited and when both the franchise and access to education were restricted largely to upper-income white males. Throughout most of America's history, women, blacks, and other minorities and lower class workers who did not own property were excluded from the franchise and from exercising most of the rights of citizenship.[18]

The concept of an informed electorate composed of citizens who intelligently consider and analyze issues before voting is also a relatively recent phenomenon. It emerged during the Progressive Era at the beginning of the twentieth century and has accelerated in the world of mass media and Internet access of our time. The extent to which the kind of knowledge that the electorate needs has changed dramatically from colonial days to the present time has been summarized by Michael Schudson:

> [I]n an age of gentlemen, the citizen's relatively rare entrances into public discussion or controversy could be guided by his knowledge of social position; in the era of rule by majorities, the citizens' voting could be led by the enthusiasm and rhetoric of parties and their most active partisans; in the era of experts and bureaucracies, the citizens had increasingly to learn to trust their own canvass of newspapers, interest groups, parties and other sources of knowledge . . . [19]

In short, the vastly expanded electorate encompassing individuals of both genders and of all classes, races, and ethnic groups, combined with contemporary expectations that a citizen's role is to analyze issues rationally and make individual electoral decisions, renders the link between effective education and the maintenance of a viable democracy more important than ever.

The United States Supreme Court agreed in its 1973 *Rodriguez* decision that our democracy "depends on an informed electorate: a voter cannot cast his ballot intelligently unless his reading skills and thought processes have been adequately developed."[20] Because its reading of the U.S. Constitution precluded an active federal role in promoting education, the Supreme Court left this responsibility to the states. The state courts have accepted this responsibility to an extent that few would have predicted in 1973, with more than two-thirds of the states that have considered sound basic education cases finding that students have a substantive constitutional right to a decent education and that it is the duty of the state courts to enforce it. Many of these courts also fully understood and articulated the critical importance of ensuring that contemporary students are provided the opportunity to develop the skills they need to become capable citizens and competitive workers. The state courts' actual follow-through in regard to enforcing their perceived responsibility in this area has, however, been inconsistent and, at times, ineffective.

A major reason some of the state courts have not consistently been able to effectuate fully successful remedies in the sound basic education cases is that they have been hamstrung by anachronistic concepts of separation of powers. As I discussed in chapter 1, in recent years, research has shown that many of the historical assumptions about the courts' alleged lack of capacity to take on this role have been grossly exaggerated, and the public and their political representatives have in practice come to embrace an active judicial role in education and many other areas. Nevertheless, allegations of judicial usurpation of legislative and executive authority still abound, and many judges are still sensitive to them. As Judge Albert Rosenblatt of the New York Court of Appeals bluntly put it, "Judges don't like to be seen as elitist or as activists."[21]

Charges of judicial activism are particularly misguided in the state court context. Historically, the pejorative use of this term arose from resistance to the role of the federal courts in school desegregation cases. The facile extension of criticisms of those highly charged federal court interventions, whatever their validity there, to the recent actions of state courts in the sound basic education cases is entirely inappropriate. These state court cases do not involve the federalism issues that overlay the separation of powers concerns in the school desegregation cases. In contrast to federal judges, who were sometimes "pictured as 'outsiders,' rendering their controversial decisions subject to more resistance than an equally controversial decision handed down by the 'local' judge,"[22] state court judges, who are usually drawn from the local political elite, are well aware of the legal and political environment of the state scene. Matthew Bosworth attributed the willingness of legislative leaders in Texas to cooperate with the state court's order in the *Edgewood* litigation in these terms:

> [An] experience these leaders had shared . . . was federal court takeover of the state prison system and state mental health facilities . . . One major difference was that in the prison and mental health cases, a federal judge was ordering improvements as opposed to the state supreme court. The respondents said that there was quite a bit of "fear and loathing" of the federal courts. Many former colleagues sat on the state supreme court, by contrast, and the state

court had to face the same electorate the legislature did, producing more of a "comfort zone" on the part of the legislature.[23]

Judith Kaye, former chief judge of the New York Court of Appeals, agrees that state court judges have a firmer democratic pedigree: "[S]tate courts are generally closer to the public, to the legal institutions and environments within the state, and to the public policy process. This both shapes their strategic judgments and renders any erroneous assessments they may make more readily redressable by the People."[24]

In contrast to federal judges who are appointed for life, thirty-nine of the fifty states elect some or all of their judges either in garden-variety partisan elections or in a variant of a retention election.[25] Moreover, the constitutions that state judges are called upon to interpret are capable of relatively easy amendment, rendering their decisions subject to a form of "majoritarian ratification."[26]

A final and highly significant distinction between federal courts and state courts is that, as discussed in chapter 2, in key areas of state responsibility like education and welfare, state constitutions incorporate "positive rights" that call for affirmative governmental action in contrast to the "negative restraints" of the federal constitution.

As Judge Albert Rosenblatt explains,

The federal constitution was never designed as a rights-driven document. Although we call it the "Bill of Rights," this part of the federal constitution was not designed to give anybody "rights." It was designed to allay the states' concern that the federal government could take rights away from citizens. It was designed as a check on the Congress. The First Amendment says the Congress shall not pass any law abridging freedom of religion or establishing a national religion, and so forth. The state constitutions, on the other hand, are in part structural and in part rights-driven. New York's constitution, unlike the federal constitution, included an article that dealt with education, another article that dealt with the needy, and so forth. . . . This is healthy. These matters are in a sense local and regional, and we cannot and should not expect the federal government and the federal constitution to get into all facets of American life. The state constitutions are different—they concentrate on different things, and it should not be a surprise that the state constitutions are the sources of expanded educational opportunities. The New York constitution provides for free education as a constitutional right of New Yorkers that does not exist in the federal constitution.[27]

State judges have a clear duty, therefore, to enforce the affirmative rights bestowed by the state constitution.

Rosenblatt, a middle-of-the-road jurist who shuns the "activist" label, spelled out the implications of this positive constitutional command in response to Supreme Court justice Clarence Thomas's comment that judges should not be "social engineers":

> When there's a constitutional command, as in New York, Massachusetts, and every other state where children are entitled to a sound basic education at least or its equivalent, and it is not being honored by the legislators—you may say because of lack of political will or maybe because they're too responsive to the voters—it falls on the judiciary to do it. I would not call that "social engineering," I would call it fidelity to the constitutional command, and judges don't do it cheerfully. They do it with a sense of balance and proportion, and when the time comes to do it they have done it in virtually all, or in the great majority of instances.[28]

Indeed, the overwhelming majority of the state courts have recognized that education is a positive right and that the courts have a responsibility to remedy constitutional violations in this area.

Nevertheless, in spite of their understanding that they must uphold the constitution and protect students' educational rights, many of the judges in sound basic education cases have refrained from instituting the kind of comprehensive remedies that are necessary to vindicate these rights. The courts' boldness often disappears at the remedy stage because judges recognize the complexity of the task and sometimes doubt their expertise or their institutional capacity to oversee wholesale educational reform. The trepidation that the Nebraska Supreme Court expressed about venturing into the "Stygian swamp"[29] of remedial oversight in a sound basic education case reflects this exaggerated apprehension that many judges feel about getting involved in remedial oversight in these cases.

It may be that courts have been held—and have held themselves—to too high a standard in assessing their capability to manage remedies in these cases. As Neil Komesar has pointed out, all government institutions are imperfect, and the fact is that neither the legislative nor the executive branches on their own have made much headway to date in ensuring the meaningful educational opportunities guaranteed to all children by the state constitutions. Critics and commentators often allege that "courts have not produced the desired reforms"[30] without considering whether the task at hand can indeed better be performed by a legislature, a state education department, or another governmental or private agency. Comparative institutional analysis, the approach Komesar utilizes to evaluate institutional functioning,[31] widens the discussion of judicial capability by asserting that "[i]n the relevant comparative institutional world, courts may be called upon to consider issues for which they are ill equipped in some absolute sense because they are better equipped to do so in a relative sense."[32] Most of the courts that have invoked the "political question" doctrine in declining to accept jurisdiction of an education adequacy case, as discussed in chapter 2, have done so after focusing on the courts' limitations but without undertaking any comparative institutional analysis of the difficulties the other branches would face in confronting these problems.

Komesar has analyzed in depth whether courts, legislatures, or the market provide the best forum for resolving specific public policy issues like land use and violation of property rights. For him, the key question in choosing among imperfect alternatives is "deciding who decides."[33] In the present context, however, whatever the philosophical or policy arguments that might be made, as a practical matter, that question has already been answered. The vast majority of state courts have already decided in their rulings in the sound basic education litigations that specific constitutional provisions compel them to take responsibility for ensuring that all students are provided the opportunity for a basic quality education. The important issue that needs to be considered in this arena, therefore, is how courts that have taken on this responsibility can craft remedies that effectively vindicate students' constitutional rights. Comparative institutional analysis can provide important insights that respond to this question.

Courts have inherent strengths that are particularly well suited to shepherding the implementation of the kind of reforms that are needed for success in sound basic education cases. As discussed in chapter 2, standards-based reform is a well-conceived, comprehensive approach for radically improving our education system so that all students can be given a meaningful opportunity to develop the skills they need to compete in the global marketplace and to become capable citizens. It requires a coordinated, long-range set of reforms based on the articulation of challenging academic content standards, assurance of adequate funding, the training of competent teachers, revisions of curriculum, provision of adequate textbooks and other instrumentalities of learning, and development of accurate assessment techniques, all to reflect and effectively implement the core standards. As evidenced by the inconsistent and uncoordinated implementation of the NCLB,[34] the political branches have a poor track record in meeting the national need for effective implementation of their own standards-based reform policies.

Sustained implementation of standards-based reforms requires a principled, long-range commitment to equity and effective institution building. Governors and legislators live in a "sound bite" culture. Although they may be fervently committed to a policy goal, they are often distracted from following through to ensure that a policy they favor is effectively implemented over a sustained time period by a wide range of competing short-term political demands and media pressures. In addition, the growing trend toward imposition of legislative and executive term limits exacerbates this problem. Joyce Elliott, the former chair of the education committee of the Arkansas House of Representatives, has attributed some of the problems the Arkansas legislature had in complying with court orders in that state's sound basic education litigation to this factor:

> We are term limited and can only serve two three-year terms. By the time we got around to fashioning a remedy for this case, in the house of representatives of one hundred people, we had only two people who had been there more than four years. It was very tough going because of this.[35]

Compared with elected officials, courts are "an independent body and are relatively insulated from political pressure."[36] Judges are oriented to delve deeply into issues and to explore and deal with them in depth, even when they reveal difficult and politically thorny problems. They have "staying power" and an ability to respond flexibly to changed circumstances that legislatures and executive agencies lack.[37]

Komesar also emphasizes that judicial intervention is especially justified when there is a substantial malfunction in the democratic processes of one or both of the other political branches.[38] Such a democratic malfunction often occurs in decision making on educational finance and sound basic education issues. Legislatures in most states are heavily dominated by suburban majorities, and, therefore, the legislative process, left to its own natural political propensities, will tend to create education finance systems that strongly disfavor urban and rural school systems.[39] The multifaceted pressures of poverty, which require representatives from these areas to seek assistance from the state legislature for welfare, housing, transportation, criminal justice, and other such needs, also detrimentally affect their bargaining power when it comes to educational funding:

> While legislators from mostly white, middle-income districts can focus their energy on passing school funding measures that benefit children and teachers within their legislative districts, legislators from predominantly urban areas have greater difficulty organizing themselves around a single issue. . . . To garner sufficient legislative support for the non-educational programs that are of great importance to urban voters, large city legislators [are] under pressure to accept school funding packages that place large city districts at a disadvantage.[40]

This is a prime example of the type of legislative malfunction that John Ely highlighted as deserving of judicial intervention in *Democracy and Distrust,* his classical constitutional text on justifications for judicial intervention.[41] Ely argued that although generally the political branches should determine social policy, the judiciary should intervene to correct malfunctions in the political process. Such a malfunction occurs when, "[t]hough no one is actually denied a voice or a vote, representatives beholden to an effective majority are systematically disadvantaging some minority out of simple hostility or a prejudiced refusal to recognize commonalities of interest and thereby denying that minority the protection afforded other groups by a representative system."[42]

Because of legislatures' tendency toward political malfunction in the area of education finance, courts have an important and continuing role to play in ensuring effective implementation of funding and programmatic reforms if America is to meet the educational challenges it faces. This does not mean, however, that courts can accomplish this task alone. Experience has shown that if constitutional rights in this area are to be upheld, it will be through the combined efforts of all three branches of government. In the complex administrative environment in which we now live, courts, legislatures, and administrative agencies must work together to solve major social problems successfully. Although one of the branches may initiate a reform or take prime responsibility for policy implementation in a particular area, successful policy making today often needs the extensive, complementary involvement of all three branches of government.

For example, extensive desegregation in the South was not achieved

until Congress assisted the courts by passing Title VI of the 1964 Civil
Rights Act and Title I of the 1965 Elementary and Secondary Education Act (ESEA), which provided a carrot (Title I's substantial federal
funding) and a stick (Title VI's cutoff of federal funding for failure to
comply with school desegregation decrees). The combination of forceful decisions by the Supreme Court, passage of Title VI and the ESEA,
and vigorous enforcement by the Office for Civil Rights of the Department of Health Education and Welfare in the 1960s had dramatic results. Although more than 98 percent of black students in the states of
the deep South had been attending schools that had 90 percent or more
black students in 1964, by 1972 less than 9 percent were in such segregated facilities.[43]

Similarly, the extensive rights to educational opportunity now enjoyed by students with disabilities were originally developed as part of
the remedies ordered by federal courts in two constitutional litigations.[44]
These remedial procedures were then codified by Congress into a major
federal statute,[45] which is now being broadly implemented by the Office
for Civil Rights in the United States Department of Education, state education departments, and scores of federal and state courts.

Effective implementation of remedies in sound basic education cases
has also occurred when the three branches of government have worked
together harmoniously to accomplish that end. Bert T. Combs, lead
counsel for the plaintiffs in Kentucky's *Rose* case (and a former Kentucky governor) attributed the success of that endeavor to the effective
collaboration among the three branches of government: "Legal histori-
ans will note that Kentucky's School Reform Law is a classic example
of how this democracy of ours can work for progress when heads of the
three coordinate branches of government lay aside their egos and pride
of turf and work together."[46]

This pattern of effective "colloquy"[47] among the branches has also
occurred in other states such as Vermont and Massachusetts, where, as
George Brown has noted,

> the school finance cases represent development of a new form of public law
> litigation: the dialogic as opposed to the managerial model. The state ju-
> diciary is taking a track different in two ways from the federal judicial ap-
> proach. They are less managerial and more advisory . . . what is transpiring
> is a multi-faceted dialogue between these courts and legislatures, across state
> judicial systems . . . .[48]

In these school finance cases, there has been a pattern of "implicit dialogue" between the branches of state government that is noticeably different from the remedial pattern that occurs in federal court remedial interventions.

Although Brown and other commentators[49] have recognized that this positive pattern of interinstitutional dialogue sometimes occurs in state court education finance decisions, they have not developed a practical conceptual framework that can regularize and advance these practices. Comparative institutional analysis can provide important insights for developing a functional model that can maximize the potential for productive dialogues among the three branches of government at the remedial stage of a sound basic education case. Such a model would focus on how the strengths of each of the branches of government can best be utilized to effectuate long-lasting reforms that can provide all students with meaningful educational opportunities.

The empirical studies of the comparative functioning of the executive, legislative, and judicial branches that I undertook in the 1980s with my colleague Arthur Block are relevant in this regard. As discussed in chapter 1, we reached a number of conclusions concerning the comparative institutional strengths and weaknesses of the judicial, legislative, and executive branches in implementing educational policy reforms, and our findings have been largely confirmed in the years since. Although I do not, of course, claim that the comparative institutional analysis that we undertook in a limited number of case studies at a certain point in time constitutes a definitive analysis of comparative institutional functioning, our findings can provide a starting point for developing a comparative institutional remedial model, which can then be the subject of critical analysis and further empirical study.

The key conclusions we reached were that the rational-analytic decision-making mode of the courts was effective for articulating fundamental principles, while the legislatures' mutual adjustment decision-making mode was better equipped to develop specific policies through broad political compromises, and the administrative agency's pragmatic-analytic decision-making approach was most useful for understanding and reflecting grassroots implementation needs.[50] In regard to fact finding, we determined that legislative hearings tended to be "window-dressing" occasions with little relevance to actual decisions, whereas judicial fact finding was relatively efficient and administrative fact finding was the most efficient mechanism when it was fully invoked. Administrative agencies were most effective in formulating comprehensive educational reform plans, but courts were relatively effective in this regard when the resources of the affected parties were utilized by the courts. Courts, as noted above, also have significant compliance monitoring staying power, in contrast to administrative agencies, which have relatively ineffective compliance monitoring power; legislative oversight and statutory modifications have some influence on remedial enforcement.[51]

Komesar's analysis of the major functional distinctions between courts and legislatures complements our findings. He emphasizes three major characteristics of the judicial process: higher threshold access costs, limited scale, and judicial independence.[52] For example, his emphasis on judicial independence explains the source and significance of the judicial orientation toward a principled analysis of issues:

> From a social standpoint, the greater insulation of judges from the various pressures, produced in part by the presence of all the formalities, provides an important source of comparative advantage for the adjudicative process. This independence provides judges with the opportunity to shape social decisions without some of the biases and pressures that distort other institutions.[53]

On the other hand, Komesar's emphasis on the higher threshold costs of access to the judicial process highlights a major comparative disadvantage of the judicial process, namely, that "judges are far less able to initiate decision making than legislators. Legislators can resolve a social issue without anyone officially and formally bringing the issue to their attention."[54] Initial access to the judicial process is not a major issue in regard to sound basic education cases since courts in forty-five of the fifty states have already considered the issue. The question of continuing access is, however, significant because lack of resources may limit plaintiffs' abilities to continue to pursue compliance remedies in a long-standing litigation or to initiate a new suit if a court has prematurely terminated jurisdiction. The fact that judicial proceedings have a limited scale is a reminder that judges alone do not have the tools and resources to solve major social problems: they can be effective only in a productive dialogue with the other branches.

The greater access costs and limited scale of judicial operations also mean that courts can only take on a small number of public policy responsibilities. The question of which policy areas merit the scarce amount of available judicial attention is of major importance generally for comparative institutional analysts. It is less significant in the present context since most courts have interpreted state constitutions as compelling courts' attention to sound basic education issues, and these courts have already agreed that this a high-priority area meriting substantial time and effort. The key question at this point is how this involvement can be improved.

Our findings on comparative institutional functional capacities could substantially assist courts—and legislatures, state education departments, and executive agencies—in the practical tasks of developing workable remedial processes. Clearly, the courts' principled approach to issues and their long-term staying power are essential for providing continuing guidance on constitutional requirements and sustained commitment to meeting constitutional goals. Legislatures, however, are better equipped to develop specific reform policies, and executive agencies are most effective in undertaking the day-to-day implementation tasks of "explaining what is required, why it is required and how it can be done well, and then checking that districts and schools can and do carry out those requirements."[55] When disputes arise on whether specific mechanisms are, in fact, meeting constitutional requirements, judicial fact-finding mechanisms should be invoked, although there is a problem in assuring access to this process for all of the affected interests.

Although most state courts understand the importance of upholding the constitutional right to a sound basic education and acting to counter legislative malfunctions at the liability stage of a lawsuit, too few take these institutional factors into account at the remedy stage. To achieve a successful remedy, however, these comparative functional factors must be an integral aspect of the formulation of a remedy. The reality is that to implement a successful remedy in a case involving complex institutional reforms courts need to deal over a multiyear period with the complexities of the implementation of wide-ranging standards-based reform and both the strengths and the weaknesses of the operations of the other branches of government. In the next chapter, I will propose a model for judicial oversight of legislative and executive actions through all four of the remedial phases necessary for sustained success in sound basic education cases. This model is based on the insights of comparative institutional analysis as well as on practical examples of techniques that have worked in past cases of this type.

CHAPTER FIVE

Implementing Successful Remedies: A Model for Constitutional Compliance

John Rawls has rightly declared that "the fundamental criterion for judging any procedure is the justice of its likely results."[1] Once a court has found that a state education and/or educational finance system is constitutionally invalid, it has a responsibility to ensure that the remedies that are put into effect cure the constitutional infirmities and provide meaningful educational opportunities for all students. At the outset of the remedial process, therefore, the court should inform the governor, the legislature, and the public at large of its constitutional expectations. This was precisely what the chief justice of the Arizona Supreme Court did at that stage of his state's sound basic education litigation. He wrote,

> This case . . . involves the meaning and application of a state constitutional clause that gives the children of Arizona a fundamental constitutional right to education and that places on the legislature the corresponding obligation to enact laws necessary to establish and maintain a system that will transform that right from dry words on paper to a reality bringing to fruition the progressive views of those who founded this state . . . Parents, their children, and all citizens need to know what rights the constitution gives our children, and the legislature needs to know the extent of its obligation in effectuating those rights. This court exists primarily for the purpose of resolving such issues.[2]

These words convey a message regarding the full scope and significance of the case and properly set the stage for the three branches to
jointly develop an effective remedy.

For the reasons that I discussed in detail in chapter 3, fully effectuat-
ing children's constitutional rights requires the state to develop challenging standards, an education finance system that ensures adequate funding
levels, effective instructional programs and accountability mechanisms,
and appropriate and accurate mechanisms for assessing improvements
in student performance. Given the courts' inherent constitutional responsibilities and their comparative institutional advantages, a successful remedial system should involve a specific court role in regard to each
of the four areas necessary for success in sound basic education cases. A
model approach for promoting successful remedies for sound basic education, therefore, would emphasize the courts' responsibilities to

1. Ensure that the state has adopted challenging academic content and performance standards that define in concrete terms the content of a sound basic education. Such standards would provide the basis for the organization
   and assessment of reforms to improve teacher training, upgrade curriculum, ensure adequate funding, and afford appropriate instrumentalities of
   learning.
2. Require states to determine the actual cost of providing all students the opportunity for a sound basic education and to adopt state education finance
   systems that ensure that the adequate resources are provided to students in
   all schools.
3. Ensure that the state develops and implements instructional programs and
   accountability mechanisms that will provide all students with meaningful educational opportunities.
4. Assess the extent to which student performance has improved as a result of
   these reforms.

Consistent with the comparative institutional perspectives developed
in chapter 4, the court should make clear that the legislative and executive branches will retain the power and duty to develop appropriate policies and practices in each of these areas but that the court will review
their performance as necessary to ensure that reasonable efforts are being made and acceptable results are being achieved.

Some may object that empowering courts with broad remedial responsibility will vastly expand the day-to-day intervention of the courts into the policy domains of the other branches. But vesting in the courts ultimate authority and final responsibility for constitutional compliance does not mean that the courts need to undertake active oversight in each of these areas on a continuing basis. On the contrary, clarification of the courts' role and of their expectations that constitutional compliance must be achieved may well reduce rather than increase the actual incidents of judicial intervention in many cases.

Where courts have issued strong principled orders that make clear that the executive and legislative branches must get the job done, but that leave the policy-making details to the other branches, effective compliance has generally occurred. Matthew Bosworth noted, for example that in Texas,

> [T]he legislature took the court decisions quite seriously and acted in basic accordance with the Court's directives . . . [due to] the lack of an effective alternative because of Court threats, and second, ideological agreement with the basic principles of the court orders on the part of most of the leadership . . . many leaders truly believed that the Court had identified a problem that needed correcting . . . [The Court was] a catalyst—nothing was going to happen without the Court.[3]

The best evidence of the feasibility of the successful-remedies approach I am advocating is that in many cases, and in each of the enumerated categories, some courts have already successfully overseen legislative and regulatory actions in the recommended manner. My aim in setting forth a comparative institutional methodology is to build on these experiences and to try to persuade more courts to utilize these practical and productive mechanisms on a regular basis. The balance of this chapter will describe past successful efforts of courts to carry out the recommended successful-remedies responsibilities in each of the categories and will draw from these experiences specific suggestions on how all state courts might operate more successfully in each of these domains in the future. This discussion will demonstrate that courts, working cooperatively with legislatures, governors, and executive agencies in a manner consistent with the separation of powers and their comparative institutional strengths, can ensure that all children actually do receive their constitutional right to a sound basic education.

Challenging Standards

Challenging academic content and performance standards have been successfully developed in most states through a productive dialogue among courts, legislatures, and regulatory agencies that adheres closely to the expectations of the successful-remedies model. The courts have generally effectively carried out their responsibility to articulate broad constitutional principles highlighting the citizenship and workforce goals of public education; at times, existing legislative standards have provided the courts substantive insights on contemporary needs that have assisted them in formulating these constitutional concepts. The courts' constitutional standards have established parameters for legislative and executive efforts to develop specific content and performance requirements that will induce schools to meet these broad goals. These specific expectations and outcome measures have provided courts the tools and "manageable judicial standards" they need to develop appropriate remedial mechanisms in this area.

The fact that state academic standards have influenced the courts' development of remedial standards in some cases does not mean, as some commentators have assumed, that there is an expectation in sound basic education cases that the courts will simply adopt these standards per se as the constitutional requirement.[4] What has actually occurred in most states is a more nuanced and more significant dialogic interplay between the branches that is largely consistent with the functional division of labor anticipated by the successful-remedies model. This process has not generally resulted in extensive judicial remedial intervention because rarely have any disputes emerged that have required hearings or other forms of judicial involvement in the development and implementation of the standards.

These dynamic dialogues between the branches have taken many forms, but from an analytical perspective, most fit into one of two basic categories: (1) cases in which the courts have been the prime movers in articulating the operative concepts of sound basic education that were then further developed into operational expectations and standards by the legislative and/or executive branches; and (2) cases in which standards originated by the legislature have substantially influenced the courts' development of their constitutional concepts and facilitated the development and evaluation of specific remedies.[5]

The first category of interaction has been the most prevalent. In these cases, the courts have tended to describe a basic quality education in broad, principled terms as preparing students to "function productively as civic participants" and to "compete in the global economy."[6] They often then explicitly call upon the other branches of government to "develop and adopt specific criteria implementing these . . . broad constitutional guidelines."[7] The prime example of this pattern occurred in Kentucky where the court first articulated constitutional guidelines for an adequate education that were then developed into specific statutory and regulatory concepts by the legislature.

The Kentucky Supreme Court in its 1989 adequacy ruling held that an "efficient" system of education must have as its goal to provide each and every child with at least the following seven capacities:

1. Sufficient oral and written communication skills to enable students to function in a complex and rapidly changing civilization;
2. Sufficient knowledge of economic, social, and political systems to enable the student to make informed choices;
3. Sufficient understanding of governmental processes to enable the student to understand the issues that affect his or her community, state, and nation;
4. Sufficient self-knowledge and knowledge of his or her mental and physical wellness;
5. Sufficient grounding in the arts to enable each student to appreciate his or her cultural and historical heritage;
6. Sufficient training or preparation for advanced training in either academic or vocational fields to enable each child to choose and pursue life work intelligently; and
7. Sufficient levels of academic or vocational skills to enable public school students to compete favorably with their counterparts in surrounding states, in academics or in the job market.[8]

The legislature responded to this judicial guidance by enacting the Kentucky Education Reform Act (KERA), one of the most sweeping education reform measures in American history. KERA set forth six specific learning goals based on those constitutional requirements, required the Department of Education to develop those goals into more specific expectations and a model curriculum, mandated specific educational innovations including state-funded preschool and a statewide school technology system, prohibited a number of corruption-prone district practices, mandated a minimum local tax effort, and added major new funding to equalize what districts were able to raise.[9]

The Kentucky constitutional goals have proved quite influential. They have been adopted by other state supreme courts that have similarly used them as general guidelines for their legislatures to utilize in developing specific, appropriate adequacy standards.[10] Legislatures in other states, like Arkansas, have followed the *Rose* guidelines, even without a specific directive from their own state courts to do so.[11]

In Montana, the court held that the present educational finance system was unconstitutional because the legislature had not defined "quality education," the key constitutional term, before determining its funding allocations. "Unless funding relates to needs such as academic standards, teacher pay, fixed costs, costs of special education, and performance standards, then the funding is not related to the cornerstones of a quality education," the court said.[12] The Montana court also refused to accept the state's position that good test scores were all that was required for a showing of quality.[13] In asserting that an educational system is about more than test scores, the court noted that extracurricular activities were important and that their value would not necessarily be reflected in test scores. In addition, although the court accepted the state's assertion that Montana students were performing well on tests compared with students from similar states, it said there was no guarantee that their success would continue.[14] The legislature promptly followed up on these constitutional expectations by enacting legislation that defined a "basic system of quality public schools."[15]

The Washington Supreme Court was especially sensitive to the functional distinctions between the respective roles of the courts and the legislature. After specifying that the state constitution's education clause "embraces broad educational opportunities needed in the contemporary setting to equip our children for their role as citizens and as potential competitors in today's market as well as in the market place of ideas,"[16] it expressly declined to assume the legislature's responsibility for developing these general guidelines into more specific operative categories:

> [Plaintiffs] also suggest the need for additional judicial guidelines for matters less fundamental than those discussed heretofore. However, in light of the judicial guidelines already set forth and considering the need for the Legislature to rethink and retool much of the present educational system, so that it may mesh as a working whole, we decline respondents' invitation.[17]

The Washington legislature then adopted the Basic Education Act that set forth detailed staffing ratios and salaries and all of the other specific categories that had been identified by the plaintiffs.[18]

The Supreme Court of North Carolina explicitly directed the trial court to consider the "[e]ducational goals and standards adopted by the legislature" to determine "whether any of the state's children are being denied their right to a sound basic education."[19] The trial judge then reviewed the standards in a number of subject areas and concluded that they did provide students a reasonable opportunity to acquire the skills that constituted a sound basic education as defined by the Supreme Court. The chief justice of that court, when later interviewed, explained that courts gain a sort of democratic legitimacy in their educational adequacy rulings by respecting legislatively enacted standards: "Courts can look at what the legislatures have done, and do so recognizing that they have had the opportunity to hear from everybody and to thrash it out in open hearings, unconstrained by the case and controversy limitations. It does give the judge some guidelines and, at least, reassurance."[20]

The North Carolina Supreme Court did, however, also influence the manner in which the state's standards were implemented, since it upheld the trial court's determination, after extensive analysis of the standards, that Level III proficiency on standardized end-of-grade and end-of-class tests would be considered the operative constitutional standard for adequacy in regard to test scores.[21]

At times, legislatively enacted state academic standards have strongly influenced, without fully determining, the content of the constitutional standards that were ultimately formulated by the state courts. New York is the prime case in point. There, the New York Court of Appeals in its initial decision on the motion to dismiss set forth a "template" that described its initial concept of what the constitutional requirements should encompass. The template emphasized the skills that students would need to "function productively as civic participants capable of voting and serving on a jury."[22] It was then the trial court's responsibility to consider in depth the implications of this proposed constitutional concept and to flesh out precisely what skills would be required to meet this general standard.

The trial court heard extensive testimony regarding the content of the learning standards in seven academic subjects that had recently been adopted by the New York State Board of Regents. Evidence based on these standards guided the court's understanding of the specific levels of reading comprehension, mathematical understanding, and knowledge of science, economics, civics, and other subjects that students would need to be "capable voters" and "competitive workers" in the twenty-first century. This evidence clearly influenced the court's definition of the requirements for a sound basic education.[23] In articulating that definition, however, the court specifically held that the Regents' standards exceeded constitutional requirements[24] and that, in any event, "the ambit of a constitutional right [cannot be defined] by whatever a state agency says it is."[25]

This position was affirmed by the New York Court of Appeals.[26] Based on the trial court's opinion and the extensive evidence that supported it, the Court of Appeals added to its initial constitutional concept the requirement that the skills students need to function as capable citizens and competitive workers must exceed the minimal sixth to eighth grade level and must be at a "meaningful high school" level of academic functioning. Because all of the parties and amici involved in the case agreed that the current Regents Learning Standards and the related graduation requirements did encompass such a "meaningful high school" level of attainment—indeed, the trial court had found that the Regents Learning Standards exceeded such a level—the court did not need to elaborate further on possible differences between the constitutional and the regulatory requirements.[27] Should a future legislature or Board of Regents water down their standards and/or their high school exit requirements to a point that might arguably be below the constitutional minimum, the court could be called upon to consider enforcement action.[28]

Similarly, in Idaho, where a dispute arose over whether the constitutional "thoroughness" clause included a state obligation to ensure adequate capital facilities for schools, the court took notice of the fact that relevant state statutes obligated the state to ensure proper facilities and stated,

> Balancing our constitutional duty to define the meaning of the thoroughness requirement of art. 9 § 1 with the political difficulties of that task has been made simpler for this Court because the executive branch of the government has already promulgated educational standards pursuant to the legislature's directive in I.C. § 33–118.[29]

Overall then, in most cases the courts have tended to articulate broad constitutional guidelines in order to spur legislatures that have not adopted detailed academic content and performance standards on their own to do so. However, in situations in which a legislature had already adopted adequate substantive standards, the courts sometimes looked to those standards for empirical indications of contemporary schooling requirements and have strongly considered the state's experience in ultimately formulating the final constitutional requirements. In virtually every case, the courts looked to the legislatures and state education departments for the operational standards and regulations that could implement their broad constitutional concepts.[30] Thus, the development of challenging academic standards is an area in which the type of interbranch colloquy called for in the successful-remedies model already is the operative general practice.[31] The result of this colloquy has been that standards-based reforms have been reconceptualized "as a form of governance bound to a state's greater constitutional duty to provide students with an adequate education"[32] and consequently there has been greater precision and a higher level of validity in regard to both constitutional concepts and legislatively enacted state academic standards.

Adequate Funding

State legislatures and education departments tend to put substantial effort into developing clear expectations and specific standards for student performance but substantially less effort into ensuring that all schools have adequate resources to provide students a meaningful opportunity to meet these standards. One of the "poignant" facts that the New York Court of Appeals emphasized in its *CFE* ruling was that while the Regents Learning Standards required all students to pass a science examination that was based in part on a laboratory experience, almost one-third of New York City's high schools "have no science laboratory whatsoever."[33] As Peter Shrag put it,

> There's incontrovertible logical, ethical, fiscal and legal, [*sic*] in the tight two-way link between standards and adequate resources. If a state demands that schools and students be accountable—for meeting standards, for passing exit exams and other tests—the state must be held equally accountable for providing the wherewithal to enable them to do it.[34]

Accordingly, one of the specific requirements courts should set forth in their remedial orders is a clear direction that the state determine the actual cost of providing a sound basic education. In a number of states, such a directive has been issued and has been implemented through appropriate judicial/legislative interchanges. Effective judicial oversight to ensure that the appropriate amount of funding is actually made available to all school districts has, however, been accomplished less often.

The best way to determine the actual amount of funding that is needed to provide all children the opportunity for a sound basic education is to undertake a detailed analysis of the costs of the resources that are needed to implement the state standards successfully. Courts have specifically ordered such cost studies in Wyoming, Ohio, New York, and a number of other states, and these precedents have been the catalysts for a plethora of other cost studies. Utilizing a variety of professional methodologies, such studies have been carried out, often without explicit courts orders, in at least thirty-nine states. Although there is ongoing discussion about the relative advantages and disadvantages of each of the various methodologies, the focus of all of these studies is on matching funding to student needs. The transparency of these procedures is a vast improvement over past practices under which funding allocations were often determined through backroom political deals and had no bearing on actual costs or student need.[35]

The courts' approach to cost studies has been remarkably consistent, with an effective functional division of responsibility among the branches. None of the courts that have ordered these studies have specified a methodology or constrained the policy prerogatives of the political branches in conducting the studies. For example, the Wyoming Supreme Court's order merely directed the state to determine the cost of the "basket of goods and services" needed to provide all students with a proper education,[36] leaving it to the state to define the basket and the methods for determining its costs. Similarly, the New York Court of Appeals succinctly directed the state to "ascertain the actual cost of providing a sound basic education in New York City."[37]

Most of the legislatures have also generally responded appropriately to these directives. For example, in Wyoming, the legislature promptly developed a work plan to respond to the court order and delegated responsibilities to six joint interim committees to follow through on the plan.[38] After the legislature established a basket of educational goods and services based on a common core of knowledge and skills, and student performance standards related to them, it hired a consultant to undertake a detailed analysis of the cost of an adequate education based on this basket.[39]

Where allegations of bias or manipulation have arisen, the courts have held hearings that have played a critical role in ensuring the professional integrity of the studies. For example, in Ohio, the court unearthed "evidence of a conscious consideration by the State [to manipulate the consultant's] methodology with an intent to lower the base cost of calculation."[40] In Texas, the court similarly found that legislative leaders had directed their consultant to remove discussion of higher performance targets from their report because "the higher costs associated with the higher performance levels would be the focus of attention."[41] The courts' ability to comprehend the complex educational finance issues raised by these studies confirms our previous findings regarding the effectiveness of judicial fact-finding procedures. Judicial scrutiny has not only ensured the integrity of the studies directly reviewed by the courts, but it has provided guidance to the development of professional practice in the field as a whole, as the "battles of the experts" in the courtroom have been the focus of the professional dialogue on the state of practice in the emerging field.[42]

Cost studies, to the maximum extent possible, should, of course, base their funding estimates on the cost of providing services efficiently and in accordance with current best practices. One example of how this can be done is Oregon's Quality Education Model (QEM). The QEM is a mechanism for determining both the amount of money and the effective educational practices that will lead to high student performance in accordance with established state standards. In Oregon, a Quality Education Commission was established by the governor and the legislature in 1999. Since then, the commission has developed a detailed set of educational prototypes and cost analyses and has regularly updated the model and issued reports on a range of cost analysis and best-practice recommendations based on its model.[43] It is not, however, reasonable to base cost estimates on politically inspired cost-reduction targets or speculative notions of efficiency that have never actually been realized in practice.[44]

Overall, the experiences to date indicate that the courts have played an important role in initiating and ensuring the integrity of the sound basic education cost studies, without infringing on legislative and executive policy prerogatives. In fact, by validating the integrity of these studies, judicial oversight has enhanced the value of the legislature's policy decisions.[45] Since cost studies have been shown to be critical mechanisms for establishing the amount of funding actually needed to provide all students a meaningful educational opportunity, courts should not shrink from encouraging legislatures to undertake these studies and from resolving serious controversies that may emerge regarding the validity of the studies or their use.

Some courts, however, have summarily determined that reviewing cost studies is not an appropriate role for the courts without considering the importance of judicial scrutiny to the integrity of the process for ensuring adequate funding to meet constitutional requirements. In New York, for example, a panel of special masters appointed by the trial court (two of whom were, in fact, former appellate judges) provided the Court of Appeals with a thorough record regarding allegations of improper weightings and manipulations of a cost-effectiveness screen in the state's cost study. Instead of reviewing that record and making a final determination on these issues (and thereby providing important guidance to the state for future cost studies), the court summarily rejected the referees' report and plaintiffs' allegations.[46] The court also rejected the special masters' recommendation that, because economic conditions and student needs constantly change, the court should require the state to ensure that appropriate procedures are in place for undertaking new costing-out analyses on a regular basis in the future.[47]

In addition to ensuring that adequate levels of funding are made available, courts also have a constitutional responsibility to verify that the state has in place funding formulas and other mechanisms to ensure that the requite amount of funding is actually made available to all local school districts. The colloquy among state courts, policy makers, and scholars has in recent years resulted in an effective "consensus that a foundation plan based on a generous notion of educational adequacy, a required minimum tax rate, and some kind of educational cost adjustment that provides extra funds for high need districts forms the core of an acceptable reform of state education finance."[48]

Here again, most courts have made clear that the policy determinations that enter into the revision of a complex state education finance system should be undertaken by the political branches. They generally assume that their main responsibility is "to get the process moving,"[49] by declaring the old system unconstitutional and deferring to the legislature, usually with a deadline date, to determine specifically how to revise the state's education finance system to meet constitutional requirements. For example, the New York Court of Appeals directed the state to

"[r]eform the current system of financing school funding... by ensuring...
that every school in New York City would have the resources necessary
for providing the opportunity for a sound basic education" but imposed
no specific guidelines regarding the content of those reforms.[50] Where it
has been determined after a reasonable period of time that the legislature has failed to respond or has adopted reforms that do not meet constitutional requirements, some courts have set forth concrete guidelines
or suggestions to focus attention on the need for specific action. Still,
they tend to leave the definitive policy-making responsibilities with the
other branches. For example, in *Hull v. Albrecht,*[51] after finding that the
state had failed to meet constitutional strictures regarding uniformity in
the funding of capital facilities, the Arizona Supreme Court set forth examples of several ways that the legislature could meet the constitutional
requirements, including equalization of local property taxes, instituting
a statewide tax, or redrawing of district lines to minimize disparities in
property values among the districts. The court made clear, however, that
"[w]hich approach to take, of course, is up to the legislature."[52]

Although many courts review the legislatures' initial compliance efforts, they often terminate jurisdiction before a sufficient period of time
has passed to assess the actual implementation of the new statutory
scheme. In some states, this has led to the filing of new cases and new
rounds of litigation to review major revisions that the legislature has adopted and that plaintiffs claim will undermine the equity and adequacy
of the initial reforms.

Kansas provides a notable case in point. The major confrontation between the Kansas Supreme Court and the legislature was actually pre-
ceded by three rounds of litigation. Each time a trial court ruled the
state education finance system unconstitutional, the legislature initiated
some reforms and the court terminated its jurisdiction; then the reforms
unraveled, leading to another round of litigation. Thus, at issue in the series of *Montoy* cases in 2003–2005 was whether the state education finance system the court had approved a decade earlier was still constitutional. If the court had retained jurisdiction during this period, it is less
likely that the original reforms would have unraveled and the dramatic
"gunfight at the K-12 Corral," as one commentator described the 2005
judicial-legislative confrontation, may well have been avoided.[53]

Courts may also have an important role to play in ensuring that adequate funding is available during times of economic stress or recession.

Although state and national economies obviously go through economic cycles, students' basic educational opportunities should not be subjected to the vicissitudes of economic events. Ideally, once a cost study has determined the amount of money necessary to ensure students in a state a sound basic education, the legislature should establish a mechanism that can assure stable funding for the future at that level, with necessary inflationary adjustments. Vermont established such a system as part of its legislative response to the state supreme court's sound basic education decision. Vermont state law now requires that dedicated revenues from the statewide education property tax and state lottery, Medicaid reimbursement funds, and one-third of the revenues raised from sales and use tax be deposited into a state education fund. In addition, an annual general fund appropriation, with an inflationary adjustment, is also added to the education fund. The money for this education fund cannot be used for any purpose other than education, and a strong stabilization reserve fund has been established to ensure that surpluses are carried forward and that the education fund has sufficient assets even in times of economic decline.[54] As a deepening recession gripped the nation's economy and caused state governments in many parts of the country to cut basic education funding at the end of 2008, education funding in Vermont remained strong and stable.[55]

Maintenance of adequate basic educational funding levels, even in the face of economic downturns, is a constitutional necessity.[56] Because ensuring a sound basic education is an affirmative obligation of state government under most state constitutions, it clearly follows that once a state has satisfied a court mandate to determine and fund the actual cost of providing a sound basic education, it must permanently maintain that level of funding. A child only has one opportunity to learn reading during his or her critical early school years, and a teenager only has a single chance to obtain a meaningful high school education. The resources must be in place to ensure the uninterrupted provision of a sound basic education throughout a child's schooling years. Economic exigencies may induce policy makers to develop more efficient ways to provide a constitutionally adequate level of educational services, but the burden should be on them to demonstrate that costs can be reduced without a negative impact on educational opportunities before a court permits them to reduce funding below the levels that they had previously attested were necessary to meet constitutional norms.

Effective Program Implementation and Accountability Systems

Even if challenging standards are developed and adequate funding is made available, effective educational programs need to be developed and effectively implemented if students are actually to receive the opportunity for a sound basic education. Successful program development and implementation is especially important for schools attended by low-income and minority students, which historically have been underfunded and need to build up their capacity to overcome past deficiencies and to meet their students' extensive educational needs. A court that fails to consider these issues during the remedial process surely "abdicate[s] its responsibilities."[57]

Overseeing the development and implementation of educational programs and accountability mechanisms is a responsibility that many judges have shunned because they assume that it will require them to "make the subtle judgments inherent in education policymaking."[58] But under a proper comparative institutional framework, courts need not and should not directly undertake such policy-making responsibilities. Some courts have specifically focused on the appropriate comparative institutional responsibilities of the three branches of government in the implementation of education reforms. A particularly constructive framework in this regard was articulated a number of years ago, by the U.S. Court of Appeals for the Fifth Circuit.

The major issue before that court in *Castaneda v. Pickard*[59] was whether the language remediation program the school district had implemented satisfied the requirements of the federal Equal Educational Opportunity Act of 1974. The court developed a three-stage process for reviewing the district's development and implementation of an educational program that would comply with the statutory requirements. In essence, under the *Castaneda* procedures the court's role would be to

1. "[A]scertain that a school system is pursuing a program informed by an educational theory recognized as sound by some experts in the field, or, at least deemed a legitimate experimental strategy . . . "
2. Determine "whether the programs and practices actually used by a school system are reasonably calculated to implement effectively the educational theory adopted by the school."
3. Ensure that "after being employed for a period of time sufficient to give the

plan a legitimate trial, [the plan] produce[s] results indicating that the language barriers confronting students are actually being overcome . . . "[60]

This *Castaneda* framework for judicial oversight properly balances the principled oversight responsibilities of the courts and the policy-making prerogatives of the political branches in a manner that is remarkably consistent with the functional strengths and weaknesses of the branches as identified by comparative institutional analysis. It utilizes the courts' staying power to make sure that the political branches carry out their responsibilities to provide meaningful programs to all students on a sustained basis, but, so long as the school officials are using sound professional judgment to develop and implement effective plans, all of the detailed policy-making and administrative functions are left in their hands.

The *Castaneda* approach is fully consistent with constitutional separation of powers precepts. The framers of the Constitution emphasized a "blended" concept of separation of powers.[61] Their central concern was not a tight compartmentalization of responsibilities, but rather the avoidance of excessive concentration of power in one of the political branches. As James Madison put it in the "Federalist No. 47," the key issue was whether "the whole power of one department is exercised by the same hands which possess the whole power of another department."[62] The *Castaneda* procedures delineate a responsible, functional division of labor among the three branches of government that avoids excessive concentration of power in the judiciary or any other branch, and it provides an appropriate and effective balancing of responsibilities for the remedial stage of sound basic education litigations in the state courts.

Consistent with the *Castaneda* framework, in the sound basic education context, the policy decisions about educational programming and spending oversight should be the domain of the legislative and executive branches. The manner in which this division of labor should function— and has already functioned well in a number of sound basic education situations—has been described in terms of a form of "democratic experimentalism" by professors James Liebman and Charles Sabel as follows:

The reform grows out of and contributes to a new form of collaboration among courts, legislatures, and administrative agencies on the one side and between these organs of government and new forms of public action on the others . . .

The core architectural principle of the emergent system is the grant by higher-level authorities . . . to lower level ones of autonomy to pursue the broad goal of improving education. In return, the local entities . . . provide the higher ones with detailed information about their goals, how they intend to pursue them, and how their performance measures against their expectations.[63]

Some judges, like John Greaney of the Massachusetts Supreme Judicial Court, believe that to ensure an effective remedy the court needs to bring all the parties and the educational experts together to hammer out a solution directly under the court's auspices.[64] Most judges, however, adopt a perspective that is consistent with *Castaneda*'s policy allocation approach, one that, as Albert Rosenblatt, former judge of the New York Court of Appeals put it, "say[s] in effect, to the governor, the legislature, 'This is your job; do it. We have confidence you're going to do it.'"[65]

The North Carolina Supreme Court acted in accordance with this perspective when it reversed an attempt by the lower court to impose a specific remedial program after finding that a sound basic education required the state to take steps to overcome the impact of poverty early in children's lives. The court held that "there is a marked difference between the State's recognizing a need to assist 'at-risk' students prior to enrollment in the public schools and a court order compelling the legislative and executive branches to address that need in a singular fashion."[66] Accordingly, the court vacated the specific requirement that the state provide prekindergarten classes for all of the at-risk prospective preschool enrollees and left to the state's discretion the choice of particular preschool interventions that it would implement to meet this newly articulated constitutional requirement.

This first stage of the *Castaneda* remedial process rarely constitutes a major issue in the sound basic education context. The program selection decision at issue in the *Castaneda* case itself involved highly controversial decisions regarding the efficacy of bilingual versus English immersion programs. In sound basic education cases, however, there usually is little disagreement about the programmatic issues involved. Both parties usually concur that for students from disadvantaged backgrounds to receive a sound basic education, improvements involving issues like teacher quality, effective leadership, class size reduction, and adequate facilities and instrumentalities of learning need to be made. In fact, few courts have actually reviewed programmatic decisions of state legislatures or state education departments in this area. On the contrary, in

two instances in which plaintiffs asked the courts to mandate a particular programmatic approach—that is, broad-based use of educational
vouchers—the courts specifically declined to do so on the grounds that
such policy decisions should be left to the legislature and/or the state education department.[67]

One of the few state courts that has been actively involved in programmatic oversight has been the New Jersey Supreme Court. In its *Abbott II* decision, the court had ordered the state to ensure not only that
funding was "substantially equal" between poorer urban districts and
affluent suburban districts but also that additional funds be provided for
supplemental educational programs that would meet the special needs of
students in the poorer urban districts.[68] Seven years later, having determined that, despite further admonitions from the court, the department
of education and the commissioner had failed to develop and implement the special supplemental programs and services that the children
in these districts required, the court took a proactive stance. It ordered
the commissioner to submit programmatic proposals in a wide variety of
areas for review by a special master and the trial court.[69] Following the
review, which largely affirmed the validity of the commissioner's proposals, the court, consistent with the *Castaneda* procedures, authorized and
directed him to implement the whole-school reform, full-day kindergarten, and a half-day preschool programs he had largely devised "as expe-
ditiously as possible."[70]

Recalcitrant education departments and legislatures do often respond
effectively to appropriate judicial programmatic oversight. In Arkansas,
for example, as discussed in chapter 3, the court felt compelled to appoint special masters on three occasions to respond to plaintiffs' allegations that the legislature had not taken appropriate actions to remedy
the constitutional defects that the court had found in its previous decision. Each time that the masters were appointed, the legislature quickly
enacted major reform legislation. The masters then largely approved
the legislative actions and deferred to the legislature's judgment on the
key policy issues.[71] The Arkansas court then "join[ed] the Masters . . . in
their praise for the work done by the General Assembly in the field of
education."[72]

Because there is relatively little controversy about program content in
the sound basic education cases, it is the second stage of the *Castaneda*
process, the actual implementation of the programmatic reforms that
the legislature or the state education department have developed, which

tends to be a more significant problem in these cases. For example, although standards-based reform is a durable, pervasive reform approach, most states have failed to systematically put this reform approach to which they are committed, and which is important for realizing constitutional ends, into effect.[73]

> On the one hand, standards-based reform and related accountability policies appear to have generated significant changes in the U.S. education system. All states have enacted standards-based reform and accountability policies, and the federal government has become perhaps more involved in education policy that at any other point in its history in its efforts to encourage and shape the development of these policies. . . . On the other hand, several serious problems have emerged. Educational personnel at various levels appear to have lacked necessary technical knowledge and skills. . . . A number of administrative and instructional personnel similarly appear to have lacked the financial and physical resources needed to support the instructional changes in all schools and to support a well-functioning infrastructure for the administration of accountability systems required by No Child Left Behind. . . . Educators and administrators have sometimes lacked the political will to change their instructional and administrative practices to support student learning in a way that reflects challenging standards, especially in schools in high-poverty areas.[74]

Judicial oversight would help overcome these problems and would likely prompt more serious and sustained implementation of these reforms.

The real issue here is not a lack of judicial capacity to undertake such reviews but a general reluctance to do so. For example, although the Arkansas Supreme Court in the case discussed above emphasized that the masters had concluded that "much needs to be done to fully implement the system, such as the adoption of rules, commission appointments, training, and development of assessment instruments,"[75] nevertheless, even after making this strong statement about the implementation work that still needed to be done, the Arkansas Supreme Court, held that

> [I]t is not this court's constitutional role to monitor the General Assembly on an ongoing basis over an extended period of time until the educational programs have all been completely implemented or until the dictates of *Lake View III* have been totally realized. Accordingly, we release jurisdiction of this case and the mandate will issue.[76]

The one issue that sometimes does invoke judicial concern at the implementation stage is whether the local school districts are actually receiving sufficient funding to implement the programs that will meet the students' needs. A striking example in this regard occurred in New Hampshire where the court found that the statutory scheme permits a school district to provide less than an adequate education as measured by the state's minimum school approval standards "when the local tax base cannot supply sufficient funds to meet the standards."[77] The Court made clear that "[e]xcused noncompliance with the minimum standards for financial reasons alone directly conflicts with the constitutional command that the State must guarantee sufficient funding to ensure that school districts can provide a constitutionally adequate education,"[78] and it invalidated the state statutes that permitted that result.

If the constitutional mandate for providing all students the opportunity for a sound basic education is truly to be honored, courts need more generally to retain jurisdiction and to be available to ensure that programs are adequately funded and effectively implemented. Even where seemingly appropriate programmatic reforms have been formulated and a new funding system has been put into place, it is important that the courts oversee the adoption and implementation of effective programs and an effective accountability system.

The New Jersey Supreme Court is one of the few courts that has included such specific requirements in its orders and has retained jurisdiction to review the state's implementation efforts when they have been challenged. For example, as discussed above, in its Abbott V order,[79] the court directed the state to implement, among other things, preschool programs for all students in the plaintiff districts, extensive facilities improvements, and many other programmatic improvements. When questions arose regarding the implementation of these sweeping changes, the court promptly accepted jurisdiction and quickly resolved the issues.[80] Similarly, the district court in Alaska, after holding that the state had a constitutional responsibility "to identify those schools that are not according to children a meaningful opportunity" and to provide "a concerted effort to remedy that situation," heard evidence about the state's efforts in this regard. It determined that the State Education Department was not providing sufficient oversight and assistance to schools in chronically underperforming school districts because, among other things, it had failed to ensure that each school district's curriculum is aligned to the state's standards, had not addressed the specific strengths and weaknesses of each chronically underperforming district, and had failed to address high teacher turnover and teacher inexperience.[81]

Most other courts, however, do not include specific accountability measures in their orders, and the few that do generally decline to enforce them. For example, the New York Court of Appeals included in its *CFE II* order a requirement that "the new scheme should ensure a system of accountability to measure whether the reforms actually provide the opportunity for a sound basic education."[82] Both the plaintiffs and the defendant governor asked the courts to enforce this provision by insisting that the New York City Department of Education, which was slated to receive billions of dollars of court-ordered funds, develop a comprehensive plan and annual reports that would detail how these funds would be spent and what results had been achieved. Although a panel of referees and the lower court had endorsed this request,[83] it was ultimately denied by the Court of Appeals, based on an abstract separation of powers concern that the courts' involvement in this case must be terminated as soon as possible.[84] After the court terminated its jurisdiction, the New York legislature did adopt a Contract for Excellence law that requires New York City and other school districts receiving large funding increases to meet certain programming and accountability requirements.[85] These Contract for Excellence requirements cover only a portion of the *CFE* funds, and the effectiveness of these provisions, and the degree to which they will be enforced without any possibility of judicial monitoring, are open questions at the time of this writing.

Ironically, some opponents of judicial involvement in sound basic education cases rebuke the courts for mandating sizeable increases in education funding without taking any steps to ensure that the money is actually spent effectively,[86] while at the same time others argue that the courts are inappropriately supervising school finance systems for many years and should terminate their involvement in these litigations as soon as possible.[87] Courts have a unique capacity for ensuring that effective accountability measures are put into effect, not by micromanaging the day-to-day operations of a school system, but by making sure that legislatures, state education departments, and school districts do their jobs well. The increased levels of information made available through the standards-based reforms adopted by most states provide judges readily available tools for undertaking these responsibilities. For these reasons, courts should utilize their staying power and maintain their jurisdiction long enough to ensure that effective programming *and* effective accountability systems have been put into place.

Improved Student Performance

In the past, few courts have considered it part of their remedial responsibility to review the validity of state assessment systems and to consider the extent to which increased funding and other reforms have actually resulted in improved student performance. Generally, courts terminate their jurisdiction long before the funding and accountability measures that are needed to ensure constitutional compliance have fully taken effect.

Analyzing the results after reforms have been in effect for a sufficient period of time is the third stage of the *Castaneda* remedial review procedures, and it should be considered an essential component of a constitutional compliance process in sound basic education cases. The purpose of this review is not to determine whether all students have achieved certain definitive results but to examine the extent to which they have been given a reasonable opportunity to progress by evaluating the effectiveness of reforms that the state has implemented. Moreover, putting policy makers on notice that outcomes will be considered after a reasonable implementation period is likely, in and of itself, to have a significant positive effect in motivating the legislators and administrators to fully implement and follow through on the programs they have developed to provide students an opportunity for a sound basic education.

Recently several second-generation cases have arisen in which plaintiffs have asked courts to issue additional remedial orders in long-standing litigations in order to ensure full constitutional compliance. These cases have presented courts with the opportunity to review in depth the outcomes of the original litigations and to determine whether the outcomes indicate that constitutional compliance has been achieved or whether, as plaintiffs requested, further judicial action needs to be taken at the present time. The Massachusetts case of *Hancock v. Commissioner of Education*[88] is particularly noteworthy in this regard since all parties there agreed that the state had phased in a new foundation funding system, implemented a far-reaching Education Reform Act that increased school spending by over $ 6.5 billion, and substantially improved the educational performance of most students in the state.[89] Plaintiffs claimed, nevertheless, that more needed to be done because many low-income and minority students in a number of districts were still not being adequately served.

The evidence in the case focused on four "focus districts" that were chosen to represent the sixteen low-income and minority districts that had brought the suit. A majority of the justices accepted the trial judge's findings that, although statewide results were impressive, "the goals of education reform . . . . [c]learly . . . have not . . . been fully achieved."[90] Specifically,

> In all four focus districts, public school students who required special education, and students who had limited English proficiency, came from low-income families, or were members of racial or ethnic minority groups, performed at substantially lower levels on the MCAS examinations than did their peers in the focus districts. The pass rates for these targeted populations on the 2003 grade ten MCAS mathematics examination were twenty-three per cent in Brockton, twenty-five per cent in Lowell, fifteen per cent in Springfield, and twelve per cent in Winchendon, compared with a Statewide average of fifty per cent.[91]

Despite evidence that constitutional compliance had not yet been achieved for these students, the high court terminated its jurisdiction and left unfettered responsibility to the other branches. The chief justice explained that

> The presumption exists that the Commonwealth will honor its obligations . . .
> I am confident that the Commonwealth's commitment to educating its children remains strong, and that the Governor and the Legislature will continue to work expeditiously "to provide a high quality public education to every child."[92]

Justice John Greaney disagreed and dissented. He opined that since the state had failed to provide all of its students "a reasonable opportunity to acquire an adequate education,"[93] the court needed to continue its oversight. His view was that "[t]he problem is of such magnitude that the collective involvement of all three branches of government is needed. . . . In view of the enormity of the task, to remove the court from the process entirely is a great misfortune and mistake."[94]

Justice Greaney's statement is clearly correct. If, as the court acknowledged in *Hancock*, constitutional compliance has not yet been achieved, the integrity of the constitutional process requires the courts to ensure that constitutional mandates are respected, and comparative institutional analysis dictates that the principled approach and staying power of the court will be necessary to complete the job. One of the decisive functional advantages of courts is that they strive to complete tasks that they have undertaken. Aggrieved parties expect to be made whole, and courts endeavor to do so to the best of their ability. Legislators and administrators, by way of contrast, tend to react to the crises or policy priorities of the day, their attention shifts as events (and election results) unfold.

In the area of school desegregation, the U.S. Supreme Court has held that a court should terminate its jurisdiction only after the court has determined that the school board has "complied in good faith with the . . . decree since it was entered, and [that] the vestiges of past discrimination had been eliminated to the extent practicable."[95] An analogous test should be applied in state court sound basic education cases. A decree should not be terminated until there has been a determination that the state has complied in good faith with the court order and that the opportunity for an adequate education has been provided to all students "to the extent practicable."

In *Hancock*, the majority of the Supreme Judicial Court implicitly determined that the state had complied in good faith with the prior *McDuffy* order because of the substantial increases in educational spending and the effective implementation of standards-based reforms that had been accomplished over the previous decade. Before reaching this conclusion, however, the court should have directly addressed the two issues that most concerned the lower court and the dissenters. The first was the fact that, although a cost study had been undertaken in the 1990s, no current analysis of the school districts' actual needs had been undertaken by the legislature.[96] Second was the trial judge's finding that the state education department lacked sufficient funding to carry out its statutory duties of evaluating and providing corrective measures to low-performing schools and districts.[97] These issues raised serious questions about the long-term sustainability of the reforms.

The Massachusetts Supreme Judicial Court also did not determine whether the state had provided educational opportunities to the low-income and minority students in the focus districts and elsewhere in the state "to the extent practicable." Especially because the court had acknowledged that test scores of these students were unacceptably low, the court should not have terminated its jurisdiction without further consideration of the implications of the extremely low tests scores of students in the focus districts. At the least, the court had an obligation to define constitutional expectations for student success and provide the legislature, the governor, and the state education department principled guidance on this issue.

Similarly, a Kentucky trial court recently dismissed plaintiffs' suit for additional funding in order to maintain progress toward constitutional compliance in that state.[98] The court held that it had the power and duty to determine whether current funding levels are adequate and that objective outputs such as test scores should be the main determinant of adequacy. Nevertheless, the court dismissed the complaint after summarily determining, without a trial, and without any explanation, that although the state's long-term proficiency goals have not yet been met, the current rate of progress of Kentucky students was sufficient.[99] Here, as in *Hancock,* the court did not articulate any constitutional notion of sufficient progress that would guide the state's future efforts. In fact, the court indicated that it would revisit the issue if evidence were presented that indicated that the rate of progress toward the educational goals had proved inadequate, but it did not give the parties any guidance on what rate of progress would be considered adequate.

Clearly, determining the relationship between the reasonableness of state efforts to provide opportunities for an adequate education and indicators of student performance is a complex undertaking. It requires consideration of such questions as whether compliance requires total elimination of racial achievement gaps or a substantial narrowing of that gap. If the gap has not been sufficiently reduced at present, what rate of progress and what continuing rates of progress should be expected? If substantial compliance but not total elimination of the achievement gaps is acceptable, should consideration be given to the sufficiency of the resource inputs that have been provided and to whether effective accountability systems are in place in defining that standard? Further, if sufficient instructional inputs have been provided and reasonable accountability mechanisms have been put in place and results still are not satisfactory, does the state have an obligation to provide "instruction plus"[100] and to deal with students' health, nutrition, and family support needs in order to afford all students a meaningful educational opportunity? Deciding these issues requires a sensitive weighing of constitutional principles and factual evidence regarding actual rates of student progress and student proficiency, the adequacy of funding levels, and the efficacy of programmatic reforms and accountability mechanisms that have been put into place.

The courts' responsibility to assess student performance raises even more profound issues. Both the majority and the dissenting justices in *Hancock* framed their arguments in terms of results on standardized test scores. But should a court rely solely on these results when critics have raised profound questions about the validity of these tests, whether they are aligned with the subject matter content required by the state's academic standards, and the extent to which test preparation and outright cheating distort the outcomes?[101] Moreover, in the constitutional context, don't courts have an obligation to determine whether students are receiving the full range of knowledge and skills they need to become capable citizens and competitive workers?[102] To do so, student outcomes need to be assessed broadly, not only in terms of basic reading and math skills, but also in regard to competencies like basic academic knowledge in all relevant subject areas, critical thinking and problem solving, preparation for skilled employment, social skills and work ethic, and citizenship and community responsibility.[103] Since testing and sampling techniques are available to assess these broader categories of skills, shouldn't courts consider them before deciding whether students are receiving the opportunity for a sound basic education?[104]

If the courts do not answer these questions—or induce the legislative and executive branches to enter into a dialogue with them to determine the answers no one will. Legislatures rarely undertake a serious policy review of the levels of performance that should and can be expected to result from a rigorous reform process; rather, they tend to set unrealistic achievement targets for political reasons. For example, Congress's definition of compliance for purposes of the No Child Left Behind Act is 100% of the students in the United States being proficient in meeting challenging state standards by 2014.[105] Even the prime sponsors of the bill know this goal is unattainable. Senator Edward M. Kennedy, one of the congressional architects of the law, recently acknowledged that "the idea of 100 percent proficiency is, in any legislation, not achievable."[106]

Consistent with the expectations of comparative institutional analysis, the sustained presence of the courts is needed to ensure that a proper focus on important and attainable outcome expectations is established for meeting constitutional expectations. Although courts should properly look to the legislatures and state education departments to define proficiency in terms of state content standards and to create the assessment mechanisms for determining how well students are progressing toward proficiency goals, it is the court's responsibility to ensure that legislators and administrators are asking the right questions and are providing well-considered, attainable, and constitutionally acceptable answers to them.

How long must a court retain jurisdiction to ensure that the legislative and executive branches have attempted to remedy constitutional deficiencies "in good faith" and have provided meaningful educational opportunities to all students "to the extent practicable"? Some practical guidelines are suggested by the concrete issues that arose in the *Hancock* case. At the least, a constitutional concept of what the state is expected to achieve must be articulated, some reasonable amount of progress consistent with the constitutional expectation must be demonstrated, and the state must be committed to ongoing processes like periodic assessments and cost analyses to ensure sustained implementation of the reforms. How long it will take to meet such benchmarks will, of course, depend on the complexity of the issues being considered and the degree of cooperation or resistance that a court encounters in a particular state. In some states, the criteria for success may be satisfied relatively quickly, while in others, some form of oversight might be needed for a much longer period of time.

The actual mechanisms that courts might use to maintain jurisdiction and oversight will, of course, vary, depending on practices and procedures in that state. In New Jersey, on many occasions, the Supreme Court retained jurisdiction, and the full court quickly considered the controversies that arose. In Arizona and Wyoming, the trial courts were given definitive authority to act promptly to resolve issues that arose during the remedial process, and in Arkansas, as I discussed in chapter 3, the Court appointed two special masters to carry out these responsibilities. Whatever the means permitted or preferred in a particular state, the important point is that the courts must make clear that there will be prompt and definitive judicial procedures to resolve any major disputes that may arise at any stage of the remedial process.

Retention of jurisdiction in sound basic education cases until basic reforms are implemented and prove effective also is a sensible use of judicial resources. In Arkansas, the state supreme court's decision to terminate jurisdiction after issuing its initial remedial order meant that the case had to be reopened and additional hearings held on three separate occasions when compliance issues arose. Such a scenario does not promote effective judicial oversight or efficiently utilize judicial resources. The Montana trial court judge, in rejecting a motion to terminate jurisdiction clearly understood this point: "The Court must be mindful to use its judicial resources wisely. At this stage of the proceedings, it does not appear to the Court to be a wise use of its resources to have the parties begin a new lawsuit that would take months, if not years, to prepare and weeks to try."[107]

In short, as James Ryan has explained, "The simple truth about funding litigation is that it requires continued court involvement in order to succeed over the long run." To ensure a successful remedy, in most situations, I would expect that ten to twenty years of technical judicial jurisdiction would be the norm.[108] Justice Greaney agreed with this estimate and explained why:

Ten years might be just a minimum; it might be 20 years, and the courts have to be prepared to do it long term. The mental health litigation cases lasted 15–20 years, fair housing cases lasted 15–20 years. These are structural societal problems and take a long time to fix. I think we can stay in and we should stay in, and if 10 years is what it takes, fine, if 20 years, fine and so forth.[109]

Although jurisdiction should be maintained for an extended period, courts do not need to be involved in active oversight activities most of that time. In Massachusetts, the court had maintained nominal jurisdiction over the prior *McDuffy* case for twelve years at the time it decided *Hancock,* as it had authorized a single judge "to retain jurisdiction to determine whether, within a reasonable time, appropriate legislative action has been taken."[110] The single judge (who happened to be Justice Greaney), for all of the years prior to the filing of the *Hancock* motion, had never actually been called upon to take any active role in implementing the prior order.[111] Entry of a *Hancock* order that would have delineated the final actions the state needed to take probably would have required the court to retain jurisdiction for a few more years in order to ensure that a cost study was undertaken (and commitments made to do so periodically in the future), that state education department funding was properly in place, and that adequate programs that were resulting in improved achievement in the focus districts were now in place.[112] These additional efforts would have allowed for a successful termination of the litigation.

Although the successful-remedies model may strike some readers as far-reaching, in effect, the model simply recommends that all courts undertake the commonsense compliance procedures that some courts have successfully utilized in the past. Almost no one can deny the need to formulate challenging standards, ensure adequate funding, develop and implement effective programs and accountability mechanisms, and achieve improved student performance. Upon reflection, most people would also probably agree that these critical reforms will not be carried out on a sustained basis without some extensive judicial oversight. In short, if we believe that children are constitutionally entitled to the opportunity to a sound basic education—and if we believe that the nation's economic vitality and democratic culture depend on a sound school system—adoption of the successful-remedies model is an obligation and not merely an option.

CHAPTER SIX

Confronting the Political Realities

I have argued in the preceding chapters that success in sound basic education cases is critical to achieving our national goals of equity and excellence in education. Effective remedies in these cases require the adoption of challenging standards, adequate funding, effective programmatic reforms and accountability systems, and improvements in student achievement as measured by accurate assessment systems. This proposed successful-remedies model draws on the actual experiences of numerous state courts that have fruitfully carried out many of the functions advocated by the model. No court has, however, yet implemented this model in full.

Although a reader who has followed my argument this far may agree that the theory and the design of the successful-remedies model respond aptly to all of the major implementation issues, a key question that undoubtedly will arise is whether in the end this approach can pass the reality test. In an era when "judicial activism" retains a negative connotation, can we credibly call for courts to oversee the implementation of an enormous educational reform process and to retain jurisdiction over a ten- to twenty-year period?

I believe this is a realistic role for courts, and I will discuss three main reasons for this.[1] First, this model calls for less active judicial involvement than meets the eye. Second, the comparative institutional approach upon which the model is built is consistent with the widely shared view among social scientists that effective social reform requires a functional division of labor among the three branches of government. Third, empirical evidence demonstrates that the productive colloquy among the branches that is at the core of this model has worked well at times and can function even more effectively if courts and educational advocates take specific actions to foster a supportive political culture. The rest of this chapter will elaborate on each of these points.

Extent of Judicial Involvement

Turning first to the issue of the extent of actual judicial involvement, although the successful-remedies model vests continuing oversight responsibilities in the state courts, it eschews the micromanaging and extensive judicial policy making that are the major concerns of critics of judicial activism. As discussed in the previous chapter, under the model, it is the state legislatures and state education departments that develop the substantive standards, undertake the cost analyses, develop the programmatic reforms and accountability systems, and assess the results. In essence, the court's' main responsibility is to make sure that the other branches do their job.

The frequency and the magnitude of actual judicial involvement in the implementation process will depend directly on the actions—or inactions—of the political branches in a particular state. Clear advance notice by the court of its expectations, its determination to enforce children's constitutional rights fully, and its articulation of a credible process for doing so may preempt the political grandstanding that often occurs when the judiciary's oversight role and its response to resistance are in doubt. The successful-remedies model, when presented as an effective and essential mechanism for actually achieving the state's commitment to eliminating achievement gaps, may "change perceptions of what education reform [can] be accomplished,"[2] and the active cooperation of the other branches of government that is needed to put the model into effect may be readily achieved.

Indeed, it is often the uncertainty about whether, when, and how courts will exercise their jurisdiction during the remedial process that creates delays and exacerbates confrontations. In New York, for example, after the legislature failed to meet the court's deadline for enacting reforms, it took the plaintiffs over two years to get a definitive final ruling from the state's highest court on the extent of the defendants' compliance obligations. During that time, political confrontations and media wars mounted, and no action whatsoever was taken by the legislature. But only a few months after a definitive ruling was issued by the court,[3] major reforms to the state funding system and an extensive new accountability system were adopted.

Lack of judicial resolve and absence of a clear strategy for judicial oversight are often what provoke resistance. Ohio provides an extreme example. There, over a period of five years, the Ohio Supreme Court had issued a series of decisions holding that the state was not providing its students a thorough and efficient education and had obtained partial compliance responses from the legislature. In 2002, after finding that recent legislative actions had still fallen short of constitutional requirements, the court reiterated that "the constitutional mandate must be met"[4] but then quickly made clear that it nevertheless would cease enforcing its own constitutional ruling.[5] Not surprisingly, for years, therefore, there was mounting political confrontation and no further serious attempts to reform Ohio's grossly inadequate school finance system.

If, instead of announcing to the other branches that it would *not* enforce the children's constitutional rights that it again held were being violated, the Ohio Supreme Court had expressed a resolve to see the process through to a successful conclusion, the legislature, which had partially complied, would likely have completed the process. Furthermore, the court's indication, consistent with comparative institutional analysis, that it would give great deference to good faith program implementation and accountability initiatives of the political branches may also have induced the plaintiffs to seek to work with the legislature and/or the administrative officials to deal with problems that arise rather than to resort to the courts.

Courts and Effective Social Reform

In contrast to those who fear an inordinate judicial influence on educational policy making, skepticism about the viability of the successful-remedies model may also come from those who claim that enhanced judicial oversight is likely to be unproductive because the courts, in fact, have little real impact on social reform. The best-known proponent of this view, Gerald Rosenberg, has argued that the widely held perception that courts have been "powerful, vigorous and potent proponents of change" is "an overstatement of the role of the courts, and a "mystification of the judiciary."[6] In particular, Rosenberg and other critics claim that *Brown* and other Supreme Court decisions have had minimal impact on the advancement of civil rights in the United States.[7]

Certainly it is true, as I have argued throughout this book, that courts alone cannot bring about major social change and that complementary supportive action by the executive and legislative branches is necessary for thoroughgoing reform to take hold. For example, as I discussed in chapter 4, effective enforcement of *Brown*'s desegregation mandate did not occur until Congress provided substantial federal funding to school districts to assist them in meeting the educational needs of economically disadvantaged students, and also empowered the federal Department of Health, Education and Welfare to cut off federal funding to any school district that discriminated on the basis of race, color, or national origin. Taken together, this carrot and stick approach meant that substantial amounts of federal funds had been made available, and these funds could also be withheld if schools districts were found to be violating the desegregation orders of the federal courts.[8]

Rosenberg's critique has engendered a vigorous response from social scientists who maintain, consistent with comparative institutional analysis, that although courts cannot on their own bring about major social change, their role in the process is essential. Michael McCann, in a major empirical analysis of the equal pay movement, has demonstrated how the "indirect effects" of litigation and the legal discourse that courts provide define and advance social reform agendas.[9] Kevin J. McMahon and Michael Paris, in a close analysis of the Montgomery bus boycott, showed that Rosenberg's assumption that the *Brown* decision had little to do with inspiring and maintaining the Montgomery bus boycott was wrong, and that the vision provided by the Supreme Court's decision in *Brown* was a sine qua non for both the initiation and successful conclusion of this landmark civil rights event.[10] And writing specifically as a "rejoinder to Rosenberg," Douglas S. Reed has described the "meaningful effects [state] courts have had on school finance.[11]

In short, Rosenberg is attacking a straw man when he faults the courts for not singlehandedly bringing about dramatic social changes. He "neglects the repetitive, dialogic nature of the interactions between courts, legislatures, agencies, and other social processes, as well as the political synergy that some litigation engenders."[12] Actual social reform processes necessarily involve dynamic interactions among all three branches. From this perspective, the successful-remedies model I am advocating is merely a specific mechanism for more successfully organizing that dialogue in the context of implementing remedies in sound basic education cases.

Rosenberg, despite his generally skeptical view of the role of the courts, does acknowledge that under certain circumstances courts can be effectual. Among these "conditions for court efficacy" is that "courts may effectively produce significant social reform by providing leverage, or a shield, cover, or excuse, for persons crucial to implementation who are *willing to act*."[13] The state courts have been effective in many sound basic education litigations precisely because these conditions, which rarely occurred in the major desegregation cases, do often prevail in this sector. Matthew Bosworth, who undertook an empirical study of fiscal equity and education adequacy cases in Kentucky, Texas, and North Dakota, which he deemed to be largely successful, concluded that state courts can be effective catalysts for reform because they provide "a shield" that allows legislators "to solve the problems in the educational system without the usual political constraints, specifically those against raising taxes."[14]

Most legislators, in fact, expect the courts to oversee their response to a finding of unconstitutionality. Although a few legislators may grandstand and rail against the court, the majority, even if they originally opposed the position that the court has now endorsed, tend to accept their responsibility under established constitutional separation of powers principles to accept the court's judicial review role. As Arkansas representative Joyce Elliott explained,

[T]here were some who thought the court should absolutely go away. But as a body, we recognized, whether we liked it or not, that the court had a right to be in this. There was an expectation that they would hold our feet to the fire once they had said that this whole process was unconstitutional. In fact, I can't imagine them not doing that, considering our history of not having funded education. It would have been a travesty if they had not returned once there was a problem.[15]

Bosworth similarly noted that in North Dakota, "nearly all state policymakers concerned in any way with education paid attention to the Court ruling and took it seriously"[16] and that in Kentucky, "once the Court decision was issued, it was very clear that the legislature would have to make some kind of response; massive resistance was never considered."[17] Although there is an underlying racial component in many (but not all) sound basic education litigations, opposition is less intense because the public and their political representatives recognize that "state court interventions in school finance [are] the result of real problems within a state's educational system . . . Typically, lawmakers will regret that the policy problem has been 'legalized,' but they will not deny the existence of the problem or attribute the judicial decision to the meddling of 'outside interests.'"[18]

Moreover, in contrast to the overwhelmingly resistant attitudes toward school desegregation of most southern whites at the time the Supreme Court issued the *Brown* decision, public opinion in regard to fiscal equity and sound basic education cases tends to support in principle, rather than oppose, the types of changes courts seek to implement. This means that the courts' role in these cases is to harness and enhance generally supportive public attitudes rather than to try to reshape highly resistant public opinion. State and national polls have revealed a consistent willingness of large majorities of the American public (59–75 percent) to pay higher taxes for education, especially if there is a reasonable expectation that the money will be spent well.[19] People also are becoming sensitized to the enormous detrimental implications of the growing gap between the rich and the poor in our society.[20]

Political opposition to education finance reform is also lessened when the issues occur in the adequacy rather than the equity mode. "Leveling up" basic educational spending, rather than capping or recapturing high levels of expenditure in affluent districts, is a significant factor in building public and political support for reforming state funding formulas. As William H. Clune has explained,

> History has demonstrated that . . . recapture of local tax revenues from local districts . . . has been the single greatest practical problem with judicial decrees of fiscal neutrality. . . . Wealthier districts have proven the most determined foes of fiscal neutrality in constitutional litigation. Much of the delay and uncertainty in reaching stable legislative solutions has revolved around the rich districts.[21]

This is not to say, of course, that the state courts encounter no resistance to their decrees in sound basic education cases. There has been substantial opposition to the state courts' stances in New Jersey, New Hampshire, Kansas, and a number of other states. What is significant in these situations, however, is that, when the courts in these states stood firm and insisted on constitutional compliance, ultimately they have prevailed. One of the most dramatic examples occurred recently in Kansas where, as Richard E. Levy explained in an article that was quite appropriately entitled "Gunfight at the K–12 Corral: Legislative vs. Judicial Power in the Kansas School Finance Litigation,"

> Following the court's decision in Montoy III, the Governor called the Legislature back for a special session devoted to school finance. During the session, many legislators (and the Attorney General) sharply criticized the court's decision. Of particular concern was the court's statement that the Legislature "shall" provide a specified dollar amount, which opponents of the court's decision regarded as a usurpation of the Legislature's exclusive authority to make appropriations. Various constitutional amendments were proposed in response, including amendments that would prohibit the courts from ordering or redirecting appropriations, prevent judicial enforcement of school funding provisions in the Constitution, and change the manner of selecting judges. Some legislative leaders indicated that they would not address the funding issues until a constitutional amendment was approved for submission to the voters . . . Emotions were running high as the special session dragged on into July—past the court's deadline—and the Legislature appeared to be at an impasse. The state requested an extension, which was denied, and on July 2, 2005, the court entered an order directing the parties to appear on July 8, 2005, to show cause why the court should not enjoin the expenditure [and thereby shut down all public schools statewide] . . . The Legislature recessed for the July 4 holiday with no solution in sight. When legislators returned from the recess, however, the logjam had broken. By the time of the show-cause hearing, a funding proposal that met the minimum amount indicated by the court (S.B. 3) was approved, and efforts to amend the Constitution fell short. At the show-cause hearing, the court concluded that the Legislature had satisfied the mandate of Montoy III for the coming year, but retained jurisdiction in light of the need for further action in the following legislative session.[22]

Despite Alexander Hamilton's oft-quoted expectation in Federalist No. 78 that the judiciary would always be the least powerful branch because it "has no influence over the sword or the purse," when the moral suasion of their principled stances does not induce compliance, the courts' ability to impose significant sanctions has repeatedly overcome

resistance from the other branches. Courts have the power to find public officials in civil contempt for failing to comply with judicial orders
and to fine or even jail these officials until compliance is forthcoming.[23]
As illustrated by the Kansas example, they also can mandate the clos-
ing down of the entire state public school system until the unconstitutionality of the state's education finance system has been cured. In addition to the Kansas Supreme Court, courts in at least three other states,
New Jersey, Arizona, and Texas, have threatened similar funding shut-
downs, and each time that threat has resulted in prompt compliance by
the other branches.[24]

In sum then, the combination of widespread respect for the state
courts' responsibility to enforce affirmative constitutional rights to a basic quality education and the effective compliance sanctions the courts
can wield when necessary provides courts with both the carrots and the
sticks they need to carry out the kind of limited but muscular judicial
oversight they require to implement the successful schools model. The
greatest remedial challenge that courts have experienced in practice,
however, has been sustaining constitutional compliance over time.

Fostering a Supportive Political Culture

Although there is considerable underlying public support for constitutional compliance when the issue is brought to the fore, that support
tends to be episodic. In most states, the usual political processes tend
to revert to inequitable funding patterns largely because of the domi-
nance of affluent suburban districts in state legislatures.[25] Their interest in maximizing funding for their constituents—combined in many circumstances with an underlying racist resistance to providing substantial
support to urban school districts with majority nonwhite populations—
tends over time to cause court-ordered fiscal equity reforms to unravel.
Thus, when it comes to funding for public education, there is an "inequitable equilibrium" resulting from the distribution of political power in
most states. According to Jeffrey Metzler, who coined this term,

> [W]hile an outside event, such as an adverse court ruling, may temporarily
> upset this equilibrium, in many cases the system will gradually return to its
> equilibrium point, or something close to it. Thus, while a state may change
> its basic approach to education funding in response to outside pressure, the

legislature often manipulates that approach in order to restore the previous equilibrium.[26]

Such reversions to inequitable financing systems have occurred in a number of states like Washington and Kansas.[27] A related problem, which, as discussed in the previous chapter, has occurred in states like Massachusetts and Kentucky, is that state funding levels that reasonably support a sound basic education erode over time to inadequate levels because of inflation or appropriation reductions.

To achieve lasting reforms, Metzler argues that "courts and reformers must dig deeper, and they must focus on changing the political dynamics that perpetuate the inequitable equilibrium of school finance."[28] In other words, to achieve permanent constitutional compliance in a fiscal equity or sound basic education case, courts need to consider not only the legal and structural features of the remedial decree but also the broader political and cultural context that will influence the long-range implementation of the decree.

As discussed in chapter 4, an important aspect of the court's proper role from a comparative institutional perspective is its principled perspective on major values issues and its ability to communicate "the public values of the Constitution."[29] By maintaining jurisdiction over an extended period of time and, during that time, repeatedly articulating the relevant constitutional values, courts can help influence public attitudes and positively shape the direction of the political culture. As Alexander M. Bickel noted, their "insulation and the marvelous mystery of time give courts the capacity to appeal to men's better natures, to call forth their aspirations, which may have been forgotten in the moment's hue and cry."[30] The courts' conscious use of this important educative function can help immeasurably in creating a supportive political culture for constitutional compliance. As Judge Rosenblatt of the New York Court of Appeals recognized, "Our order was out there. There were signals to the political branches that this was warranted and that the judges were not simply issuing a decree that is pie-in-the-sky, unrealistic, or arrogant. Then the public support began to mount as it should."[31]

The U.S. Supreme Court and many of the lower federal courts clearly had such an educative function in mind during the early years of the desegregation era. The moving language of the *Brown* decision, with its ringing statements that "segregation in education itself results in the Negro children, as a class, receiving educational opportunities which are substantially inferior to those available to white children . . . "[32] and that "Separate educational facilities are inherently unequal"[33] were plainly intended to raise the level of political discourse and to positively influence political and social attitudes. Although the Court's decision in *Brown II* to allow desegregation initially to proceed with "all deliberate speed"[34] allowed many southern states to delay implementation, by the early 1960s the Court did decide that "[t]he time for deliberate speed has run out . . . [t]he burden on a school board today is to come forward with a plan that promises realistically to work, and promises realistically to work *now*."[35] Thus, the Supreme Court's language and guidance to lower courts underscored the urgency of overcoming the initial resistance to the desegregation mandate.

The federal trial courts were also clearly aware of their need to influence the local political culture in order to obtain compliance, and they often devised creative remedial mechanisms like involving citizens as active participants in developing and implementing the decree in order to do so. As the judge in the Lansing, Michigan, case put it,

> The court recognizes that the issues involved are of particular interest and vital significance to all Lansing area citizens. Therefore, this opinion is aimed at communicating the factual and legal bases for the court's decision, not only to the parties and reviewing courts, but also to the community. For it is the hope of the court that a sincere civic involvement in implementing the terms of this decision will help improve the school system and strengthen the community, for citizens of all races, and their children.[36]

The courts' efforts during the initial years of the desegregation era did clearly affect the hearts and minds of citizens in the South and throughout the country. For example, from 1954 to 1963, the percentage of white southern parents objecting to sending their children to a school with some black children declined from 61 to 15.[37] Over time, however, the U.S. Supreme Court retreated from its efforts to influence public attitudes on issues of racial integration. This retrenchment culminated in the 2007 decision in the *Seattle* litigation,[38] discussed in the introduction of this book, which unfortunately represents a use of the educative power of the court to support values that undermine, rather than further, the goal of effective racial integration in the schools.

Some have argued that it was precisely the Supreme Court's unwillingness to communicate a consistent message of support for school desegregation and to encourage continuing active jurisdiction of these cases in the lower courts that eventually undermined possibilities for sustained large-scale racial integration.[39] In any event, state courts involved with fiscal equity and sound basic education issues are not faced with the intense level of racial animosity and the deep-seated resistance to a mandate for revolutionary social change that many of the federal courts confronted with school desegregation. The state courts can and should have a more substantial and more sustained impact on shaping the political culture on these questions.

The fact that the prime educational policy of the nation and of most states, which was enacted with broad public support, is to create an educational system that will enable all students to meet challenging academic standards makes the courts an ally rather than an opponent of the policy stances that the legislature and most of the public want to pursue. A strong judicial stance at the remedy stage of a sound basic education case can, therefore, constitute a clarion call that gives constitutional stature to this broadly supported public policy direction, and provides a principled counterweight to the particular interests that push toward a reversion to inequitable equilibriums. The successful-remedies model can become a map of the steps that need to be taken to achieve these important goals to which the state is already firmly committed.

The weighty support for thoroughgoing reform articulated by the Kentucky Supreme Court and the dramatic Kentucky Education Reform Act reforms that flowed from the case have helped build a deep-seated supportive culture in Kentucky that is still evident today, twenty years after the court's decision in the case. As Susan Perkins Weston and Robert Sexton have noted, continuation of the court-initiated reforms is now a deeply rooted bipartisan value:

> In the new emphasis on schools that are not on track for 2014 . . . it is worth noting that the leading voices of concern about those weaknesses come from a state Board of Education appointed entirely by our Republican governor, based on their concern to ensure success as defined in regulations adopted almost entirely by previous Boards appointed by Democrats.[40]

As discussed above, although courts have an important role to play, they cannot singlehandedly bring about and maintain substantial social reform. Clearly, "the long-term viability of court-ordered changes [also] depends on local constituency support."[41] Continuing advocacy for full implementation of the reforms associated with a court decree by education groups and supportive civic organizations is also critically necessary. Kentucky's sustained commitment to fiscal equity and education adequacy was substantially fueled by the ongoing advocacy over more than two decades of the Prichard Committee, a blue ribbon citizens' education advocacy group. It and other educational, civic, and business groups have supported "ongoing public dialogue about the relationship between a richer civic life, a more vibrant economy and proper investment in learning for all children."[42] As Weston and Sexton, leaders of this group, have explained, "Active public engagement maintains a vigorous public discourse on the importance of deep investment in education. The same engagement demonstrates that strong political forces are ready to push for that investment to continue.[43]

Significantly, in addition to Kentucky, extensive public engagement processes have occurred in many of the other states where notable successes at the remedy stage of fiscal equity and sound basic education cases have been achieved. For example, in the state of Washington, the legislature's enactment of the Basic Education Act in 1977, even before the appeal of the sound basic education case had been decided by the state supreme court, was heavily influenced by the statewide activities of a grassroots citizens group, the Citizens for Fair School Funding.[44] Arizona's adoption of an extensive capital funding scheme followed an innovative statewide education finance summit to which the State Superintendent of Public Instruction invited fourteen legislators as well as representatives of fifty education, business, and parent organizations, shortly after the state supreme court's decision was announced, as well as an ongoing, active lobbying campaign by the plaintiffs and their attorneys.[45]

My colleagues and I at the Campaign for Fiscal Equity (CFE) in New York initiated a major statewide public engagement campaign to build broad-based support for reform when we began to prepare for the trial in the case. We were concerned that any remedial order the court might ultimately issue on behalf of New York City's public school students would encounter substantial resistance from suburban and upstate legislators who traditionally had blocked efforts to provide more funding to the predominantly minority New York City schools. We decided, therefore, to reach out, using a public engagement process, to school boards, unions, and business and civic groups throughout the state. Our aim was both to forge a statewide coalition for reform and to neutralize to the extent possible active resistance to equitable remedies from the affluent districts. Because I think that this public engagement campaign had a significant positive impact on both the outcome of the court case and the subsequent adoption of far-reaching reform legislation, I will describe the process in some detail.[46]

Public Engagement in New York State

The public engagement process was initiated shortly after the Court of Appeals issued its 1995 *CFE I* order that denied the state's motion to dismiss and set the case down for trial. To help prepare for the trial and to begin to think strategically about possible remedies, we initiated a series of three all-day conferences for our core New York City constituents. Representatives of approximately one hundred education advocacy, parent, and community groups participated in these events.

The first major issue we considered was whether the goal of the litigation should be strict dollar equity in spending, which could require substantial fund transfers between rich and poor districts, or specific educational improvements for city students, without regard for the level of expenditure elsewhere. The main themes that dominated the discussion were the philosophical concern for the equal worth of every student, the fiscal concern that raising new resources might meet taxpayer resistance, and the political concern that redistributing funds among school districts might provoke major confrontations between the city and the surrounding suburbs. In the end, despite the political and philosophical appeal of the equity arguments, the group overwhelmingly endorsed an adequacy approach that eschewed a "Robin Hood remedy" and sought to increase funding for New York and other underfunded districts throughout the state, while endorsing the maintenance of current funding levels for other districts.

This key strategic decision allowed the public engagement process to broaden into a full statewide dialogue the next year. CFE worked to build coalitions with residents of urban, rural, and suburban districts throughout the state. This entailed promoting sustained conversations about directions for reform, not only with residents of poor urban and rural areas, who constituted CFE's natural allies, but also with residents of affluent communities whose political support (or at least attenuated opposition) we deemed to be an essential part of the political equation.

Accordingly, CFE's statewide public engagement campaign commenced the next year with a series of sixteen forums held in all parts of the state, which were organized with the assistance of the statewide school boards association, the statewide teachers organization, the League of Women Voters, the Urban League, the state Parent Teacher Association, and other major statewide and local educational and civic organizations. CFE explicitly invited the participants at these events to help develop the specific proposal for defining a sound basic education that CFE would present to the trial court.

The definition of a sound basic education that CFE presented to the court, and that was largely adopted in *CFE II*, resulted from the public engagement process,[47] as did CFE's basic remedial strategies. CFE's public engagement methodology was based on the principle that there were no predetermined positions and that final positions should be developed by maximizing consensus through ongoing discussion and refinement of initial positions. The emphasis was on finding positions that virtually all participants could support or that, at the least, they could live with. Participants were also told that by participating in these public engagement events, they were not necessarily endorsing the resulting documents or positions or CFE's position in the litigation.

The expanded series of forums in later years focused on formula reform and accountability issues, and sponsorship was expanded to include additional statewide and local groups, and especially business organizations. Particularly significant was the willingness of the statewide Business Council to become a cosponsor, even though the group was on record as opposing plaintiffs' position in the case (primarily because of a fear that a plaintiff victory would lead to higher taxes); the Council decided to join in the discussions because it had concluded that plaintiffs would probably succeed in court and that, therefore, it would be in its interest to have a role in the discussions about remedies and formula revisions. It challenged CFE's stated commitment to open dialogue at these events by insisting that voucher alternatives, which CFE's board opposed, be specified as one of the remedial alternatives that would be considered at the forums. CFE did agree to this condition.[48]

By explicitly disavowing a Robin Hood remedy, and assuring residents of the affluent suburbs that the CFE case would not take resources away from their schools or threaten the quality of their children's education, the public engagement forums held in these areas allowed the participants to consider whether they had a moral obligation to help minority students in the inner cities obtain the kind of quality education their own children were already receiving. More often than not, the response was a vigorous interracial discussion of how city schools could actually be improved and what accountability methods could be developed to ensure that additional state funding was used effectively.

The success of this strategy is illustrated by the strong media support that CFE's public engagement process garnered, not only in New York City, but also in affluent suburban areas like Westchester County. The editorial position of the Westchester *Journal News* was that

> This "public engagement process" is an exciting one. It includes hundreds of parents, teachers, administrators, advocates and representatives of civic, religious, business and labor groups from across the state exchanging ideas on critical issues, including how funding reform can dovetail with state Board of Regents' effort to raise academic standards. . . . The plan . . . is to offer participants an opportunity to directly influence reform positions [CFE] will present to the court. That in itself is refreshing. After years of watching state officials . . . avoid this admittedly difficult but vital area of reform, it's high time the fiscal inequities of the education system were addressed. And the fact that the public isn't being bypassed is heartening.[49]

CFE's lawsuit, occurring in the media capital of the country, generated an enormous amount of interest and media coverage. Trial developments, the initial decision, the appeals, and negotiations in the legislature resulted in hundreds of news stories, editorials, and columns, as well as dozens of television and radio interviews, call-in shows, and commentary. CFE consciously used the media's interest in these confrontations to focus attention on its public engagement activities and its commitment to a principled statewide solution to the problem of funding inequities. CFE also actively promoted press awareness of public engagement events and encouraged attendance by the media. Press advisories were issued in advance, and meetings were arranged as often as possible with the editorial boards of local newspapers and/or television stations the day before the event.

After the court issued its basic liability decision in 2003, CFE organized the statewide Sound Basic Education Task Force to develop remedial proposals regarding cost analyses, funding reform, and accountability, each of the remedial issues that the court had directed the state to consider. About forty-five statewide organizations, including all of the major education, parent, business, and union groups interested in education issues, as well as representatives of the state education department, the New York City Department of Education, and the state school boards association, took part in these deliberations. The governor had appointed an official commission to develop recommendations to respond to the court order, but CFE took the position that the membership of the official commission was not representative of the groups that had strong interests in these issues, and it formed the task force to ensure that the full range of necessary issues would be considered and that there would be broad and diverse input into the process.[50]

The commission's official recommendations, although largely accepted by the governor, were rejected by the legislature. Because this impasse meant that the court's deadline for compliance was not met, CFE immediately brought the compliance issues back to the courts. The trial court quickly appointed a panel of three special masters to consider both the commission's recommendations and the proposals drafted by the task force. The trial court accepted the special masters' recommendation that the actual cost of a sound basic education in New York City would require $5.6 billion in increased funding, to be phased in over four years, a finding that was consistent with the task force's recommendation.[51] This position was largely affirmed by the intermediate appeals court, but was ultimately rejected by the New York Court of Appeals, which in its *CFE III* decision in 2006 held that "the constitutional floor" would be $1.93 billion, the low point in the range of cost figures the commission had recommended.[52]

The interplay of the politics of social reform with the judicial process in the actual outcome of a litigation was well illustrated by the next major development in the CFE situation. In the 2007–2008 Education Budget and Reform Act, the legislature did not adopt the Court of Appeals' minimal "constitutional floor" appropriation, but instead it adopted a funding increase for New York City of $5.4 billion (and an additional $4 billion for high-needs districts elsewhere in the state) that was consistent with the recommendations of the task force's cost study. In addition, the legislature adopted some of the formula reforms the task force had recommended and an extensive Contract for Excellence accountability plan that was, in part, based on the task force's accountability proposal.[53]

The fact that the new governor, Eliot Spitzer, was a Democrat and that he replaced George Pataki, the Republican governor, who had vehemently opposed CFE's position from the first, was obviously a major factor in this outcome. Interestingly, however, Spitzer had been the attorney general who had led the state's vigorous opposition to the CFE plaintiffs for the previous eight years, and political pressure from CFE and its statewide allies clearly played an important role in the position he took on the CFE remedy. During the gubernatorial campaign (which concluded shortly *before* issuance of the Court of Appeals' final CFE III decision), Spitzer had been pressed to take a position on the CFE funding issue. He agreed to support the trial court's $5.6 billion remedy and ultimately kept that pledge, even after the Court of Appeals endorsed a substantially lower number.

CFE's experience demonstrates that public engagement activities undertaken by plaintiffs and/or education advocacy organizations[54] can significantly influence a state's politics and its political culture. Even though Governor Pataki had consistently opposed CFE's position in court, while the case was pending and even before the court's final ruling, he had supported substantial increases in education funding because of the strong political pressures for equity and adequacy that had been unleashed by the case. School funding was a major issue in the gubernatorial and legislative campaigns throughout this period.[55]

Although courts obviously should not take political stances in determining constitutional liability, once they have found a constitutional violation and issued a remedial decree, they have a strong interest in promoting implementation of their order, and they should take note of the positive impact that public engagement dialogues can have on effective implementation of their remedial decrees. Courts should take appropriate steps, consistent with their constitutional role, to promote positive public engagement dialogues. For example, state courts in sound basic education litigations can encourage public participation in the remedial hearings that they hold to the maximum extent possible. As Bob Wise, former governor of West Virginia commented, "There was merit to the many hearings of Judge Recht in West Virginia because it gave the public a chance to understand what it was about."[56] Existing rules regarding involvement of amici curiae should be liberally applied and new procedures developed that will allow courts both to maximize the information available to them on the remedial issues under consideration and, at the same time, to engage the interested public in understanding and supporting the court's ultimate decisions.

Some state courts have devised new and creative mechanisms for directly involving the public—and the legislative and executive branches—in a positive constitutional dialogue on compliance issues that may arise. A noteworthy example is the procedure adopted by the New Hampshire Supreme Court in the *Claremont* litigation. It issued an invitation to "the public, legislators, members of the bar and anyone who wants to comment on the plan to do so."[57] These comments needed to be in writing, but they did not have to be in a technical legal form. The court selected a group of lawyers and nonlawyers to present oral argument from the list of those who had submitted comments.[58]

Another significant example of an innovative judicial mechanism for promoting broad constitutional dialogue on sound basic education issues occurred in the remedial phase of the *Rose* case in Kentucky. There, the trial court drew upon extensive expert testimony and a post-trial amicus brief filed by the Prichard Committee, which had brought to the trial judge's attention the significant national education reform initiatives, including the emphasis on educational standards. After issuing his liability decision, the trial court judge postponed his decision on the appropriate remedy for six months. During that time, a select committee he had appointed held five hearings around the state—one of which was attended by the governor and all of which were covered extensively by the press—and then enumerated five student outcomes that it believed would constitute a sound basic education. The select committee's recommendations were substantially adopted by the trial court, and their key elements were also included in the final decision of the state supreme court.[59]

Sustained judicial oversight is also important for countering the "inequitable equilibrium of education finance" and ensuring long-term constitutional compliance. Recent events in New York illustrate this point. Although the state's political culture was markedly influenced by CFE's public engagement process, the Court of Appeals' abrupt termination of its jurisdiction in 2006 undermined the prospects for enduring adherence to constitutional requirements. Despite the major legislative breakthrough that was achieved in 2007, formula reform was far from complete. One region of the state (Long Island), whose solidly Republican bloc of state senators had extensive influence in the Senate majority's caucus, was able to obtain an exception to general reform principles of the new reform formula and maintain its traditional "share" of total state aid. Thus, although funding levels were substantially raised, the "inequitable equilibrium" quickly began to reassert itself.

The economic recession that began in 2008 is also posing a substantial threat to continued constitutional compliance. Although the Budget and Reform Act had delineated a four-year phase-in period with precise amounts of increased aid per year pledged to students in New York City and fifty-five other high-needs districts around the state, when the economy began to sour during the second year of the phase-in, New York City cut its contribution for that year, and no one was able to hold the mayor and the chancellor accountable for failing to keep their funding commitments. As the economy faltered further and as year three approached, the governor[60] was able to propose cutting the actual funding level below constitutional minimums and deferring the phase-in of the promised increases for another four years, without having to justify these radical challenges to constitutional compliance in any judicial forum.

Although some accommodation must be made to severe economic circumstances, drastic budget cuts are currently being implemented in New York and in many other states with little principled consideration for constitutional mandates or children's deep needs for educational continuity. The substantial federal aid that has resulted from the American Recovery and Reinvestment Act of 2009 has mitigated the immediate impact of these cuts, but at the time of this writing the possibilities for continued progress toward assuring students' rights to a sound basic education in New York are in peril.

Whether or not the New York Court of Appeals, had it retained jurisdiction, would have countermanded any of the actions of the mayor, the governor, or the legislature, the mere availability of judicial review would have had an impact on planning and negotiations; the court's active guidance might even have been sought and appreciated in dealing with the unprecedented demands of the 2008–2009 budget crisis. Plaintiffs, of course, always have the option of returning to court by initiating a new case, but the reality—as all of the political players know—is that trial procedures and appeals in New York consume years, not months, and the current budget crisis likely would be long gone before the court would have even been in a position to weigh in on the decisions.

Conclusion

Not only in New York but in many of the other states whose highest courts have held that large numbers of students are being denied their constitutional right to a quality basic education, the courts have terminated their jurisdiction before they have ensured that appropriate remedies are in place and that lasting constitutional compliance has been achieved. Since "for most practical purposes, remedies control the value of constitutional rights,"[61] millions of students in these states continue to be denied the meaningful educational opportunities to which they are entitled. Judges must, of course, be sensitive to separation of powers precepts, but the fact is that if the courts are not committed to completing the job of establishing and sustaining meaningful educational opportunities in education adequacy cases, the other branches are not likely to do so on their own.

The state courts have already strongly entered the fray by initiating and advancing an important constitutional dialogue with the executive and legislative branches on formulating and ensuring children's right to a sound basic education. The judges have not dictated these constitutional concepts from on high or created educational reforms on their own. The extensive interchanges between the courts and the political branches in developing substantive standards for academic achievement and effective techniques for determining the cost of a sound basic education exemplify the effective and proper role that courts can and should pursue in "interpreting our shared understandings as they are expressed through our institutions, laws and social practices . . . "[62] If the standards-based reforms that are at the core of our national educational policy and have been universally extolled as being critical for maintaining our democratic institutions and the nation's competitive position in the global economy are to succeed, the courts must continue to pursue the new pathways they have opened up and insist that reforms the states have instituted to provide meaningful opportunities to all of their students are effectively implemented and the promised results actually achieved.

The successful-remedies model proposed in this book essentially adopts the best practices that many state courts have already put into practice and combines them with the insights of comparative institutional analysis to promote the degree of effective cooperation among the three branches of government that is necessary to meet the nation's broadly accepted educational objectives. It does so by establishing clear expectations that in order to comply with the constitutional mandate to provide all students a quality basic education, legislatures and executive agencies must (1) develop and implement challenging academic content and proficiency standards; (2) provide adequate funding to all schools; (3) put in place effective programs and accountability systems; and (4) demonstrate that student achievement has improved to the extent practicable.

On their own, courts cannot achieve the thoroughgoing reforms that are needed to provide all students a basic quality education. But by issuing comprehensive remedial decrees and overseeing constitutional compliance, they can make sure that the other branches do their jobs. Moreover, through their educative role in promoting the values of their state constitution, and by encouraging positive public dialogues, courts can also help move the political culture in a compliant direction. In some states, judges have not been able to maximize their potential clout for overseeing constitutional compliance because judicial experiences at the remedial stage are not regularly reported and, to a large extent, each court has to reinvent the wheel in developing a strategy, step by step, as it deals with remedial challenges as they arise. For that reason, I have tried in this book to encapsulate the positive precedents that have emerged in remedial implementation in states throughout the country over the past few decades and to provide an empirically based strategic perspective for courts—and governors, legislators, and the general public—to consider in future situations.

A lot is riding on how conscientiously the courts are willing to carry out this constitutional responsibility. Even opponents of judicial intervention in these cases agree, "The principled cause of [sound basic education] is noble in character."[63] They claim that courts lack the legitimacy or the capacity to take on these tasks, but experience demonstrates that, unless the courts clearly articulate the public values of the state constitution and ensure that the legislative and executive branches fully carry out their responsibilities to put those values into effect, the nation's stated commitment to equity and excellence and the critical national goals of providing meaningful educational opportunities for all children to meet the global economic challenges will not be met. Although, at times, issues in these cases can involve difficult "political thickets," ultimately judges must accept the fact that, as the U.S. Supreme Court held in analogous circumstances, "a denial of constitutionally protected rights demands judicial protection; our oath and our office require no less of us."[64]

A Separation of Powers Dialogue

The following discussion on the role of the courts in "sound basic education" or education adequacy cases took place at the symposium entitled "Equal Educational Opportunity: What Now?" convened by the Campaign for Educational Equity at Teachers College, Columbia University, on November 13, 2007.

The participants in this conversation were

John M. Greaney, associate justice, Supreme Judicial Court of Massachusetts. Judge Greaney has been on the court for twenty years and participated in both of the Massachusetts education adequacy decisions, voting with the majority of the court to uphold the position of the plaintiffs in *McDuffy v. Secretary*, 615 N.E. 2d 516 (Mass. 1993), and dissenting from the court's decision to dismiss the compliance issues raised by *Hancock v. Commissioner of Education*, 822 N.E. 2d 1134 (Mass. 2005).

Albert M. Rosenblatt, former judge, New York Court of Appeals. Judge Rosenblatt participated in *Campaign for Fiscal Equity v. State of New York*, 801 N.E.2d 326 (N.Y. 2003) ("CFE II"), in which he was the only judge appointed by defendant Governor George Pataki to uphold plaintiffs' position. In *Campaign for Fiscal Equity v. State of New York*, 861 N.E.2d 50 (N.Y. 2006) ("CFE III"), he joined the majority that provided plaintiffs partial relief for their compliance claims but wrote a separate concurring decision. Judge Rosenblatt reached mandatory retirement age and left the court of appeals in December 2006. He is now counsel to the firm of McCabe and Mack in Poughkeepsie, New York, and also teaches at the New York University Law School.

Joyce Elliott, former chair of the education committee, Arkansas House of Representatives. Elliott served three terms as a representative from Little Rock and participated in formulating the legislative response to the compliance orders of the Arkansas Supreme Court in *Lake View School District No. 25 v. Huckabee*, 144 S.W.3d 741 (Ark. 2004), 189 S.W.3d (Ark. 2004), 210 S.W.3d 28 (Ark. 2005), No. 01-836 Ark LEXIS 776 (Ark. 2005). Term limit requirements compelled her retirement from the house of representatives in 2006. She is now a state senator from District 33, Pulaski County, Arkansas.

Robert Wise, former governor of West Virginia. Governor Wise served nine terms as a member of the U.S. House of Representatives and subsequently served as governor of West Virginia from 2002 to 2005. In that capacity, he signed the final papers that terminated the long-pending West Virginia adequacy litigation, *Pauley v. Kelly* 225 S.E.2d 859 (W.Va. 1979) in 2003. Governor Wise is now the executive director of the Alliance for Excellent Education.

The moderator was Jay Worona, General Counsel, New York State School Boards Association.

Q. Please describe your personal involvement with education adequacy litigations.

JUDGE GREANEY: I am the only judge still on the Supreme Judicial Court who participated in both the *McDuffy* case, where we got into the business of education, and the *Hancock* case, where we got out of the business. The *McDuffy* case was essentially an interpretation of a single word in the Massachusetts constitution, which was written by John Adams, not Sam Adams (Sam was making beer while John wrote our Constitution). The magistrates were instructed to "cherish education" throughout the commonwealth at the time, so the analysis came down to the meaning of the word "'cherish.'" Was it mandatory or aspirational? If it was aspirational, as you all know who work in this field, it doesn't mean much. It bespeaks a hope, and we will just say to the legislature and the executive, "Do the best you can." If the word was mandatory, courts can get involved, issue judgments, enforce them, and consider broad relief. In the *McDuffy* case, we decided it was mandatory. If you ever want to read a wonderful bit of history, read the decision; we looked at dictionaries, books, and sources from 1780 to figure out the meaning of the somewhat ambiguous word.

We then turned the case over to a single justice. We're somewhat unique in Massachusetts because we sit as appellate judges at the top of the system and also as trial judges. When we do a blockbuster decision, such as the education decision, or gay marriage, which we did a few years ago, we turn the case over to one of our seven judges, the single justice acting as the trial judge, and say, "Okay, you fix it." In the *McDuffy* case, the single justice didn't have to fix it because the legislature and executive were poised at that time to pass the Education Reform Act. They passed the act and appropriated, over the long term, somewhere between 10 and 13 billion dollars.

I want to stress one important thing. In Massachusetts, we are unelected judges. We serve until age seventy. So if there's any backlash, which there really wasn't over *McDuffy*, we cannot be removed. They can do certain other things, but they can't get rid of us. I'll fast forward to the *Hancock* case, which originated in the early 2000s. A new set of plaintiffs came back and said, "*McDuffy*'s been helpful, the legislature has been helpful, but it's not working in a lot of our school districts. We need another look at this." I then was the single justice to whom the *Hancock* case had been assigned, and I picked one of our trial judges to do a study of this issue, actually to hold a trial. This is one unique thing that courts can do that other agencies cannot. We can hold actual trials, take evidence, and make findings of fact that are unassailable, if they're based on the evidence.

This judge compared four "focus" school districts that were in tough shape with other "comparison" districts that were in pretty good shape. She found disastrous results in the focus districts. The key fault was with the foundation budget, which she said had to be reformulated. When her recommendation got to my court, a majority decided to end the litigation.

The decision was a vote of 3-2-2. Three judges said that the state was progressing adequately; the legislature was working as hard as it could; and there were a lot of good results. These three had been seeing this litigation process evolve, and I think they felt it was too long term, draining too much of the courts' resources, and that we in the court really could not get it done.

Two other judges were new to the court, and, if the membership changes, even in an unelected court like ours, results can change. They wanted the *McDuffy* decision overruled. It was their position, basically, that the education clause had been misconstrued, and, even if it hadn't been misconstrued, the remedy was so daunting that the court should not have been involved in the first place. One of them used the word "judicial imagination" in characterizing the decision in *McDuffy*.

Then there were two judges, myself and a colleague, who dissented; we wanted to forge on. That's where the case is now, except that the three left a little narrow opening that might allow the case to come back—indicating, in other words, that if it comes back, that 3-2-2 might change to 5-2.[1]

JUDGE ROSENBLATT: In the minds of many Americans, judges are judges, and most people don't distinguish between the federal and state judiciary. It's important here that we do because there are two sets of constitutions in our country: the federal Constitution and the state constitutions. State constitutions are actually older than the federal Constitution, at least in those states that were in existence when the federal Constitution was drafted. New York's constitution was ten years old when the federal Constitution was drawn in Philadelphia in 1787.

Between the two sets of constitutions, there's a difference not only in chronology but also in focus and outlook, which is important in school litigation. The federal Constitution was never designed as a rights-driven document. Although we call it the "Bill of Rights," this part of the federal Constitution was not designed to give anybody "rights." It was really designed to allay the states' concern that the federal government could take rights away from citizens. It was designed as a check on the Congress. The First Amendment says the Congress shall not pass any law abridging freedom of religion or establishing a national religion, and so forth.

The state constitutions, on the other hand, are in part structural and in part rights-driven. New York's constitution, unlike the federal Constitution, included an article that dealt with education, another article that dealt with the needy, and so forth. This crested in 1894 with the education article, but, even before that, in 1795, Governor Clinton was speaking about the importance of education in the state. I think this is very healthy. These matters are in a sense local and regional, and we cannot and should not expect the federal government and the federal Constitution to get into all facets of American life. The state constitutions are different—they concentrate on different things, and it should not be a surprise that the state constitutions are the sources of expanded educational opportunities. The New York constitution provides for free education as a constitutional right of New Yorkers that does not exist in the federal Constitution.

Litigation began twenty-five or so years ago in New York with some school districts pointing out that they were less advantaged than others. Our court decided we were not in the business nor would we enter the business of trying to even out the funding in all the school districts. We recognized that there were certain school districts that were wealthier, and if they wanted to enhance and expand the education they offered, that would be all right, provided there's a baseline for all districts, which we called a "sound basic education."

A second lawsuit was then brought, the *Campaign for Fiscal Equity* case, in which the proponents alleged that students in New York City were not getting a sound basic education, in contrast to other districts in which maybe they were. It was a troublesome litigation to us because, as judges, this is not something that we do every day of the week. We had to go through voluminous records and reports in order to determine, in the face of competing submissions, whether or not it was true that those in New York City were not getting the baseline sound basic education. By a very slim vote we determined that they were not. We then indicated to the legislature that they needed to take certain actions, and that set off another round of litigation, which happily ended in a political forum. This points out that this business is not one that lies strictly in the judicial arena, nor should it.

The judges are there when articles of a state constitution are called on by litigants, but the courts do not enter these litigations on their own initiative. They get drawn into them when lawsuits are brought; the courts in most instances do not see themselves as proactive. Judges are more reactive; in areas like this the judges will respond to litigation that's brought and do the best they can to adjudicate it, which is what ultimately happened in *CFE II*.

GOVERNOR WISE: As a governor, you look at these things with the same enthusiasm as a root canal. Every balance of powers situation tests you every possible way because it is a pressure on the legislative branch, executive branch, and the judiciary. I've been involved in the West Virginia educational equity litigation, called the *Pauley* case, in every possible way except the judicial ruling. I was an expert witness in 1980–81, on behalf of the plaintiffs; then I was elected to the state legislature when it was deciding whether it was going to appropriate some of the funds; and then twenty years later as governor of the state of West Virginia, I signed the final agreement.

Having said that, let me take a little different tack, because this business is also very political, and I don't say "political" in a pejorative way. This is a political process as well as a judicial process because, whatever the court feels constrained to do by the arguments brought before it, ultimately it will be the legislature and the executive that will carry it out. That becomes even more significant, when, as in my case, the state was in the worst recession since World War II in terms of state revenues.

Let me suggest a few concepts here. First of all, in analyzing these cases, remember that there are other processes involved besides the judicial one. There is the relationship of the governor with the two other branches, and there are also relationships within the executive branch. My observation—and I've not spoken with Governor Spitzer[2] about this—is that when he was attorney general he was required to represent Governor Pataki's viewpoint, with which I'm not sure he was totally comfortable. I know in one case in which I was involved—not the education case—my attorney general, who was elected on his own, was filing an amicus brief individually, opposing me, while his junior attorney was in court representing me.

The kind of evidence that is put forth in the judicial proceedings is also important. That evidence can help educate the legislative and executive branches. For instance, during my transition from plaintiffs' witness to signing off on behalf of the executive branch twenty-some years later, as a nation and in our state, we went from an input basis to an outcome measurement, looking much more at standards and accountability. Now we ask about the results and outcomes of these education dollars. We ask about the relationship between early-childhood and secondary education. And we ask about the economic impact of greater education spending.

The court may hand down its ruling, but it's going to be the legislature and governor who have to go find the monies, particularly if the ruling deals with taxes. In the last six months, Professor Henry Levin and his colleagues at Teachers College issued an economic analysis that indicates that you get a strong return on investment for dollars put into improved education. This is very important when you're going have to go in front of the voters.

REPRESENTATIVE ELLIOTT: Because of my background, I was not one of those legislators who had antipathy for the court. I had been involved in these educational opportunity cases since 1957. When I started first grade, the Little Rock Central High School desegregation confrontation was happening. I had always been a rather precocious politician. I was aware that there were soldiers at the high school, and the only thing I thought was that this is not equal—where were *my* soldiers? I was also one of those freedom-of-choice kids who had the experience of sitting in the classroom and being one of the only black kids in class and experiencing the horror of it.

When I started teaching, I ended up in a school district that had a federal desegregation case. So, by the time I got to the legislature and we got a state education equity case, I had lived through enough to know that as much as I'd like to believe that people would just do the right thing, I had not seen the right thing done except through the courts.

At the time I was elected to the Arkansas legislature, we had an ongoing case from a part of the state that's called the Delta, which is very rural and poor. In the legislature everybody thought this case was the worst thing that ever happened. We had a prior case, the *Alma* case, that resulted in a funding formula that nobody could decipher. I think that happens in most of these cases. So that led to the case from the Delta, known as *Lake View*, and nobody paid attention until finally the judge ruled that this indeed was a horror story. It was appealed, and the plaintiffs won again.

When it got to the legislature, there were legislators who said, "So what if we don't do anything? What can they do to us?" I was one of two or three legislators who was saying, "Halleluiah, gentlemen," because I thought the courts should not have gotten out of the business in the first place, since the formula from the first case didn't work.

We were lucky in that we had an attorney general who was very good. He had previously been in the legislature for twenty-two years, he was very popular, and he was going to run for governor. He gave us some guidance in getting it done. We are term limited and can only serve two three-year terms. So by the time we got around to fashioning a remedy for this case, in the house of representatives of one hundred people, we had only two people who had been there more than four years. It was very tough going because of this. But with some guidance from the attorney general and more guidance from the court— the case was reopened several times, and we redid the formula with special masters, which was a good process—we got out of court for the last time just a few months ago.

Q. Is it the role of the courts to ensure that the remedy that is ordered will truly vindicate the constitutional rights of children?

GOVERNOR WISE: Clearly this is the role of the court. The court is there to interpret the constitution and resolve matters brought before it when people are seeking redress. What I observed in our proceeding as it unfolded over twenty years was that the court pushed, but it stopped short of provoking a constitutional crisis whenever it could. The legislature was always trying to stay just far enough ahead of Judge Recht to avoid a contempt citation and yet, at the same time, perhaps not giving everything. So over the fifteen to twenty years, the judge was able to get the legislature and the governors to move significantly, but at the same time, the legislature could say, "You can't tell us fully what to do."

Where the court runs short, I believe, is in its ability to enforce. The reason I ran for public office stemmed from a matter that was indirectly related to the *Pauley* case. As an attorney, I went to court representing plaintiffs against the coal companies to force them to pay the taxes that they were supposed to pay—which went to education. I won my case. I thought it was now written in stone. But it lasted only six months until the next legislative session when the companies got the legislature to change the law to say what they wanted it to say. They were able to beat it back, not judicially, but in the legislative process.

JUDGE ROSENBLATT: The courts have the obligation because the courts have no choice. When a litigation is filed, the courts must decide it, and the courts do so seriously, even if not necessarily cheerfully. In the context of the separation of powers, there are those among us who say the judges are the ones that can be counted on "to do the right thing." That kind of makes me feel good as a judge to know that one has the confidence of people here who are passionately interested in education and its advancement, but I would point out that it is not an easy business and that it has connotations that should not be taken lightly.

The reason the legislators are not willing to "do the right thing" is that the voters don't want them to. We live in a democracy, and we always have to bear in mind that when the voters don't want something to happen and the judges are called upon to do something, then what they are doing in a sense is antimajoritarian, antidemocratic. It can be challenged and attacked as elitist, and we want to be careful about that because judges don't like to be seen as elitist or as activists. They don't want to be seen as people who have jobs protected by life tenure, by appointment, that will enable them to beat the heck out of the taxpayers. When we go into conference and talk about these things, we're not indifferent. Even though we're not up for the vote, we do ask questions like, "What are the folks at Morgantown going to think about this?"

One of our outstanding judges came from a little town called Livonia, and he used to say, "You know, I'm not sure the folks in the post office in Livonia would be too happy about this." So it's on our mind. I wouldn't want anybody to think that the judiciary should be seen as immune from contact with the public, indifferent, and haughty, that they're the only ones who know how to do the right things. There is a balance there, and we try to be very sensitive to what the legislators think because they represent the voters, which is another way of saying, the population.

Q. U.S. Supreme Court Justice Clarence Thomas, in the Louisville case, said that judges should not be "social engineers." What are your thoughts about that?

JUDGE ROSENBLATT: When there's a constitutional command, as in New York, Massachusetts, and every other state where children are entitled to a sound basic education at least or its equivalent, and it is not being honored by the legislators—you may say because of lack of political will or maybe because they're too responsive to the voters—it falls on the judiciary to do it. I would not call that "social engineering." I would call it fidelity to the constitutional command, and judges don't do it cheerfully. They do it with a sense of balance and proportion, and when the time comes to do it, they have done it in virtually all or in the great majority of instances. We did it in New York, and happily in New York it worked out okay.

JUDGE GREANEY: The question as I understand it is, "Do courts have an obligation to get involved in these cases?" I differ a little from my brother. I say, maybe. First of all, you have to take a hard look at the education provision in your constitution, and if it's aspirational, and not mandatory, then I think a court has got to back away and say, "This is something that is not enforceable by the court."

I think that some states have overstepped their boundaries on this and, as a result, have encountered a lot of resistance. The bedrock of any involvement by the courts has to be a very principled decision that is not vulnerable to attack on legal scholarship grounds. So the first question is whether the courts should get involved.

Moving on from that, if, as in Massachusetts, it was accepted that we have a mandatory provision, a second question has to be asked. That is, can we remedy this if there is massive resistance? In a lot of constitutional cases, not necessarily educational cases, but other cases involving constitutional issues, we say, "Well, sure, it looks like there's a right here, but I don't think we, as judges, can enforce it." There's a very bedrock principle of equity law that says you can have a right without a remedy, and that comes into play at this point.

Now, if you answer those two questions affirmatively, namely, there is a mandate, and we can remediate it in a positive way, then I think the court has an obligation to get involved. Unlike my brother from New York, we don't ask those questions in our conferences about what they are going to think about this. Is the mayor of Boston or the postmaster up in Longmeadow going to get mad? We don't ask those questions. It's here. We think we can fix it. Bring it on.

JUDGE ROSENBLATT: I wouldn't want to be misunderstood as someone who was concerned about taking the temperature of everybody in the community, as if we in the New York Court of Appeals put it to a plebiscite. We wouldn't do that, but I'd be lying if I told you I was utterly indifferent to the plight of the people who have to pay taxes. Before we told the legislature we had to spend billions of dollars, it did cross my mind that this has enormous financial implications. It's not like a royal decree: I've got a lifetime job; you have to do it. I didn't do things that way.

REPRESENTATIVE ELLIOTT: Once the courts had found our system to be unconstitutional, we as a legislature expected that they would oversee what we had decided as a remedy. The court was very careful not to prescribe to us exactly what to do. What they'd say was, "Here is what's wrong. We're not going try to tell you just how to fix it, but fix it." I look at that like what I did when I was teaching, and I handed a student back a paper. I would say, "Here are some issues that you have; maybe you need to take a look at coherency or stream of consciousness or whatever." I didn't say, "You have to do it exactly like this." And that student expected me to look at it again and say whether or not he or she had remedied what I had pointed out.

That's the way our legislature as a whole looked at this case in Arkansas, though, as I mentioned earlier, there were some who thought the court should absolutely go away. As a body, I would definitely say we recognized that, whether we liked it or not, the court had a right to be in this. There was an expectation that they would hold our feet to the fire once they had said that this whole process was unconstitutional. In fact, I can't imagine them not doing that, considering our history of not having funded education. It would have been a travesty if had they not returned once there was a problem.

I should point out that once the court had terminated the case, another district—an affluent district as far as Arkansas goes—brought another case because they were a growing district and said they were not funded well either. So that reopened the matter, and, at that point, we were found guilty as a legislature for not having done what we said we were going to do. Basically, we set ourselves up to have the court oversee what we were doing, and we got what we asked for, rightfully so.

Q. Michael Rebell has indicated that he believes that ten to twenty years of continuing court jurisdiction may be necessary to get the job done. Do you agree?

JUDGE ROSENBLATT: In the *CFE* case, the prospect of a lengthy litigation was a concern. I was on the side that made the finding that New York City was underfunded, and I voted to issue the directive to the state legislature. We were warned by the dissenter that could lead to years and years of litigation, twenty years' worth, and we said, "No, do it anyway." We did it in the most deferential way, saying that we didn't have the means, ability, or knowledge to tell the legislature how to fix the problem. But we told the state to take a year to go about bringing the system up to the level we articulated as a sound basic education, however it felt was appropriate. We came to the right conclusion, notwithstanding the possibility of two decades of litigation, which happily did not happen.

JUDGE GREANEY: I think if you get into this area, it's a long-term prospect. You just cannot back away. I heard this morning that New Jersey's been involved in litigation for thirty-seven years. We were involved for fourteen years, before we backed out.

The desegregation cases have been going on since 1950, and they are still going on. [U.S. Supreme Court Justice] Sandra Day O'Connor, before she stepped down, said in one of her last opinions,[3] we know it can't go on forever, but we think the affirmative action cases [in higher education, which had already gone on for twenty-five years] should go on for another twenty-five years. Now, when you put the two figures together, she's talking about fifty years of court involvement in affirmative action.

I think you're talking about similar periods in these education cases. Ten years might be just a minimum; it might be twenty years, and the courts have to be prepared to do it long term. The mental health litigation cases lasted fifteen to twenty years; fair housing cases lasted fifteen to twenty years. These are structural societal problems and take a long time to fix. I think we can stay in, and we should stay in, and if ten years is what it takes, fine; if twenty years, fine, and so forth.

REPRESENTATIVE ELLIOTT: I don't pretend to have an answer for how long the courts should remain involved, but I will point out that inevitably when educators have discussions about this issue, there's always a consensus that this is a long-term issue, and we won't fix it tomorrow. Yet for some reason, most legislators want the courts to bow out after a short term.

We have a pride about ourselves as legislators. We are elected. People expect us to reflect on what they want to have done. The tension for me is the difference between representation and leadership. Anybody can be a representative, but it takes a different kind of politician to be a leader. So personally I think that there needs to be long-term oversight by the courts, but I know that is absolutely different from what the average legislature as a body would have done. For me, it just doesn't stand to reason that the courts should not exercise leadership and stay involved.

We have turnover, and if we have not done our job to bring the populace to understand that education is just as important for the person's child who lives across town as it is for mine, then the courts should. But, generally, a legislative body will get the courts out of the picture as quickly as they can.

Q. Let's further explore the question of "remedy." What can and should the state courts do in education adequacy cases?

JUDGE GREANEY: If our court had not dismissed the *Hancock* case, it would have come back to me as the single justice to implement the mandate. Let me tell you exactly what I was planning to do. I can talk about this now because the case is over.

First of all, let me say, we have a very good relationship with our legislature, although we have sometimes butted heads on other constitutional matters. We also have a good relationship with the perfectly marvelous folks in our education executive branch, and, of course, a dedicated group of teachers, students, and others up and down the line through all two hundred plus cities, towns in Massachusetts. So this would not be a case where people would be fighting you from within.

Preliminarily, I want to say that we're going to use a different vocabulary. I don't want to hear from any of you folks that we're "activists," because we're not; we're engaging in judicial restraint, we're working on a remedy that will engage us in reconciliation, and colloquy. I have an acronym, "H-A-L-O." "H" is for help. "A" is for no antagonism and how we're not going to create anarchy. "L" is long range. We've talked about that already, and outcome is the "O." We're going to work very seriously on that.

Here's what I was going to do. First, I was going to have a big meeting of all the principals in an auditorium like this. It was not going to be in the courthouse. Once the full court has laid down the direction, I think it's better to move outside of the courthouse to soften the environment. Then we would set up a kind of supernumerary council and have representatives of the department of education, the executive branch, two or three legislators; the speaker and the president of the senate will pick those folks for us, probably from their education committees, maybe someone from the ways and means committee, because we'll need money to do this—in fact, we might need a lot of money. And we're going to have representatives from labor unions, teachers unions, and so on.

I would have brought Judge Botsford in because she was the trial judge who made the three hundred pages of findings. She would be my point person and report weekly, monthly, maybe even on a daily basis to fix these problems. How do we fix these problems? Her recommendation, which I wish my court had adopted, was threefold: (1) Ascertain the actual cost of providing all public school pupils in the focus districts—we would start with those four districts—with educational opportunities as described in *McDuffy*. (2) Determine the administrative means necessary to provide meaningful educational improvement in the four focus districts and to carry out an effective implementation of these educational programs. And (3) implement whatever funding and administrative changes result from the determinations in (1) and (2).

A new cost analysis would be needed because the basis of the trial court decision, with which I agreed, was that the foundation budget needed fixing in these districts. Once we started working on this, I would also bring in experts as we need them, in a lot of areas, maybe curricula, resources, accounting, cost analysis, and so on. These would be neutral experts, not experts that the plaintiffs wanted or the defendants wanted. We would also issue regular press releases. I would bring in the public relations officer from my court and put out press releases so the public knows what we're doing, and we would have meetings with editorial boards of the newspapers.

We might have needed help from the educational institutions. There was a marvelous example in the city of Chelsea, near Boston, a few years ago. Chelsea's education system was a disaster, and John Silber, the president of Boston University, a great fellow with a lot of interest in education, offered to help fix this situation. In essence, the City of Chelsea financially went into receivership, but the school committee voted to turn over all their authority to Boston University and let them run the schools in a ten-year partnership. The legislature approved this arrangement. It wasn't 100 percent perfect, but it worked pretty well. We have about twenty to thirty colleges and universities in Massachusetts, and I would have tried try to get as many of them involved as possible, plus a whole network of state teachers colleges.

Frankly, if after a few years of effort we weren't showing progress, then I'd go back as the single justice to my six colleagues and say, "This isn't working; maybe we ought to terminate it."

Q. How would you spell success? How would you know that things are going well?

JUDGE GREANEY: I'd let my experts, the representatives from the department of education, tell me that.

Q. Is your approach consistent with separation of powers?

JUDGE GREANEY: I don't see this as any intrusion on separation of powers. It's the court basically doing what courts do, which is to decide a case that has been brought, hand down an order or judgment, and implement the mandate. The judgment would be there.

Q. Would you consider only measures of academic performance when you determine whether or not the constitutional requirement of provision of a sound education has been met?

JUDGE GREANEY: Again, I'd leave that to my experts as we worked our way through the process. I do agree that pure academic performance is not the measure of a total education. I think it was the person from Vermont who said, "I want my son to be a man or my daughter to be a woman." That's a very important component of it. Tests and measurements don't necessarily fulfill that. Coming from a background and having been trained by the Jesuits and the nuns, I know what that means, and I do think you have to have that whole person component in whatever educational plan you devise.

Frankly, if I remember the Kentucky standards,[4] I do think there's large measure of that in those standards, and we adopted those standards in *McDuffy.*

Q. Judge Rosenblatt, what is your concept of the appropriate remedy?

JUDGE ROSENBLATT: That's the hard part. As difficult as it is to issue the order, the remedy, and what one does in the event that there's noncompliance, is the really nightmarish thought. It can create a constitutional collision, a constitutional crisis, and what are the remedies that judges have when there's disobedience of a court order? Classically, it's contempt. Somebody doesn't pay the bill, we issue an order, the sheriff goes out, puts the person in jail. In theory the contempt remedy is out there, but when there had been the initial failure to meet the deadline in *CFE,* we didn't entertain any thoughts about having the police go into the governor's mansion and cart the governor off to jail; that would have been absolutely unthinkable. I don't think I'm giving away any secrets in letting the governor and the legislature know the court of appeals was not about to go down that road. They knew it and respected the court enough to know we were speaking in good conscience and fully expected there would be a political resolution, and ultimately it did result that way.

In *CFE* in theory we could have said, "Here is what we think we need, x billions of dollars, and if you do not come up with x dollars in x months, here's what's going to happen to you." There is no way we would do that in our court—almost inconceivable—because it would have shown an arrogance that the New York Court of Appeals would not use. We were saying, in effect, to the governor, the legislature, "This is your job; do it. We have confidence you're going to do it." The subtext behind that is everybody knows if and when you don't do it, then it falls to the court to create a remedy. But there's no way we would say, "This is what's going to happen to you if you don't do it." I think that would have been a disservice, an act of disrespect, and it would have been strategically bad on our part because it would have aroused and antagonized the governor and legislature needlessly, and the resolution might not have been as agreeable as it eventually turned out to be in New York.

We issued the directive with the full expectation that there would be a political solution. Frankly, I was shocked when a year went by and the New York State legislature and the governor did not agree. The relationships between the other two branches at the time were not agreeable enough to bring a harmonious solution. After another year it was resolved politically. Ultimately, there must be a political resolution with the judges in the role of pointing them in the right direction. Judges do not have budgets to make allocations. Judges don't cut checks.

What my colleague Judge Greaney said would have happened in Massachusetts is very, very alien to us in New York. It's hard for me to imagine that four judges of our court, of which there are seven, would ever vote to take over a school system. Maybe it's because we were on the edge of what we knew would be a political solution and maybe hypothetically if it got bad enough maybe the judiciary would say, "Okay, we're going to take it over," but it never reached that point because the public pressure began to mount.

One of the considerations here that we should not forget is that we all operate in a transparent society. Our order was out there. There were signals to the political branches that this was warranted and that the judges were not simply issuing a decree that is pie-in-the-sky, unrealistic, or arrogant. Then the public support began to mount as it should. The political branches eventually were able to resolve it between themselves, and though it took longer than it should have, it's a far cry from twenty years of litigation. We're grateful that the executive and the legislative branch did get together and allocate a sum of money that I think was pretty satisfactory, and I think it was really a triumph for all sides.

JUDGE GREANEY: The points I just talked about will not create the constitutional crisis alluded to, which I agree with my brother from New York we should not do. We cannot put the speaker of the house in jail. We cannot order a keeper over at the treasurer's office to start keeping a record of all the money it's collecting each day. We have to work our way through this.

Now at some point we might have to bring in superpowered mediators, a Ken Feinberg type, to work through the bumps. We did have a case a couple of years ago where there was a clear elections issue. We got in a real fight with the legislature. We said, "Okay, you're supposed to fund it under the initiative petition passed by the voters." They refused to. We then said this court is going to fund it, and we went out and seized state property and sold it. A couple of developers got some choice pieces of property for condominiums before the dispute got resolved. I don't think we would do the same thing in the area of education, but we did it there, and we did it in the same-sex marriage case.

By the way, I hope I didn't leave a misimpression. The Chelsea partnership with BU was not court ordered. It was entirely voluntary, and then the legislature did the necessary changes to allow the school committee to cede its authority.

REPRESENTATIVE ELLIOTT: In regard to remedies, I would do two things. First, a legislative remedy should involve a great deal of engagement with the general public. One of the things I've always wanted us to do as legislators and leaders of a community is to go out and have face-to-face discussions with the people to help them understand why this is important. We have to come up with a rational way to engage people rather than just criticize them for not being supportive. Help them understand what democracy means. It's going to have to be done or legislators are not going have the will, the support, or the authority to do what we need to do to continue to support our schools.

We had to raise taxes during our deliberations, when, as Governor Wise mentioned, we were in a deep recession. It was not easy to do. But it has been the only tax increase in the state that has had almost no pushback. Why did that happen? Because we took the time to make sure that the people of the state understood why we had to do that, rather than just saying that the court's making us do it.

The second thing is more difficult. We need to look at the quality-of-life issues in those very poor rural and urban places. It's more than just what goes on at school, but we don't set anything in place to address that. Whose responsibility is it to look at these issues? It's always amazed me to think education could be solved in the education committees in the legislature. We know there are housing problems; we know there are job problems. These are not resolved in the education committee. So whose responsibility is it to look at the whole issue?

A third thing I would love to do is have a section on the news every night and in the newspaper that talks about academics rather than sports. Why do sports get a whole section? Then we wonder why kids pay more attention to that. The public is more consumed with Britney Spears and Lindsey Lohan than they are with public education or the war in Iraq.

GOVERNOR WISE: Judge Greaney, it would take three days to scrape me off the wall before I would let my department heads go over to a meeting that's been called by the judiciary. By the same token, I would never have thought to ask the judiciary to come to my office on any matter. I went to see them occasionally. They came one time, but it was to discuss a matter of court administration that required legislation. I think that the total approach that you're talking about makes a lot of sense, because ultimately that's going to build the political will, but there is also a very difficult issue of how we bring it together.

Now, having said that, I happen to believe there's an educational crisis, and we know what to do about it. This is the mantra of my organization. But we have to build the will to deal with it. The court is often the one that can lay it out, be the one that starts responding to the crisis, but there will not be final resolution without public will. If there is to be a successful resolution to the court's decision, there must be public education behind it. There was merit to the many hearings of Judge Recht in West Virginia because it gave the public the chance to understand what it was about.

The court must be aware of the implications of giving the legislature and the executive branch the chance to help form the remedy and also to explain it. Do that, and then I think you do get the kind of results that you have seen in New York and we have seen in other states. Don't do that, and we see the continuing stalemates, in some of these cases.

Gaston Caperton, in 1989 as the governor of West Virginia, took the initial decision of Judge Recht saying that we were not delivering a thorough and efficient education. By the force of his personality, moving with a number of members of the legislature who were similarly inclined, he was able to take that to the necessary point, saying that's what we need to do.

My point is that what is needed is a combination of judicial impetus and the political will. If a court comes down and says, "We need $7 billion to improve education, and most likely this will require a tax increase," that gives every politician a chance to demagogue it.

To get the political will requires what I observed from a distance was done around the *CFE* case, which involved the lawsuit and the Alliance for Quality Education, the League of Women Voters, and a number of other organizations getting it to a political process. It's not a carefully orchestrated dance sometimes, but it is a number of parts that have to move simultaneously.

The court starts it, but I do believe there's a point at which you can't enforce the recommended remedy. That's why indeed it's incumbent upon all three branches to recognize that and to make the case to the public why it's essential.

Notes

Acknowledgments

1. 551 U.S. 701, 127 S.Ct. 2738 (2007).
2. 801 N.E. 2d 326 (N.Y. 2003).

Preface

1. Jose P. v. Ambach, 557 F.Supp. 1230 (E.D.N.Y. 1983); Jose P. v. Ambach, 1987 WL 6232 (E.D.N.Y., January 15, 1987). The remedial process in this case is still ongoing today, although I am no longer a counsel for the plaintiffs. A critical history of this litigation is contained in chapter 3 of Ross Sandler & David Schoenbrun, Democracy by Decree: What Happens When Courts Run Government (2003). See also, Michael A. Rebell, *Jose P. v. Ambach:* Special Education Reform in New York City, in Justice and School Systems: The Role of the Courts in Education Litigation 25 (Barbara Flicker ed., 1990).

2. Michael A. Rebell & Robert L. Hughes, *Schools, Communities, and the Courts: A Dialogic Approach to Education Reform,* 14 Yale L. & Pol'y Rev. 99 (1996).

3. No Child Left Behind Act of 2001, Pub. L. No. 107–110, § 101, 115 Stat. 1425, 1444–45, 1448 (2002) (codified at 20 U.S.C. § 6311 (2000 & Supp. II 2002)).

4. I should also note that since the CFE litigation has now terminated, and I am not currently involved in any active litigation, I do not have any ethical obligations as an attorney to represent a client's view. Although currently I work full time as an academic, I do think it important to acknowledge and explain my past experiences and their relationship to the views I express in this book. I also think that the authors of some of the works that are critical of the courts' role in the education finance cases, which I cite in this book, who have not revealed

their past involvement as paid witnesses for the defendants in many of these litigations, ill serve their readers by not making similar disclosures.

Introduction

1. 347 U.S. 483 (1954).

2. Amy Stuart Wells & Lamar P. Miller, *Brown v. Board of Education at 50: Looking Back While Moving Forward—An Introduction,* in Special Issue, Brown Plus Fifty, 107 TCHRS. C. REC. 343, 345 (2005). For other perspectives on *Brown* at fifty, see, for example, Symposium, Brown@50, 47 How. L. REV. 1 (2003–2004); Special Issue, Brown v. Board of Education, 8 AM. L. & ECON. REV. 141 (2006); Arthur Chaskalson, Brown v. Board of Education: *50 Years Later,* 36 COLUM. HUM. RTS. L. REV. 503 (2005); Michael Heise, Brown v. Board of Education, *Footnote 11 and Multidisciplinarity,* 90 CORNELL L. REV. 297 (2005); Symposium, *50 Years of* Brown v. Board of Education, 90 VA. L. REV. 1537 (2005).

3. 551 U.S. 701, 127 S. Ct. 2738 (2007).

4. "All of those plans represent local efforts to bring about the kind of racially integrated education that Brown v. Board of Education, 347 U.S. 483, 74 S. Ct. 686, 98 L. Ed. 873 (1954), long ago promised—efforts that this Court has repeatedly required, permitted, and encouraged local authorities to undertake." *Id.* at 2800 (Breyer, J. dissenting).

5. In Louisville, the district's goal of having all schools maintain not less than 15 percent and not more than 50 percent black students was achieved through a comprehensive plan that emphasized cluster groupings, adjustment of school attendance areas, and "managed choice;" the vast majority of students attended their "resides" school or were accommodated with their choice of magnet programs. Under the Seattle plan, the district used distance from home, presence of siblings, and other factors in addition to race to make its decisions. The vast majority of students obtained their first- or second-choice schools without race being taken into consideration.

6. Keyes v. Sch. Dist. No. 1, 413 U.S. 189 (1973).

7. Milliken v. Bradley, 418 U.S. 717 (1974).

8. Oklahoma City Public Schools v. Dowell, 498 U.S. 237, 238 (1991).

9. See Missouri v. Jenkins, 515 U.S. 70 (1995) (holding that students' academic achievement levels are not "the appropriate test to . . . decid[e] whether a previously segregated district has achieved partially unitary status.").

10. For a detailed overview of the Supreme Court's desegregation decisions, see James Ryan, *The Supreme Court and Voluntary Integration,* 121 HARV. L. REV. 131 (2007).

11. 127 S. Ct. 2738, 2839 (appendix A to opinion of Breyer, J, dissenting).

See also, GARY ORFIELD & CHUNGMEI LEE, THE CIVIL RIGHTS PROJECT HAR-
VARD UNIVERSITY, WHY SEGREGATION MATTERS: POVERTY AND EDUCATIONAL
INEQUALITY, 17–18 (2005). Available at http://www.civilrightsproject.ucla.edu/
research/deseg/Why_Segreg_Matters.pdf. (black and Latino students make
up 80 percent of the student population in high-poverty schools [high-poverty
schools defined as having 90–100 percent of student population as poor]).

   12. 411 U.S. 1 (1973).

   13. For an overview of the state court challenges to state education finance
systems, see Michael A. Rebell, *Education Adequacy, Democracy and the
Courts,* in ACHIEVING HIGH EDUCATIONAL STANDARDS FOR ALL (Timothy Ready
et al. eds. 2002). For up-to-date information on the state court litigations, see
National ACCESS Network, http://www.schoolfunding.info.

   14. Tamar Lewin & David M. Herszenhorn, *Money, Not Race, Is Fueling
New Push to Bolster Schools,* NEW YORK TIMES, June 30, 2007, at A10.

   15. See James S. Liebman & Charles F. Sabel, *A Public Laboratory Dewey
Barely Imagined: The Emerging Model of School Governance and Legal Reform,* 28 N.Y.U. REV. L. & SOC. CHANGE 183, 300–304 (2003) (discussing how implementation of education adequacy reforms can advance the national dialogue
on race and promote effective equality in education). Still, if we are to fully re-
alize *Brown's* vision for equal educational opportunity, and if we are to prepare
our students to compete effectively in the global marketplace and to function
productively as civic participants in a democratic society, ultimately, despite the
U.S. Supreme Court's recent ruling in *Seattle,* serious pursuit of racial integration of the schools in some form will need to again become a major aspect of national and state educational policy.

   Decades of experience indicate that all children, minority and majority, are
better prepared for work and civic life when they have experienced integrated
education. See generally AMY STUART WELLS, BOTH SIDES NOW. THE STORY OF
SCHOOL DESEGREGATION'S GRADUATES (2009) (tracking the experiences of students who graduated in 1980 from racially diverse schools); Janet Ward Scho-
field, *Review of Research on School Desegregation's Impact on Elementary and
Secondary School Students,* in HANDBOOK OF RESEARCH ON MULTICULTURAL
EDUCATION 597 (James A. Banks ed., 2001) (reviewing a wide array of research
on the impact of school desegregation); Amy Stuart Wells & Robert L. Crain,
Perpetuation Theory and the Long-Term Effects of School Desegregation, 64
REV. EDUC. RES. 531 (1994) (drawing together twenty-one studies on the long-
term effects of school desegregation).

   16. 127 S. Ct. 2779, note 14 (2007) (Thomas, J, concurring). Justice Anthony
Kennedy in his concurring opinion in *Seattle,* took issue with Justice Thomas
and the other three members of the plurality opinion for being "too dismissive of
the legitimate interest government has in ensuring all people have equal oppor-

tunity regardless of their race," *id.* at 2745, but it is far from clear that the limited openings for affirmative action allowed by his key swing decision can accomplish this goal.

17. Alfred A. Lindseth, *The Legal Backdrop to Adequacy,* in COURTING FAIL-URE: HOW SCHOOL FINANCE LAWSUITS EXPLOIT JUDGES' GOOD INTENTIONS AND HARM OUR CHILDREN 33, 36 (Eric A. Hanushek, ed., 2006) ("[I]gnoring separation of powers considerations, [some state courts] have approached adequacy lawsuits in such a way as to substantially usurp the power of the legislature."). See also Kenneth W. Starr, *The Uncertain Future of Adequacy Remedies,* in SCHOOL MONEY TRIALS: THE LEGAL PURSUIT OF EDUCATIONAL ADEQUACY 307, 310 (Martin R. West & Paul E. Peterson eds., 2007) (advocating "judicial humility" in cases involving educational policy issues); Joshua Dunn & Martha Derthick, *Adequacy Litigation and the Separation of Powers, in id* at 334–39 (expressing skepticism regarding judicial competence to fashion remedies in educational adequacy litigations).

18. Michael Heise, *Litigated Learning and the Limits of Law,* 57 VAND. L. REV. 2417, 2460 (2004).

19. 349 U.S. 294 (1955).

20. Abram Chayes, *The Role of the Judge in Public Law Litigation,* 89 HARV. L. REV. 1281 (1976).

21. Paul Gewirtz & Chad Goldner, Op-Ed., *So Who Are the Activists?* NEW YORK TIMES, July 6, 2005, at A19. Gewirtz and Goldner also point out that the Court's most conservative members tended to be the most "activist": Justice Thomas voted to strike down 65.63 percent of these congressional provisions, and Justice Scalia 56.25 percent, in contrast to only 39.06 percent for Justice Ginsberg and 28.13 percent for Justice Breyer. *Id.* See also Barry Friedman, *The Importance of Being Positive: The Nature and Function of Judicial Review,* 72 U. CINN. L. REV. 1257, 1261–63 (2004) (arguing that the Rehnquist Court is one of the "most activist in history").

22. Adam Cohen, *Last Term's Winner at the Supreme Court: Judicial Activism,* NEW YORK TIMES, July 9, 2007. Available at http://www.nytimes.com/2007/07/09/opinion/09mon4.html (discussing major cases in which the Roberts Court invalidated congressional actions in its first term).

23. Sol Stern, Campaign for Fiscal Equity: *The March of Folly,* in COURTING FAILURE, *supra* note 17, at 2.

24. Edwin Chemerinsky, *The Deconstitutionalization of Education,* 36 LOY. U. CHI. L.J. 111 (2004). See also Jack M. Ballkin, *What Brown Teaches Us about Constitutional Theory,* 90 VA. L. REV. 1537, 1546 (2005) (" . . . when litigation is one part of a larger strategy that includes direct action and legislative reform, the reform movement is more likely to be successful and to make progress more quickly.").

25. 42 U.S.C.A § 2000d (2000).

26. No Child Left Behind Act of 2001, Pub. L. No. 107–110, § 101, 115 Stat. 1425, 1444–45, 1448 (2002) (codified at 20 U.S.C. § 6311 (2000 & Supp. II 2002)). See also, for example, N.Y. State Bd. of Regents, ALL CHILDREN CAN LEARN: A PLAN FOR REFORM OF STATE AID TO SCHOOLS (1993) ("All children can learn; and we can change our system of public elementary, middle, and secondary education to ensure that all children do learn at world-class levels.").

27. Cecilia Elena Rouse, *Consequences for the Labor Market,* in THE PRICE WE PAY; ECONOMIC AND SOCIAL CONSEQUENCES OF INADEQUATE EDUCATION 99 (Clive R. Belfield and Henry M. Levin eds., 2007).

28. See *id.*

29. See, for example, Thomas R. Bailey, *Implications of Educational Inequality in a Global Workforce,* in THE PRICE WE PAY, *supra* note 27, at 74 (arguing that due to globalization, emerging nations are now competitive with more developed nations); THOMAS L. FRIEDMAN, THE WORLD IS FLAT: A BRIEF HISTORY OF THE TWENTY-FIRST CENTURY (2005) (discussing relationship between education and productivity).

30. A frank and highly informative separation of powers dialogue on many of the themes raised in the book among two state court judges, a former governor, and a legislative leader, each of whom was involved in a major sound basic education case, is set forth *infra* in the appendix.

Chapter One

1. See, for example, Nathan Glazer, *Toward an Imperial Judiciary?* 41 PUB. INT. 104 (1975); RAOUL BERGER, GOVERNMENT BY JUDICIARY: THE TRANSFORMATION OF THE FOURTEENTH AMENDMENT (1977). See also, PHILIP KURLAND, POLITICS, THE CONSTITUTION AND THE WARREN COURT 203 (1970) (accusing judges of acting like "Platonic Guardians").

2. See, for example, Frank M. Johnson, *The Role of the Federal Courts in Institutional Litigation,* 32 ALA. L. REV. 264 (1981); Owen M. Fiss, *Forward: The Forms of Justice,* 93 HARV. L. REV. 1 (1979).

3. Edward Levi, *Some Aspects of Separation of Powers,* 76 COLUM. L. REV. 371, 376 (1976). See also RICHARD NEALY, HOW COURTS GOVERN AMERICA (1981).

4. Abram Chayes, *The Role of the Judge in Public Law Litigation,* 89 HARV. L. REV. 1281 (1976).

5. See, for example, DONALD L. HOROWITZ, THE COURTS AND SOCIAL POLICY (1977); Eleanor P. Wolf, *Social Science and the Courts: The Detroit Schools Case,* 42 PUB. INT. 102 (1976).

6. *Id.* See also JEREMY RABKIN, JUDICIAL COMPULSIONS: HOW PUBLIC LAW DISTORTS PUBLIC POLICY (1989).

7. Chayes, *supra* note 4. See also Robert D. Goldstein, *A Swann's Song for Remedies: Equitable Relief in the Burger Court*, 13 HARV. C.R.-C.L. L. REV. 119 (1978).

8. Paul Rosen, The Supreme Court and Social Science (1972). Chayes, *supra* note 4.

9. *Id.* at 1308.

10. MICHAEL A. REBELL & ARTHUR R. BLOCK, EDUCATIONAL POLICY MAKING AND THE COURTS: AN EMPIRICAL STUDY OF JUDICIAL ACTIVISM (1982); MICHAEL A. REBELL & ARTHUR R. BLOCK, EQUALITY AND EDUCATION: FEDERAL CIVIL RIGHTS ENFORCEMENT IN THE NEW YORK CITY SCHOOL SYSTEM (1985). Although the core case study in the latter book involved OCR's enforcement activities in New York City, detailed comparative perspectives were also obtained of comparable OCR activities at the time in Chicago, Los Angeles, and Philadelphia.

11. A comparative analysis of the fact-finding capabilities of the U.S. Congress and the courts reached similar conclusions; see Neal Devons, *Congressional Fact Finding*, 50 DUKE L.J. 1169 (2001). See also Sheila Jasanoff, *Judicial Fictions: The Supreme Court's Quest for Good Science*, 38 SOC'Y 27, 28 (2001) ("Adversarial questioning of experts in legal proceedings has frequently exposed hidden interests and tacit normative assumptions that are embedded in supposedly value-neutral facts. The confrontation of lay and expert viewpoints that the law affords has emerged as a powerful instrument for probing some of the untested epistemological foundations of expert claims.").

12. See also JAMES O. FREEDMAN, CRISIS AND LEGITIMACY: THE ADMINISTRATIVE PROCESS AND AMERICAN GOVERNMENT 24 (1978) (discussing the implications of authorizing administrative agencies to combine investigative, prosecutorial and adjudicatory functions); William N. Eskridge, Jr., *Politics without Romance: Implications of Public Choice Theory for Statutory Interpretation*, 74 VA. L. REV. 275, 308 (1988) ("An agency tends to be 'captured' over time, as interest group demands grow increasingly asymmetrical and the agency loses outside political support and institutional momentum.").

13. See also Stephenson, *Legislative Allocation of Delegated Power: Uncertainty, Risk and the Choice between Agencies and Courts*, 119 HARV. L. REV. 1035, 1036 (2006) ("Court decisions [in comparison with administrative agency decisions] tend to be . . . stable over time."); GARY ORFIELD & SUSAN E. EATON, DISMANTLING DESEGREGATION: THE QUIET REVERSAL OF BROWN V. BOARD OF EDUCATION 350 (1996) ("Courts have some special strengths in removal from politics and the ability to stay with a complex issue long enough to implement change."). Legislatures generally do not purport to engage in remedial oversight of the reform processes they initiate, although oversight hearings and modification of statutory provisions in light of events could be said to constitute analogous functions. We did not, therefore, attempt to extend our comparative analysis of remedial oversight capabilities to the legislative domain.

14. 509 U.S. 579 (1995).

15. *Id.* at 590–91, n.9.

16. JASANOFF, *supra* note 11, at 29.

17. Clive R. Belfield & Henry M. Levin, *The Economics of Education on Judgment Day,* 28 J. EDUC. FIN. 183 (2002).

18. *Id.* at 205.

19. Kitzmiller v. Dover Area Sch. Dist., 400 F. Supp. 2d 707 (M.D.Pa. 2005).

20. *Id.* at 735. The Judge also remarked that "[t]hose who disagree with our holding will likely mark it as the product of an activist judge. If so, they will have erred as this is manifestly not an activist court." *Id.* at 765.

21. Margot Talbot, *Darwin in the Dock: Intelligent Design Has Its Day in Court,* THE NEW YORKER, December 5, 2005, at 66, 68.

22. James Anthony Whitson, *The Dover (PA) Evolution Case: A True Win for Education?* TCHRS. C. REC (2006). Available at http://www.tcrecord.org (identification number 12271).

23. See, for example, Jeremy Waldron, *The Core of the Case against Judicial Review,* 115 YALE L.J. 1346 (2006) (criticizing judicial review from a comparative international perspective); Aileen Kavanagh, *Participation and Judicial Review: A Reply to Jeremy Waldron,* 22 LAW & PHIL. 451 (2003) (defending judicial review from a comparative international perspective); MARK TUSHNET, WEAK COURTS, STRONG RIGHTS: JUDICIAL REVIEW AND SOCIAL WELFARE RIGHTS IN COMPARATIVE CONSTITUTIONAL LAW (2008) (arguing that social and economic rights can in many circumstances best be judicially enforced by decreasing the power of the courts).

24. See also Frew *ex. rel.* Frew v. Hawkins, 540 U.S. 431 (2004) (reiterating power of federal courts to enforce broad-ranging consent decrees in institutional reform litigations).

25. MALCOLM M. FEELEY & EDWARD L. RUBIN, JUDICIAL POLICY MAKING AND THE MODERN STATE: HOW THE COURTS REFORMED AMERICA'S PRISONS 344 (1999).

26. See 20 U.S.C. § 1415(e)(2) (2000); see also Adoption Assistance and Child Welfare Act of 1980, Pub. L. No. 96–272, 94 Stat. 500 (codified as amended in scattered sections of 42 U.S.C.) (requiring states to adopt federal standards to obtain federal funds). The Adoption Assistance and Child Welfare Act has reportedly spawned foster care litigation in at least thirty-four states. See National Center For Youth Law, Foster Care Reform Litigation Docket (2006). Available at http://www.youthlaw.org/fileadmin/ncyl/youthlaw/publications/fcrldocket06.pdf. Additionally, the Clean Air Act of 1970 establishes a right to healthy air and explicitly authorizes citizen suits. See Clean Air Act § 304(a), 42 U.S.C. §7604(a) (2000).

27. ROSS SANDLER & DAVID SCHOENBROD, DEMOCRACY BY DECREE: WHAT HAPPENS WHEN COURTS RUN GOVERNMENT 233 (2003).

28. Mark Tushnet, *Sir, Yes, Sir: The Courts, Congress and Structural Injunctions,* 20 CONST. COM. 189 (2003).

29. Chayes, *supra* note 4, at 1313. In one area, that of prison litigations, Congress has acted affirmatively to limit judicial involvement. Thus, the Prison Litigation Reform Act of 1995 (PLRA), among other things, limits the type of relief that courts can provide, makes any relief granted subject to termination after two years, and abridges the courts' authority to appoint a special master. Pub. L. No. 104–134, 110 Stat. 1321 (codified as amended at scattered sections of 18 U.S.C.). Although the PLRA has not totally eliminated prison reform litigation, see, for example, Benjamin v. Fraser, 343 F.3d 35 (2d Cir. 2003) (court continues long-standing litigation involving prisoner rights despite passage of PLRA; the latest decision in this still active case is Benjamin v. Horn, 2008 WL 4500689 (S.D.N.Y. October 7, 2008); and Wilson v. Vannatta, 291 F. Supp.2d 811 (N.D. Ind. 2003) (motion to dismiss prisoners' claim that deprivation of food, exercise and medication violated the Constitution denied), it has substantially decreased their incidence and impact. William C. Collins, *Bumps in the Road to the Courthouse: The Supreme Court and the Prison Litigation Reform Act,* 24 PACE L. REV. 651 (2005) (rate of prison civil rights filings declined from 29.3 per 1,000 prisoners in 1981 to 11.4 in 2001).

30. DONALD HOROWITZ, THE COURTS AND SOCIAL POLICY, *supra* note 5.

31. Neil K. Komesar, *A Job for the Judges: The Judiciary and the Constitution in a Massive and Complex Society,* 86 MICH. L. REV. 657, 698 (1988). Contemporary critics of the judicial role in the state court litigations continue to rely on Horowitz and ignore Komesar's important insight on the need for comparative perspectives in this area. See, for example, Joshua Dunn & Martha Derthick, *Adequacy Litigation and the Separation of Powers,* in SCHOOL MONEY TRIALS: THE LEGAL PURSUIT OF EDUCATIONAL ADEQUACY, 335–36 (Martin R. West & Paul E. Peterson eds., 2007).

Chapter Two

1. See DOUGLAS S. REED, ON EQUAL TERMS: THE CONSTITUTIONAL POLITICS OF EDUCATIONAL OPPORTUNITY (2001) (examining use of state constitutional provisions to increase educational opportunities); James E. Ryan, *Schools, Race and Money,* 109 YALE L.J. 249 (1999) (describing shift from desegregation to fiscal equity cases); Drew E. Days, *Brown Blues: Rethinking the Integrative Ideal,* in REDEFINING EQUALITY 139 (Neal Devins & Davison M. Douglas eds., 1997) (describing how increasing numbers of blacks were turning from the integrative ideal because of the difficulties in implementing *Brown*).

2. 411 U.S. 1 (1973).

3. 411 U.S. at 49. For a detailed discussion of the Supreme Court's decision

in *Rodriguez*, see Michael A. Rebell, *Education Adequacy, Democracy and the Courts*, in ACHIEVING HIGH EDUCATIONAL STANDARDS FOR ALL (Christopher Edley, Timothy Ready, & Catherine Snow eds., 1992); PAUL A. SRACIC, SAN ANTONIO V. RODRIGUEZ AND THE PURSUIT OF EQUAL EDUCATION: THE DEBATE OVER DISCRIMINATION AND SCHOOL FUNDING (2006).

4. Serrano v. Priest, 557 P.2d 929, 949–52 (Cal. 1976).

5. Robinson v. Cahill, 303 A.2d 273 (N.J. 1973); Horton v. Meskill, 376 A.2d 359 (Conn. 1977); Pauley v. Kelly, 255 S.E.2d 859 (W.Va. 1979).

6. 376 A.2d 359 (Conn. 1977).

7. George P. Richardson & Robert E. Lamitie, *Improving Connecticut School Aid: A Case Study with Model-Based Policy Analysis*, 15 J. EDUC. FIN. 169, 171 (1989).

8. See generally, RICHARD LEHNE, THE QUEST FOR JUSTICE; THE POLITICS OF SCHOOL FINANCE REFORM (1978) (giving a detailed analysis of the history of the *Robinson* litigation). Litigation has continued in New Jersey, down to the present day, as the Robinson case was followed by Abbott v. Burke, 575 A.2d 369 (N.J. 1990), which has at the time of this writing resulted in no fewer than nineteen follow-up compliance orders by the New Jersey Supreme Court.

9. Serrano v. Priest, 557 P.2d at 940 n.21.

10. Mark Schaur & Steve Durbin, *"Protecting" School Funding*, SACRAMENTO BEE, June 28, 1993, at B14. William A. Fischel argued in *Did Serrano Cause Proposition 13?* 42 NAT'L TAX J. 465 (1989) that Serrano removed any incentive for residents in affluent districts to oppose Proposition 13. Fischel has also argued more generally that court orders that increase the level of education funding dampen voter support for public education. William A. Fishel, *How Judges Are Making Public Schools Worse*, CITY J. 30 (Summer 1998). Richard Briffault rejects this contention, stating that the significance of local control lies in opportunities for accountability and participation; he also argues that an overemphasis on local funding for education distorts fiscal support for education as school districts seek to minimize tax rates in order to attract or keep wealthy property owners. Richard Briffault, *The Role of Local Control in School Finance Reform*, 24 CONN. L. REV. 773 (1992).

11. The states in which defendants prevailed were as follows: Arizona: Shofstall v. Hollins, 515 P.2d 590 (Ariz. 1973); Illinois: Blase v. State, 302 N.E.2d 46 (Ill. 1973); Michigan: Milliken v. Green, 212 N.W.2d 711 (Mich. 1973); Montana: Woodahl v. Straub, 520 P.2d 776 (Mont. 1974); Idaho: Thompson v. Engelking, 537 P.2d 635 (Idaho 1975); Oregon: Olsen v. State, 554 P.2d 139 (Or. 1976); Pennsylvania: Danson v. Casey, 399 A.2d 360 (Pa. 1979); Ohio: Board of Educ. (Cincinnati) v. Walter, 390 N.E.2d 813 (Ohio 1979); Georgia: McDaniel v. Thomas, 285 S.E.2d 156, 167 (Ga. 1981); New York: Board of Educ. (Levittown Union Free Sch. Dist.) v. Nyquist, 439 N.E.2d 359 (N.Y. 1982); Colorado: Lujan v. Board of Educ., 649 P.2d 1005 (Colo. 1982); Maryland: Hornbeck v. Somer-

set County Bd. of Educ., 458 A.2d 758 (Md. 1983); Oklahoma: Fair Sch. Finance Council of Okla., Inc. v. State, 746 P.2d 1135 (Okla. 1987); North Carolina: Britt v. North Carolina State Bd. of Educ., 357 S.E.2d 432, aff'd mem. 361 S.E.2d 71 (N.C. 1987); and South Carolina: Richland County v. Campbell, 364 S.E.2d 470 (S.C. 1988).

Plaintiff victories occurred during that period, as indicated, *supra* notes 4–5, in California, New Jersey, Connecticut, and West Virginia, as well as in the following states: Washington, Seattle Sch. Dist. No. 1 v. State, 585 P.2d 71 (Wash. 1978); Wyoming, Washakie County Sch. Dist. No. 1 v. Herschler, 606 P.2d 310 (Wyo. 1980); and Arkansas, Dupree v. Alma Sch. Dist. No. 30, 651 S.W.2d 90 (Ark. 1983).

12. Specifically, plaintiffs have won the liability or motion to dismiss decisions of the highest state courts or final trial court action in "adequacy" cases in the following twenty states: Alaska: Kasayulie v. State No. 3AN-97-3782 (Alaska Super. Ct. Sept. 1, 1999); Arizona: Roosevelt Elementary Sch. Dist. No. 66 v. Bishop, 887 P.2d 806 (Ariz. 1994); Arkansas: Lake View Sch. Dist. No. 25 v. Huckabee, 91 S.W.3d 472 (Ark. 2002); Idaho: Idaho Schs. for Equal Educ. Opportunity, 976 P.2d 913 (Idaho 1998); Id. Schs. for Equal Educ. Opportunity v. Evans, 850 P.2d 724 (Idaho 1993); Kansas: Montoy v. State, 120 P.3d 306 (Kan. 2005); Kentucky: Rose v. Council for Better Educ., 790 S.W.2d 186 (Ky. 1989); Maryland: Bradford v. Md. State Bd. of Educ., No. 94340058/CE189672 (Cir. Ct. 2000); Massachusetts: McDuffy v. Sec'y of the Exec. Office of Educ., 615 N.E.2d 516 (Mass. 1993); Montana: Columbia Falls Elementary Sch. Dist. No. 6 v. State, 109 P.3d 257 (Mont. 2005); Helena Elementary Sch. Dist. No.1 v. State, 769 P.2d 684 (Mont. 1989); Missouri: Comm. for Educ. Equal. v. State, 878 S.W.2d 446 (Mo. 1994) (final trial court decision; appeal dismissed on procedural grounds); New Hampshire: Claremont Sch. Dist. v. Governor, 703 A.2d 1353 (N.H. 1997); New Mexico: Zuni School District v. State, No. CV-98-14-ll (McKinley County Dist. Ct. Oct. 14, 1999); New Jersey: Abbott v. Burke, 575 A.2d 359 (N.J. 1990); New York: Campaign for Fiscal Equity, Inc. v. State, 801 N.E. 2d 326 (N.Y. 2003); North Carolina: Hoke County Bd. of Educ. v. State, 599 S.E.2d 365 (N.C. 2004); Ohio: DeRolph v. State, 667 N.E.2d 733 (Ohio 1997); South Carolina: Abbeville County Sch. Dist. v. State, 515 S.E.2d 535 (S.C. 1999); Texas: Edgewood Indep. Sch. Dist. v. Kirby, 777 S.W.2d 391 (Tex. 1989); Vermont: Brigham v. State, 692 A.2d 384 (Vt. 1997); and Wyoming: Campbell County Sch. Dist. v. State, 907 P.2d 1238 (Wyo. 1995). This list does not include follow-up decisions at the compliance stage, many of which are discussed in the chapters that follow.

During this time, defendants have won final liability decisions in "adequacy" cases in the following states: Alabama: Ex parte James, 836 So. 2d 813 (Ala. 2002); Arizona: Crane Elementary Sch. Dist. v. State of Arizona, No. CV 2001-016305 (Ariz. Ct. App. 2006) (adequacy of services to English language learners and at-risk students); Florida: Coal. for Adequacy & Fairness in Sch. Funding, Inc. v. Chiles, 680 So.2d 400 (Fla. 1996); Illinois: Committee for Educational Rights v. Edgar, 672 N.E.2d 1178 (1996); Lewis v. Spagnolo, 710 N.E.2d 798 (1999); Nebraska: Neb. Coal. for Educ. Equity & Adequacy v. Heinman, 273 Neb. 531 (2007); Oklahoma: Okla. Educ. Ass'n v. State ex rel. Okla. Legislature, 158 P.3d 1058 (Okla. 2007); Oregon: Pendleton Sch. Dist. v. State, 200 P.3d 133 (Or. 2009); Pennsylvania: Marrero v. Commonwealth, 559 Pa. 14 (1999); and Rhode Island: City of Pawtucket v. Sundlun, 662 A.2d 40 (R.I. 1995).

Currently, additional cases are pending at the trial court or appeals stages in eight states: Alaska, Colorado, Connecticut, Illinois, Indiana, Missouri, South Dakota, and Washington. For up-to-date information about the status of these cases see, the Access Web site, http://www.schoolfunding.info.

13. Arizona: Roosevelt Elementary Sch. Dist. No. 66 v. Bishop, 877 P.2d 806 (Ariz. 1994), distinguishing Shofstall v. Hollins, 515 P.2d 590 (Ariz. 1973); Idaho: Idaho Schools for Equal Educ. Opportunity v. Evans, 850 P.2d 636 (Idaho 1993), distinguishing Thompson v. Engelking, 537 P.2d 635 (Idaho 1975); Maryland: Bradford v. Maryland Bd. of Educ., No. 94300058/CE 189672 (Cir. Ct., October 18, 1996), distinguishing Hornbeck v. Somerset County Bd. of Educ., 458 A.2d 758 (Md. 1983); Montana: Helena Elementary Sch. Dist. No. 1 v. State, 769 P.2d 684 (Mont. 1989), modified, 784 P.2d 412 (Mont. 1990), reversing Woodahl v. Straub, 520 P.2d 776 (Mont. 1974); New York: Campaign for Fiscal Equity v. State, 655 N.E.2d 661 (N.Y. 1995), distinguishing Levittown v. Nyquist, 439 N.E.2d 359 (N.Y. 1982), North Carolina: Leandro v. State, 488 S.E.2d 249 (N.C. 1997), distinguishing Britt v. North Carolina State Bd. of Educ., 357 S.E.2d 432, aff'd mem. 361 S.E.2d 71 (N.C. 1987); Ohio: De Rolph v. State of Ohio, 677 N.E.2d 733 (Ohio 1997), distinguishing Board of Educ. City Sch. Dist. of Cincinnati v. Walter, 39 N.E.2d 813 (Ohio 1979). See also Seattle Sch. Dist. No. 1 v. State, 585 P.2d 71 (Wash. 1978) (declaring state education finance system unconstitutional and overruling Northshore Sch. Dist. v. Kinnear, 530 P.2d 178 (1974).

14. Georgia Const. art VIII, § 1.

15. N.Y. Const. art XI, § 1. The specific language in this constitutional provision states that "the legislature shall provide for the maintenance and support of a system of free common schools, wherein all of the children of this state may be educated. The New York Court of Appeals has interpreted the concept of "educated" in this provision to mean a sound basic education. Levittown, 439 N.E.2d at 368–69 (1982). See also Campaign for Fiscal Equity v. State (CFE I), 655 N.E.2d 661, 665 (N.Y. 1995) (holding that New York State constitution's education clause requires a sound basic education). Other courts have interpreted similar provisions in their constitutions to have substantive contemporary content. See, for example, Leandro v. State, 488 S.E.2d 249, 257 (N.C. 1997) (holding that "North Carolina Constitution requires that all children have the opportunity for a sound basic education . . ."); Tennessee Small Sch. Syst. v. McWherter, 851

S.W.2d 139, 150–51 (Tenn. 1993) (holding that education clause requires a system that "generally prepare[s] students intellectually for a mature life."); Fair Sch. Fin. Council of Okla. v. State, 746 P.2d 1135, 1149 (Okla. 1987) (holding that education clause requires "a basic, adequate education").

16. N.J. Const. art. IV, § 1. Cf. Idaho Const. art. IX, § 1 (a "general, uniform and thorough system" of education.); Ky. Const. § 183 (an "efficient system of common schools throughout the state.").

17. Mont. Const. art. X, § 1.

18. See generally, LAWRENCE CREMIN, AMERICAN EDUCATION: THE NATIONAL EXPERIENCE 1783–1876 (1980); C. KAESTLE, PILLARS OF THE REPUBLIC: COMMON SCHOOLS AND AMERICAN SOCIETY 1780–1860 (1983).

19. See, Mass. Const. part 2, chap. 5, § 2; see also Brigham v. State, 692 A.2d 384, 675; N.H. Const. art. 83.

20. McDuffy v. Secretary of Educ., 615 N.E.2d 516, 545 (Mass. 1993). Accord: Claremont Sch. Dist. v. Governor, 635 A.2d 1375, 1381 (N.H. 1993).

21. Attempts to categorize the constitutional language in the state constitutions in terms of their relative strength have proved unavailing. For example, William E. Thro, in *The Role of Language of the State Education Clauses in School Finance Litigation,* 79 EDUC. L. REP. 19 (1993), set forth four basic categories related to the relative strength of the educational clauses, which he then organized according to which states employed which type of language: (1) seventeen states simply mandate free public education; (2) twenty-two states "impose some type of minimum standard of quality"; (3) six states require a "stronger and more specific educational mandate" than the states in items (1) or (2); and (4) four states regard education as an "important, if not the most important, duty of the state." *Id.* at 23–24. His predictions regarding the likely outcome of court cases based on his categorizations have, however, been belied by the actual decisions. For example, on the basis of Thro's categorization, plaintiffs should have won the cases in Maine, Rhode Island, and Illinois, which they lost, and they should have lost the cases in New York, North Carolina, and Vermont, which they won.

22. Brigham v. State, 692 A.2 at 680. See also Serrano v. Priest, 487 P.2d. 1241, 1258–59 (Cal. 1971) (education is "crucial to . . . the functioning of democracy [and to] an individual's opportunity to compete successfully in the economic marketplace . . .); Claremont Sch. Dist. v. Governor, 703 A.2d 1353 (N.H. 1997) (defining constitutional duty in terms of preparing "citizens for their role as participants and as potential competitors in today's marketplace of ideas."); Robinson v. Cahill, 303 A.2d 273, 295 (N.J. 1973) (defining the constitutional requirement as "that educational opportunity which is needed in the contemporary setting to equip a child for his role as a citizen and as a competitor in the labor market."); Campaign for Fiscal Equity, Inc. v. State, 655 N.E.2d 661, 665 (N.Y. 1995) (defining "sound basic education" in terms of preparing students to

"function productively as civic participants . . . qualified to vote or serve as a juror . . . capably and knowledgeably" and "the ability to obtain competitive employment."); Edgewood Indep. Sch. Dist v. Kirby, 777 S.W.2d 391, 395–96 (Tex. 1989) (citing intent of framers of education clause to diffuse knowledge "for the preservation of democracy . . . and for the growth of the economy."); Vincent v. Voight, 614 N.W.2d 388, 396 (Wis. 2000) ("a sound basic education is one that will equip students for their roles as citizens and enable them to succeed economically and personally); Campbell County School District v. State, 907 P.2d 1238, 1259 (Wyo. 2001) (defining the core constitutional requirement in terms of providing students with "a uniform opportunity to become equipped for their future roles as citizens, participants in the political system, and competitors both economically and intellectually").

John Dinan argues in a recent law review article that the eighteenth- and nineteenth-century drafters of these state constitutional clauses saw them as being largely hortatory and did not intend to create a judicially enforceable right that could be used to overturn legislative judgments regarding an equitable, adequate, and/or uniform education. John Dinan, *The Meaning of State Constitutional Education Clauses: Evidence from the Constitutional Convention Debates*, 70 ALB. L. REV. 927 (2007). See also John C. Eastman, *Reinterpreting the Education Clauses in State Constitutions*, in SCHOOL MONEY TRIALS: THE LEGAL PURSUIT OF EDUCATIONAL ADEQUACY 55 (Martin R. West & Paul E. Peterson eds., 2007). A contrary view that holds that the state constitutions contained "rich, purposeful language" that was "intended to create the educations and the citizens they spoke about in that rhetoric" is set forth in INSTITUTE FOR EDUCATIONAL EQUITY AND OPPORTUNITY, EDUCATION IN THE 50 STATES: A DESKBOOK OF THE HISTORY OF STATE CONSTITUTIONS AND LAWS ABOUT EDUCATION (2008). The vast majority of state court judges have, however, rejected this originalist viewpoint and have held that the constitutional purpose "should be measured with reference to the demands of modern society . . . " CFE II, 801 N.E.2d at 330.

23. Lake View Sch. Dist. v. Huckabee, No. 1992-5318 (Ark. Ch. Ct., May 25, 2001).

24. Williams v. California, First Amended Complaint, ¶ 280 (No. 312236, Cal. Sup. Ct., 2000).

25. CFE II, 801 N.E.2d at 334 n.4.

26. Abbeville County Sch. Dist. v. State, Case No. 93-CP-31-0169 (S.C. Ct. Common Pleas, December 29, 2005).

27. NATIONAL COMMISSION ON EXCELLENCE IN EDUCATION, A NATION AT RISK: THE IMPERATIVE FOR EDUCATIONAL REFORM 5 (1983); see also CARNEGIE FORUM ON EDUCATION AND THE ECONOMY, TASK FORCE ON TEACHING AS A PROFESSION, A NATION PREPARED: TEACHERS FOR THE 21ST CENTURY (1986); THEODORE SIZER, HORACE'S COMPROMISE: THE DILEMMA OF THE AMERICAN HIGH SCHOOL (1989).

28. NATIONAL ASSESSMENT OF EDUCATIONAL PROGRAMS, AMERICA'S CHAL-

LENGE: ACCELERATED ACADEMIC ACHIEVEMENT (1990); see also Robert L. Linn & Stephen B. Dunbar, *The Nation's Report Card: Good News and Bad about Trends in Achievement*, 72 PHI DELTA KAPPAN 127, 131 (1990).

29. INA V.S. MULLIS ET AL., NATIONAL ASSESSMENT OF EDUCATIONAL PROGRESS 1992. TRENDS IN ACADEMIC PROGRESS, 4–5 (1994); see also U.S. DEPARTMENT OF EDUCATION, AMERICA 2000: AN EDUCATION STRATEGY (1991) (finding that U.S. schools are not developing the skills and knowledge that students need today to compete in a globally competitive economy).

30. Two additional national summits were held in 1996 and 1999; the president, most of the nation's governors, and the CEOs of major corporations as well as commissioners of education from most of the states attended these events. For a discussion of the origin of the national standards movement see MARC S. TUCKER & JUDY B. CODDING, STANDARDS FOR OUR SCHOOLS, 40–43 (1998); and DIANE RAVITCH, NATIONAL STANDARDS IN AMERICAN EDUCATION (1995).

31. Goals 2000: Educate America Act, 20 U.S.C. §§ 5801–5871 (1994).

32. 20 U.S.C.A. § 6301 et. seq. (2001).

33. For general descriptions of the standards-based reform approach, see SUSAN H. FUHRMAN, DESIGN OF COHERENT EDUCATION POLICY: IMPROVING THE SYSTEM (1993); TUCKER & CODDING, *supra* note 30; ROBERT ROTHMAN, MEASURING UP: STANDARDS, ASSESSMENT AND SCHOOL REFORM (1995).

34. Molly McUsic, The Use of Education Clauses in Litigation, 28 HARV. J. ON LEGIS. 307, 328 (1991); see also Michael Heise, *State Constitutions, School Finance Litigations, and the "Third Wave": From Equity to Adequacy*, 68 TEMPLE L. REV. 1151, 1175 (1995) ("[A]dequacy decisions do not pose a direct and immediate threat to local control of schools.").

35. For more detailed discussions of the strategic advantages of the adequacy approach, see Peter Enrich, *Leaving Equality Behind: New Directions in School Finance Reform*, 48 VAND. L. REV. 101 (1995); and Molly S. McUsic, *The Law's Role in the Distribution of Education: The Promises and Pitfalls of School Finance Litigation*, in LAW AND SCHOOL REFORM: SIX STRATEGIES FOR PROMOTING EDUCATIONAL EQUITY, 88, 114 (Jay Heubert ed. 1999). For a recent philosophical perspective on this issue, see Harry Brighouse, *Putting Educational Equality in Its Place*, 3 EDUC. FIN. & POL'Y 444, 446 (2008) ("The view in favor of adequacy gains support from the fact that few egalitarians object to all educational inequalities, even in principle, and that it seems impossible to produce strict equality of educational outcomes even if that were desirable.").

For general discussions of the shift from "equity" to "adequacy" holdings in the recent cases, see Allen W. Hubsch, *The Emerging Right To Education under State Constitutional Law*, 65 TEMPLE L. REV. 1325 (1992); Richard J. Stark, *Education Reform: Judicial Interpretations of State Constitutions' Education Finance Provisions—Education vs. Equality*, 1991 ANN. SURV. AM. L. 609; William Thro, *Note, To Render Them Safe: The Analysis of State Constitutional*

Provisions in Public School Finance Reform, 75 VA. L. REV. 1639 (1989); Alexandra Natapoff, *1993: The Year of Living Dangerously: State Courts Expand the Right to Education,* 92 WEST EDUC. L. REP. 755 (1994); and Deborah A. Verstegen & Terry Whitney, *From Courthouses to Schoolhouses: Emerging Judicial Theories of Adequacy and Equity,* 11 EDUC. POL'Y, 330, 331 (1991).

36. Deborah A. Verstegen, *Judicial Analysis during the New Wave of School Finance Litigation: The New Adequacy in Education,* 24 J. EDUC. FIN. 51, 67 (1998). See also, William H. Clune, *The Shift from Equity to Adequacy in School Finance,* 8 EDUC. POL'Y 376 (1994) (describing the thrust of the cases as calling for "a high minimum level"); Paul A. Minorini & Stephen D. Sugarman, *Educational Adequacy and the Courts: The Promise and Problems of Moving to a New Paradigm,* in EQUITY AND ADEQUACY IN EDUCATION FINANCE: ISSUES AND PERSPECTIVES, 175, 188 (Helen F. Ladd et al. eds., 1999) (stating that the cases call for a "high minimum approach [that] focuses on what would be needed to assure that all children have access to those educational opportunities that are necessary to gain a level of learning and skills that are now required, say, to obtain a good job in our increasingly technologically complex society and to participate effectively in our ever more complicated political process.").

37. James E. Ryan, *Standards, Testing and School Finance Litigation,* 86 TEX. L. REV. 1223 (2008). See also Richard Briffault, *Adding Adequacy to Equity,* in SCHOOL MONEY TRIALS, *supra* note 22 (arguing that in both theory and practice there has been a "general blurring of adequacy and equity concerns" in the cases. *Id.* at 47); William S. Koski & Rob Reich, *When Adequate Isn't: The Retreat from Equity in Educational Law and Policy and Why It Matters,* 56 EMORY L.J. (2006) (criticizing "adequacy" for including only static, nonrelational standards).

38. See discussion *infra* in chapter 3. Goodwin Liu, *Education, Equality and National Citizenship,* 116 YALE L.J. 330 (2006), while acknowledging that there is relational dimension to educational adequacy, also stresses that "citizenship requires a threshold level of knowledge and competence for public duties such as voting, serving on a jury and participating in community affairs . . . " *Id.* at 345. See also Debra Saatz, *Equality, Adequacy and Educational Policy,* 3 EDUC. FIN. & POL'Y 424 (2008) ("Educational adequacy should be tied to the requirements of equal citizenship.").

39. The one arguable exception is the affirmation, without opinion, by the Arizona Supreme Court of a lower court's summary judgment ruling that refused to provide extra resources for English language learners and other at-risk students to remedy educational disparities "caused by socioeconomic factors rather than by the financing schemes." Crane Elementary Sch. Dist. v. State of Arizona, No. CV 2001-016305, slip op. at 20 (Ariz. Ct. App. 2006). Whether this ruling should be considered an "adequacy" decision or a more focused attempt to establish specific constitutional rights for English language learners or

other at-risk groups is debatable. Note in this regard that the Arizona Supreme Court had previously held that the capital funding provisions of the state education finance system were unconstitutional. Roosevelt Sch. Dist. No. 66 v. Bishop, 877 P.2d 806 (Ariz. 1994). In any event, since the matter was decided on summary judgment, the court did not thoroughly examine the evidence through a trial process.

40. A moving description of the impact of these resource deficiencies is contained in JONATHAN KOZOL, SAVAGE INEQUALITIES (1991).

41. Coalition for Adequacy and Fairness in Sch. Funding, Inc. v. Chiles, 680 So.2d 400, 408 (Fla. 1996).

42. Marrero v. Commonwealth, 739 A.2d 110, 113–14 (Pa. 1999). In Pendleton Sch. Dist. v. State, 200 P.3d 133 (Or. 2009), the Oregon Supreme Court held that the legislature had failed to fund the public school at the constitutionally required level, but it also held that the constitutional provision at issue did not empower the court to compel them to do so.

43. Lake View Sch. Dist. No. 25 v. Huckabee, 91 S.W.3d 472, 484 (Ark. 2002).

44. Idaho Schs. for Equal Educ. Opportunity v. Evans, 123 Idaho 573, 583 (1993). See also Rose v. Council for Better Educ., Inc., 790 S.W.2d 186, 209 (Ky. 1989) ("To avoid deciding the case because of 'legislative discretion,' 'legislative function,' etc., would be a denigration of our own constitutional duty. To allow the General Assembly . . . to decide whether its actions are constitutional is literally unthinkable.").

45. 369 U.S. 186 (1962). Six of the seven cases specifically cited *Baker.* The Oklahoma decision relied on art. IV, § 1, of the state constitution, the separation of powers clause, in declaring that the educational adequacy claims raised a nonjusticiable political question, without mentioning *Baker.* See Oklahoma Educ. Ass'n v. State, 158 P.3d 1058, 1066 (Okla. 2007).

46. 369 U.S. at 217.

47. Martin Redish, *Judicial Review and the "Political Question,"* 79 N.W.U. L. REV. 1031, 1059–60 (1984). See also, Louis Henkin, *Is There a "Political Question" Doctrine,* 85 YALE L.J. 597 (1976) (arguing that although courts should give deference to the substantive decisions of the political branches, there is no justification for permitting self-monitoring of their constitutional compliance); Richard F. Fallon, *Judicially Manageable Standards and Constitutional Meaning,* 119 HARV. L. REV. 1274 (2006) (arguing that most constitutional tests would not pass muster under a strict application of the 'judicially manageable standard' concept).

48. See, for example, Goldwater v. Carter, 444 U.S. 996 (1979) (refusing to review president's termination of mutual defense treaty with republic of China without senatorial consent); Gilligan v. Morgan, 413 U.S. 1 (1973) (refusing to consider injunction against national guard actions in regard to student disruptions).

49. Nixon v. United States, 506 U.S. 224 (1993) (refusing to consider Senate procedure for impeaching a judge).

50. See, for example, Powell v. McCormack, 395 U.S. 486 (1969) (prohibiting Congress from removing one of its members from his seat in the House of Representatives due to alleged fiscal improprieties.).

51. See Wesberry v. Sanders, 376 U.S. 1 (1964) (holding that population of Georgia's congressional districts should be "as nearly as practicable" to one person, one vote); Reynolds v. Sims, 377 U.S. 533 (1964) (articulating of one person, one vote standard in regard to reapportionment of voting districts for Alabama legislature). *Wesberry* relied on article I, § 2 of the U.S. Constitution ("Representatives   shall be apportioned among the several states which may be included within this union, according to their respective numbers . . . "), while *Reynolds* relied on the Equal Protection Clause of the Fourteenth Amendment. Numerous other Supreme Court cases have applied the one person, one vote standard in a broad range of political and policy contexts. See, for example, Karcher v. Daggett, 466 U.S. 910 (1984) (striking down New Jersey congressional districts that deviated from population equivalency by less than 1 percent); Avery v. Midland Count, 390 U.S. 474 (1968) (holding that one person, one vote standard does apply to state and local governmental entities with a legislative function); Ball v. James, 451 U.S. 355 (1981) (upholding voting structure of Arizona water districts, which was based on proportion of landownership rather than one person, one vote, due to narrow, specialized function of legislative body); Board of Estimate v. Morris, 489 U.S. 688 (1989) (striking down New York City's Board of Estimate, which had equivalent representation from all five boroughs in spite of vast population differences between them).

Recently, in the related area of political gerrymandering, a plurality of the Court held that there were no "judicially discoverable and manageable standards" to govern the Court's rulings. Vieth v. Jubelirer, 541 U.S. 267, 267 (2004). This decision reversed the Court's earlier ruling in Davis v. Bandemer, 478 U.S. 109 (1986), which had held that political gerrymandering was justiciable. Justice Kennedy, although agreeing that no manageable standards had been demonstrated in the immediate case, refused in his concurring opinion to bar future courts from attempting to define standards and remedies for political gerrymandering. 541 U.S. at 309–12 (Kennedy, J., concurring).

52. Helen Hershkoff, *Positive Rights and State Constitutions: The Limits of Federal Rationality Review,* 112 HARV. L. REV. 1131, 1137 (1999). See also Robert F. Williams, *The Brennan Lecture: Interpreting State Constitutions as Unique Legal Documents,* 27 OKLA L. REV. 189, 192 (2002) ("State constitutions often contain positive or affirmative rights, while federal constitutional rights are primarily negative in nature."); Robert A. Schapiro, *Judicial Deference and Interpretive Coordinacy in State and Federal Constitutional Law,* 85 CORNELL L. REV. 656 (2000) (noting that state constitutions often establish affirmative obligations that

the government must discharge); Jonathan Feldman, *Separation of Power and Judicial Review of Positive Rights Claims: The Role of State Courts in an Era of Positive Government*, 24 RUTGERS L. REV 1057 (1993) (distinguishing "positive" separation of powers from "negative" separations of powers); Robert F. Williams, *Equality Guarantees in State Constitutions*, 63 TEX. L. REV. 1195 (1985) (describing how concepts of equality in state constitutions differ from federal equal protection concepts); cf. Frank B. Cross, *The Error of Positive Rights*, 48 UCLA L. REV. 857 (2001) (discussing the difficulties for courts in enforcing positive rights).

53. Columbia Falls Elem. Sch. Dist. No. 6 v. State, 326 Mont. 304, 310 (2005).

54. Even critics of the courts' role in sound basic education cases acknowledge that "Courts use it [the justiciability doctrine] only if they are predisposed not to enter into a controversy, deploying it or ignoring it as they choose." Joshua Dunn and Martha Derthick, *Adequacy Litigation and the Separation of Powers*, in SCHOOL MONEY TRIALS, *supra* note 22 at 326.

55. Rock v. Thompson, 426 N.E. 2d 891, 896 (Ill. 1981). A few years later, in holding that voters could challenge the authority of a political party's committee to appoint an individual to fill a vacant legislative seat, the Illinois Supreme Court also stated that

> a determination by a court that if an integral part of the legislative branch of government is permitted to proceed in a particular manner the result will be a deprivation of a constitutional right of an individual, does not constitute a lack of respect due a coordinate branch of the government, but it is an exercise of one of the duties committed to the judiciary. Kluk v. Lang, 531 N.E.2d 790, 797 (Ill. 1988).

56. Committee for Educational Rights v. Edgar, 672 N.E. 2d 1178 (Ill. 1996) (emphasis added).

57. *Id.* at 1191. Three years later, plaintiffs in Lewis E. v. Spagnolo, 710 N.E.2d 798 (Ill. 1999) attempted to distinguish *Edgar* by bringing a claim based on denial of a minimum adequate education, arguing that a denial of basic services provided a manageable judicial standard, even if high-quality education would not. Citing *Edgar,* the Illinois Supreme Court also rejected this claim on justiciability grounds. In August 2008, yet another sound basic education case was filed in Illinois, Chicago Urban League v. State of Illinois, Civ. No. 30490/08 (Cir. Ct., Cook Co.). No decision has yet been rendered in that proceeding.

Outside the area of educational adequacy, however, the Illinois courts have continued to apply the principles of *Kluk* and *Donovan* and have rejected defendants' attempts to declare a range of other issues nonjusticiable political questions. See, for example, People v. Lawton, 818 N.E.2d 326, 336 (Ill. 2004) (appellant permitted to challenge effectiveness of his attorney in proceedings under the Sexually Dangerous Persons Act); City of Elmhurst ex rel. Mastrino v. City of

Elmhurst, 649 N.E.2d 1334, 1341 (Ill. App. 1994) (taxpayers allowed to seek injunction to prevent city from paying for alderman's legal defense in a libel case); Roti v. Washington, 500 N.E.2d 463 (Ill. App. 1989) (city council members could file action for declaration that council resolutions were improperly enacted).

58. Neeley v. W. Orange-Cove Consol. Indep. Sch. Dist., 176 S.W.3d 746, 778–79 (Tex. 2005). As Richard Fallon points out, "a judicially manageable standard is an output in any case in which a court successfully devises a test that can thereafter be used implement a constitutional provision." Fallon, *supra* note 47, at 1283. As will be discussed further in chapter 4, adoption by legislatures and state education departments in Illinois and by most other states of standards-based reforms that require the states to develop specific academic content and proficiency standards render the argument based on "lack of manageable standards" especially inappropriate in sound basic education cases.

59. Dade Co. Classroom Teachers Assoc. v. Legislature of the State of Florida, 269 So.2d 684, 686 (Fla. 1972).

60. 680 So.2d 400 (Fla. 1996).

61. Allen v. Barbour Co, 2007 WL 1793874 (Ala., June 22, 2007).

62. Ex parte James v. Ala. Coal for Equity, 836 So.2d 813 (Ala. 2002).

63. 731 N.W.2d 164, 182–83 (Neb. 2007).

64. *Id.* at 183.

65. City of Pawtucket v. Sundlun, 662 A.2d 40, 59 (R.I. 1995).

66. "In most public rights cases, courts first rule on the merits, then struggle with remedial issues. Sometimes, however, worries about the difficulty of crafting remedies contribute to decisions that a category of dispute is non-justiciable." Fallon, *supra* note 47, at 1293.

67. See, for example, Molly A. Hunter, *All Eyes Forward: Public Engagement and Educational Reform in Kentucky,* 28 J. L. & EDUC. 485 (1999) (noting that immediate legislative response to court order led to substantial increases in funding for low-wealth districts).

68. KENTUCKY DEPARTMENT OF EDUCATION, RESULTS MATTER: A DECADE OF DIFFERENCE IN KENTUCKY'S PUBLIC SCHOOLS 1990–2000 REPORT ON THE 10TH ANNIVERSARY OF EDUCATION REFORM IN KENTUCKY, 72–87 (2000), available at http://www.kde.state.ky.us/NR/rdonlyres/EF0A1C1D-F709-44D3-8CC2-74E 113172B51/0/10thAnniversary Report.pdf.

69. Hancock v. Driscoll, No. 02-2978, 2004 WL 877984, at *5 (Mass. Super. Ct., April 26, 2004) (expounding on the key changes of the Education Reform Act), reversed on other grounds, 822 N.E.2d 1134 (Mass. 2005) (summarizing the background and effect of the Education Reform Act).

70. For example, on the fourth grade English Language Arts examinations, the percentage of students meeting proficiency standards rose from 20 percent in 1998 to 55 percent in 2003; on the tenth grade math examination, the percentage meeting proficiency standards over that five-year period rose from 25 to 50 per-

cent. Rennie Center for Education Research & Policy, Reaching Capacity: A Blueprint for the State Role in Improving Low Performing Schools and Districts, 9 (2005), http://www.renniecenter.org/research.

71. Michael A. Rebell & Jeffrey Metzler, *Rapid Response, Radical Reform: The Story of School Finance Litigation in Vermont*, 31 J. L. & Educ. 167 (2002) (describing the rapid passage of the Equal Educational Opportunity Act of 1997); Thomas Downes, "School Finance Reform and School Quality: Lessons from Vermont," in *Helping Children Left Behind: State Aid and the Pursuit of Educational Equity* (John Yinger, ed., 2004). (Act 60 has dramatically reduced dispersion in education spending, and initial evidence indicates that student performance has become more equal in the post–Act 60 period.)

72. These developments are described in detail by Molly A. Hunter, *Building on Judicial Intervention: The Redesign of School Facilities Funding in Arizona*, 34 J. Law & Educ. 173 (2005).

73. R. Shep Melnick, *Taking Remedies Seriously: Judicial Methods for Controlling Bureaucratic Discretion in Public Schools*, in American Enterprise Institute: From Brown to "Bong Hits": Assessing a Half-Century of Judicial Involvement in Education (2008). Available at http://www.aei.org/event/1746.

74. Malcolm M. Feeley & Edward L. Rubin, Judicial Policy Making and the Modern State: How the Courts Reformed America's Prisons, 97 (1999).

Chapter Three

1. Eric A. Hanushek & Alfred A. Lindseth, *Schoolhouses, Courthouses, and Statehouses: Solving the Funding-Achievement Puzzle in America's Public Schools*, 3 (2009). For a discussion of the issues raised by this book, see Eric A. Hanushek, Alfred A. Lindseth & Michael A. Rebell, *Forum* Education Next, vol. 9, no. 4 (Fall 2009).

2. In Iowa, within a year after a coalition of 160 school districts and individuals filed suit challenging the school funding system, the legislature passed a bill replacing the current local-option sales tax for schools with a pool of sales tax money that would be distributed on a per-pupil basis, and the suit was withdrawn. Lynn Okamoto, *House OKs Bill on School Tax Pool*, Des Moines Register, April 24, 2003, available at http://desmoinesregister.com/news/stories/c4780934/21086606.html; Press Release, Iowa Department of Revenue SF445 (June 2, 2003), available at http://www.state.ia.us/tax/news/nrSF445.html. In North Dakota, plaintiffs dropped their suit after a new funding formula enacted in response to the suit was signed into law. Dale Wetzel, *School Lawsuit Ends*, Bismarck Tribune, January 11, 2006, available at http://www.bismarcktribune.com/articles/2006/01/11/news/topnews/108347.txt.

3. In Nebraska, for example, the plaintiffs withdrew their equity complaint

after the legislature enacted major changes to the state education finance system that provided fundamental reforms that resulted in substantial increases in funding to the plaintiff districts. Jeffrey Robb, *Revamped School Finance Formula Wins Final OK*, OMAHA WORLD-HERALD, April 2, 2008.

4. See, for example, G. A. Hickrod, et al., *The Effect of Constitutional Litigation on Education Finance: A Preliminary Analysis*, 18 J. EDUC. FIN. 180 (1992) (concluding that reductions in inequity occur in states experiencing education finance litigations, whether plaintiffs prevail or not, compared with states in which there has been no litigation). See also William S. Koski & Henry M. Levin, *Twenty-Five Years after Rodriguez: What Have We Learned?* 102 TCHRS C. REC. 480, 506 (2000) ("Surely every state legislature is aware of the possibility of educational finance litigation and many have likely taken prophylactic measures.").

5. Montoy v. State, 120 P.3d 306, 308 (Kan. 2005). The constitutional confrontation is described in detail by Richard E. Levy, *Gunfight at the K-12 Corral: Legislative vs Judicial Power in the Kansas School Finance Litigation*, 54 U. KAN. L. REV. 1021 (2006).

6. The New Jersey Supreme Court recently denominated its long remedial efforts as a "success" in that "children in . . . Abbott districts . . . show measurable educational improvement." Abbott v. Burke XIX, 960 A.2d 360, 363 1 (N.J., 2008). At latest count, the New Jersey Supreme Court has issued twenty-four compliance rulings, five in *Robinson v. Cahill* and nineteen in *Abbott v. Burke*. The state's recent motion to terminate the remedies in the case because a new statewide funding formula has now achieved constitutional compliance, was granted by the New Jersey Supreme Court provided the new formula is fully funded. Abbott v. Burke XX, 2009 WL 1578814 A.2d (N.J., May 28, 2009). For details and the latest information on developments in the New Jersey litigation, see http://www.edlawcenter.org.

7. In 1982, the trial court found the school finance system unconstitutional and, with the help of the state superintendent of schools, developed a 356-page master plan for reform. Delays in implementation of the plan led plaintiffs back to court, where they obtained a ruling from the Supreme Court that the state has "a specific duty to implement and enforce the policies and standards of the Master Plan." Pauley v. Bailey, 324 S.E.2d 128, 135 (1984). Although the legislature subsequently adopted a number of reforms, the main equity reforms and educational innovations promised by the *Pauley* decision were not implemented, primarily because of resistance to increased funding.

In 1995, plaintiffs returned to court, and, a year later, the trial court in *Tomblin v. Gainer* found that the state had ignored many of the reforms the court had ordered. The court held that the state still did not provide a "thorough and efficient" system of education. In 1998, the legislature established a state office to perform school reviews, and, under a 2000 court order, the state must evaluate and report on individual schools' specific needs, including personnel, curriculum, and facilities. In January 2003, the trial court denied plaintiffs' remaining motion for an order to change specific aspects of the state's funding calculations, and declaring the new system constitutional, ended its jurisdiction. Tomblin v. West Va. State Bd. of Educ., Civ. No. 75-1268 (Cir. Ct., January 3, 2003).

8. For a detailed discussion of the Ohio litigation, see Larry J. Obhof, *De-Rolph v. State and Ohio's Long Road to an Adequate Education*, 2005 B.Y.U. EDUC. & L.J. 83 (2005). The politics of judicial elections was clearly a factor in the court's withdrawal. In Ohio, as in about half of the states, state supreme court judges are elected. The education adequacy case became a major issue in the judicial elections in Ohio in 2000 and 2002. In 2001, after a heated election in which the judge who had written the original adequacy ruling was strongly challenged, but who nevertheless retained her seat, the court issued a "compromise" ruling that clearly indicated its desire to limit its ongoing remedial involvement, despite substantial noncompliance with the previous rulings. *Id.* at 132–33. In 2002, the court terminated its jurisdiction after a new judge who was critical of the court's adequacy ruling replaced a member of the majority who had voted for the education finance reforms. *Id.* at 139–40. In Alabama, after a change in its membership following an election, the court *sua sponte* reopened Alabama Coalition for Equity v. Spiegelman, 713 So.2d 937 (Ala. 1997), a case it had decided for the plaintiffs in 1993, and after soliciting arguments from the two sides, dismissed the case, citing separation of powers and justiciability concerns. *Ex parte* James, 836 So.2d 813 (Ala. 2002).

9. See, for example, Sheila E. Murray, William N. Evans, & Robert N. Schwab, *Education Finance Reform and the Distribution of Education Resources*, 88 AM. ECON. REV. 789–812 (finding that, in a study of sixteen states, "successful litigation reduced inequality by raising the spending in the poorest districts while leaving spending in the richest districts unchanged. . . . "); William N. Evans, Sheila E. Murray, & Robert N. Schwab, *The Impact of Court-Mandated Finance Reform*, in EQUITY AND ADEQUACY IN EDUCATION FINANCE: ISSUES AND PERSPECTIVES, 72 (Helen F. Ladd et al. eds., 1999) (study of 10,000 school districts from 1972–92 found that court-ordered reform leveled up disparities and increased overall spending on education); Douglas S. Reed, *Twenty-Five Years after Rodriguez: School Finance Litigation and the Impact of the New Judicial Federalism*, 32 LAW & SOC. REV. 175 (1998) (study of eight states found increasing equity in five states in which the state supreme court invalidated the existing school finance system and greater inequities in three states in which the courts denied relief); R. L. Manwaring & S. M. Sheffrin, *Litigation, School Finance Reform and Aggregate Educational Spending*, 4 INT'L TAX & PUB. FIN. 107 (1995) (noting that litigations increase overall spending on education); BUILDING EDUCATIONAL SUCCESS FOREVER ("BEST"), GROWTH AND DISPARITY: A DECADE OF U.S. PUBLIC SCHOOL CONSTRUCTION, 36 (2006), available at http://www.21csf.org/csf-home/publications/BEST-Growth-Disparity-2006.pdf (states with successful

facility court cases spent, on average, an additional $158 dollars per pupil ($p = .04$) two years after the successful court cases compared with the states without successful cases or no cases at all); cf. Bradley W. Joondeph, *The Good, the Bad and the Ugly: An Empirical Analysis of Litigation Prompted School Finance Reform*, 35 SANTA CLARA L. REV. 763 (1995) (study of six school districts found a narrowing of disparities in education expenditures but a lowering of rate of overall increase in expenditures for education).

10. Close analyses of patterns in particular states may be more accurate gauges of these issues. The methodologies used in the large metastudies depend on judgments made about which states will be analyzed and for which time periods. These judgments also often overlook the impact of key predecessor or follow-up litigations that may substantially influence the trends that are being analyzed. See Michael A. Rebell, *Discussion: Do State Governments Matter?* in YOLANDA K. KODRZYCKI, EDUCATION IN THE 21st CENTURY: MEETING THE CHALLENGES OF A CHANGING WORLD (Federal Reserve Bank of Boston, 2002).

11. PETER SCHRAG, FINAL TEST: THE BATTLE FOR ADEQUACY IN AMERICA'S SCHOOLS, 92 (2d ed., 2005).

12. MATHEW H. BOSWORTH, COURTS AS CATALYSTS: STATE SUPREME COURTS AND PUBLIC SCHOOL FINANCE EQUITY, 85 (2001).

13. Margaret E. Goertz & Michael Weiss, *Assessing Success in School Finance Litigation: The Case of New Jersey*, in CAMPAIGN FOR EDUCATIONAL EQUITY SYMPOSIUM: EQUAL EDUCATIONAL OPPORTUNITY: WHAT NOW?, 13 (2007), http://devweb.tc.columbia.edu/manager/symposium/Files/111 Goertz NJ _case_study_draft%20_10.04.07_.pdf.

14. "First, amendments to the statute removed the list of education goals and eliminated a committee charged with monitoring the administration of school finance, as a result of which there was no longer any assurance that funding of individual districts was sufficient to provide a suitable education. Second, changes to the system of weights and removal of limits on the local option budget exacerbated disparities between districts, so that at the time of trial the per-pupil disparity between the districts with lowest and highest funding exceeded three-hundred percent. Third, the overall level of funding had fallen far below that which was necessary to provide a suitable education for each student in Kansas." See Levy, *supra* note 5, at 1041–42.

15. 411 U.S. at 42. The *Rodriguez* case is discussed in more detail in chapter 2.

16. UNITED STATES DEPARTMENT OF HEALTH, EDUCATION, AND WELFARE AND UNITED STATES OFFICE OF EDUCATION, EQUALITY OF EDUCATIONAL OPPORTUNITY, 22 (1966).

17. The major errors by Coleman and his colleagues included "fail[ure] to use available scaling techniques to validate their procedures . . . and fail[ure] to measure crucial variables now known to be associated with school effects, "as well as use of "non-standard procedures for statistical analyses that generated falsely

deflated estimated school effects." BRUCE J. BIDDLE & DAVID C. BERLINER, ED-
UCATION POLICY STUDIES LABORATORY EDUCATION POLICY REPORTS PROJECT,
WHAT RESEARCH SAYS ABOUT UNEQUAL FUNDING FOR SCHOOLS IN AMERICA,
13–14, 37 (2002), available at http://epsl.asu.edu/eprp/EPSL-0206-102-EPRP.
doc. James Guthrie sees as the major flaw of the Coleman report its failure—
because of the limitations of data at the time—to disaggregate school-based ex-
penditures per pupil from district-level expenditures per pupil. See James W.
Guthrie, *Implications for Policy: What Might Happen in American Education If
It Were Known How Money Actually Is Spent?* in WHERE DOES THE MONEY GO?
RESOURCE ALLOCATION IN ELEMENTARY AND SECONDARY SCHOOLS (Lawrence O.
Picus & James L. Wattenbarger eds., 1996).

18. JAMES S. COLEMAN, EQUALITY AND ACHIEVEMENT IN EDUCATION, 339
(1990). See also MICHAEL A. REBELL & JESSICA R. WOLFF, MOVING EVERY CHILD
AHEAD: FROM NCLB HYPE TO MEANINGFUL EDUCATIONAL OPPORTUNITY, chapter 4 (2008) (proposing specific measures to overcome the impact of concen-
trated poverty and enable all children to be ready to learn).

19. Eric A. Hanushek, *The Quest for Equalized Mediocrity: School Finance
Reform without Consideration of School Performance,* in PICUS & WATTEN-
BARGER, *supra* note 17, at 26–27.

20. Eric Hanushek, *When Reform May Not Be Good Policy,* 28 HARV. J. ON
LEGIS. 423, 434 (1991). See also Eric Hanushek, *The Impact of Differential Expenditures on School Performance,* 18 EDUC. RES. 45, 45–65 (1989).

21. Corrine Taylor, *"Does Money Matter? An Empirical Study Introducing
Resource Costs and Student Needs to Education Production Function Analysis,* DEVELOPMENTS IN SCHOOL FINANCE (1997). Available at http://nces.ed.gov/
pubs98/98212-5.pdf.

22. Rob Greenwald, Larry V. Hedges, & Richard D. Laine, *Does Money Matter? A Meta-analysis of Studies of the Effects of Differential School Inputs on
Student Outcomes,* 23 EDUC. RES. 5–14 (1994). These researchers claimed that
nine of Hanushek's basic studies were inappropriate choices and that thirty-one
other studies should have been included. In a later work, they analyzed this larger
sample in depth and concluded that "a broad range of school inputs are positively related to student outcomes, and . . . the magnitude of the effects are sufficiently large to suggest that moderate increases in spending may be associated
with significant increases in achievement." Rob Greenwald, Larry V. Hedges,
& Richard D. Laine, *The Effect of School Resources on Student Achievement,*
66 REV. EDUC. RES. 362 (1996). Hanushek replied that the Greenwald, Hedges,
& Laine analysis suffers from a narrowness inherent in their statistical methods
and is based on a very highly selected sample of results that biases their analysis
precisely toward their conclusion. See Eric A. Hanushek, *A More Complete Picture of School Resource Policies,* 66 REV. EDUC. RES. 397–409 (1996).

More recent studies concur in the view that educational expenditures are correlated with positive student outcomes. See, for example, Kristen Harknett et al., *Do Public Expenditures Improve Child Outcomes in the U.S.? A Comparison across Fifty States* 17 (Ctr. for Policy Research, Maxwell Sch., Syracuse Univ., Working Paper Series No. 53, 2003). Available at http://www.cpr.maxwell .syr.edu/cprwps/pdf/wp53.pdf (finding "particularly strong and positive effects" between additional educational expenditures and students test scores and adolescent behavior).

23. Montoy v. State, No. 99-C-1738, 2003 WL 22902963 at *49 (Kan. Dist. Ct. December 2, 2003), affirmed 112 P.3d 923 (Kan. 2005).

24. These cases are discussed in detail by Michael A. Rebell, *Poverty, "Meaningful" Educational Opportunity, and the Necessary Role of the Courts*, 85 N.C. L. Rev. 1467, 1476–87. Eric Hanushek appeared as the prime witness for the defense on this issue in a dozen of these cases. The Rhode Island Supreme Court, in City of Pawtucket et al. v. Sundlun et al., 662 A.2d 40 (R.I. 1995), was the only court that held that money does not matter. It overruled the evidentiary holding of the trial court that there was a clear causal link between insufficient funding and poor students. It relied on a vaguely referenced study that claimed that parental involvement was the most influential aspect of a child's educational opportunities and that dollars expended did not have an impact on the education a child received. *Id.* at 63 n.10. The court did not, however, discuss any specific reasons for this holding. Although it made brief mention of this issue, the court's ultimate holding was that the sound basic education issues were not justiciable (see discussion on "justiciability" in chapter 2).

25. Hoke County Board of Education v. State of North Carolina 1, 95 CVS 1158 (N.C. Gen. Ct. of Justice, Sup. Ct. Div., 2000) at 74, available at www .schoolfunding.info/states/nc/HOKEI.PDF.

26. Montoy v. State, No. 99-C-1738, 2003 WL 22902963 at *49. See also Hanushek, *The Quest for Equalized Mediocrity, supra* note 19, at 37–38 ([T]he real problem is [that nothing] in the current structure . . . moves us to better use of resources.").

27. Ken McGuire, *Mass. Students lead US on Tests*, Boston Globe, September 26, 2007. Available at http://www.boston.com/news/local/articles/2007/09/26/ mass_students_lead_us_on_tests/.

28. Thomas Downes, Jeffrey Zabel & Dona Ansel, Mass, Inc. Incomplete Grade: Massachusetts Education Reform at 15, 11 (2009). This report also found a significant reduction in achievement between the lowest-spending and highest-spending districts. *Id.* at 56.

29. Goertz & Weiss, *supra* note 13, at 16. Goertz & Weiss also report that the gap between the *Abbott* districts and all other districts was reduced by twelve points or .4 standard deviations in reading during this same time period (*id.* at

17). Although statewide results in eighth grade math and language arts were essentially stagnant between 2000 and 2005, the *Abbott* districts saw an increase in both math and language art scores of six points and one point, respectively, leading to closure in the achievement gap between the *Abbott* districts and the rest of the state of three points in math and one point in language arts (*id.* at 18).

30. Susan Perkins Weston & Robert F. Sexton, *Substantial and Yet Not Sufficient: Kentucky's Effort to Build Proficiency for Each and Every Child,* CAMPAIGN FOR EDUCATIONAL EQUITY SYMPOSIUM : EQUAL EDUCATIONAL OPPORTUNITY: WHAT NOW? (2007), http://devweb.tc.columbia.edu/manager/symposium/Files/108_KentuckyCaseStudy_Final.pdfTest score gains have also been noted in states in which court orders have only been in effect for a few years. See, for example, Jennifer Medina, *Reading and Math Scores Rise Sharply across N.Y.,* NEW YORK TIMES, June 24, 2008, and John Lyon, *State Test Scores Show Narrowing of Achievement Gap,* ARKANSAS NEWS BUREAU, June 21, 2008.

31. CFE I, 655 N.E. 2d at 666 (N.Y. 1995).

32. See, for example, CENTER ON EDUCATIONAL POLICY, ANSWERING THE QUESTION THAT MATTERS MOST: HAS STUDENT ACHIEVEMENT INCREASED SINCE NO CHILD LEFT BEHIND? (2007) (noting that test data in only twenty-five of the fifty states have consistent tests that allow results that allow for comparisons in elementary math since 2002); Goertz & Weiss, *supra* note 13, at 16 ("It is difficult to assess the impact of the Abbott decisions on indicators of student achievement because New Jersey, like most other states, has changed its assessments several times over the last 30 years.").

33. For a detailed discussion of these issues, see REBELL & WOLFF, *supra* note 18, at chapter 7. For additional discussions of problems raised by utilizing a single stakes standardized achievement test as a measure of proficiency, see, for example, JAY HEUBERT & RITA HAUSER, HIGH STAKES TESTING FOR TRACKING, PROMOTION AND GRADUATION (1999); Daniel Koretz, *The Pending Re-Authorization of NCLB: An Opportunity to Rethink the Basic Strategy,* in GAIL L. SUNDERMAN, HOLDING NCLB ACCOUNTABLE: ACHIEVING ACCOUNTABILITY, EQUITY AND SCHOOL REFORM (2008); and MONTY NEILL ET AL., NATIONAL CENTER FOR FAIR AND OPEN TESTING, FAILING OUR CHILDREN: HOW NO CHILD LEFT BEHIND UNDERMINES QUALITY AND EQUITY IN EDUCATION (2004).

34. James E. Ryan, *Standards, Testing and School Finance Litigation,* 86 TEX. L. REV. 1223, 1244–45 (2008) (footnotes omitted). The decision Ryan is analyzing is Neeley v. W. Orange-Cove Consol. Indep. Sch. Dist. 176 S.W.3d 746, 769–70 (Tex. 2005).

35. Walt Haney, *The Myth of the Texas Miracle in Education,* 8 EDUC. POL'Y ANALYSIS ARCHIVES (2000). Available at http://epaa.asu.edu/epaa/v8n41/ .

36. JAY P. GREENE & MARCUS WINTER, MANHATTAN INSTITUTE, PUBLIC SCHOOL GRADUATION RATES IN THE UNITED STATES (2002). Regulations recently

issued by the U.S. Department of Education aim to remedy this problem by standardizing graduation rate data for No Child Left Behind reporting purposes. See David J. Hoff, *Rules Mandate Uniform Graduation Rates*, EDUC. WEEK, November 5, 2008, at 15.

37. CHRISTOPHER B. SWANSON & DUNCAN CHAPLIN, URBAN INSTITUTE, COUNTING HIGH SCHOOL GRADUATES WHEN GRADUATES COUNT: MEASURING GRADUATION RATES UNDER THE HIGH STAKES OF NCLB (2003). A recent report from the Kentucky state auditor indicated that reported dropout figures in that state may understate the real problem by as much as 30 percent. Weston & Sexton, *supra* note 30, at 14.

38. See, for example, Brian Jacob & Steven D. Levitt, *Catching Cheating Teachers: The Results of an Unusual Experiment in Implementing Theory* 185, BROOKINGS-WHARTON PAPERS ON URBAN AFFAIRS 2003 (William G. Gale & Janet R. Pack eds., 2003).

39. Andrew Wolf, *An Invitation to Cheat*, NEW YORK SUN, June 12, 2007, available at http://www.nysun.com/opinion/invitation-to-cheat/56370/?print= 1876584121; Sol Stern, *Grading Mayoral Control*, July 26, 2007, available at http:// www.townhall.com/columnists/SolStern/2007/07/26/grading_mayoral_ control; *see also* THE NEW YORK STATE SCHOOL REPORT CARD: ACCOUNTABILITY AND OVERVIEW REPORT 2005–06 (P.S. 33 Timothy Dwight School), available at https://www.nystart.gov/publicweb-rc/2006/AOR-2006-321000010033.pdf.

40. For example, in addition to improving psychometric methodologies for assessing the full range of knowledge and skills that students have learned in academic subject areas, survey methodologies can be developed for assessing citizenship skills and preparation for the workplace. See RICHARD ROTHSTEIN, REBECCA JACOBSEN, & TAMARA WILDER, GRADING EDUCATION: GETTING ACCOUNTABILITY RIGHT (2008).

41. Moore v. State, Case No. 3AN-04-0756 (Alaska Sup. Ct., June 21, 2007), at 174.

42. Lake View Sch. Dist. No. 25 v. Huckabee, 91 S.W.3d 472, 511 (Ark. 2002).

43. Lake View Sch. Dist. No. 25 v. Huckabee, 144 S.W.3d 741, 742 (Ark. 2004), *per curiam.*

44. Lake View Sch. Dist. No. 25 v. Huckabee, 189 S.W.3d 1, 17 (Ark. 2004).

45. Lake View Sch. Dist. No. 25 v. Huckabee, 210 S.W.3d 28, 30 (Ark. 2005).

46. Lake View Sch. Dist. No. 25 v. Huckabee, No. 01-836, 2005 Ark. LEXIS 776 (Ark. Dec. 15, 2005).

47. Lake View Sch. Dist. No. 25 v. Huckabee, No. 01-836, 2007 Ark. LEXIS 343 (Ark. May 31, 2007).

48. Lake View Sch. Dist. No. 25 v. Huckabee, No. 01-836, 2007 Ark. LEXIS 343, at *9–10 (Ark. May 31, 2007).

49. Lake View Sch. Dist. No. 25 v. Huckabee, 210 S.W.3d 28, 29 (Ark. 2004).

Chapter Four

1. PISA 2006: Science Competencies for Tomorrow's World, OECD Briefing Note for the United States, 1 (2007). Available at http://www.oecd .org/dataoecd/16/28/39722597.pdf.

2. *Id.*

3. *Id.* at 2.

4. *Id.* at 20.

5. Bob Herbert, *Hard Road Ahead,* New York Times, News of the Week in Review, May 17, 2008, at A27. See also Report of the Secretary's Commission on Achieving Necessary Skills ("SCANS") (1991) (finding that students need much higher levels of technical skill and knowledge than they did in the past, including the ability to manage and comprehend complex texts and information); National Center on Education and the Economy, America's Choice: Higher Skills or Low Wages (1990) (comparing skill levels of students graduating from U.S. schools with graduates of other industrial nations and concluding that U.S. workers need higher level skills to be competitive).

6. Text of Policy Statement Issued at National Summit, 15 Educ. Week 13, April 3, 1996.

7. Achieve, Inc., Benchmarking the Best, 3 (1999); See also Bob Wise, Raising the Grade: How High School Reform Can Save Your and Our Nation, 11 (2008) ("Experts predict that almost 90% of the fastest-growing high-wage jobs of the future will require some postsecondary education training.").

8. National Voter Turnout in Federal Elections: 1960–2006. Available at http://www.infoplease.com/ipa/A0781453.html. See also http://elections.gmv .edu/voter_turnout.htm.

9. Robert D. Putnam, Bowling Alone: The Collapse and Revival of American Community, 63 (2000).

10. Richard Desjardins & Tom Schuller, *Introduction: Understanding the Social Outcomes of Learning,* in Measuring the Effects of Education on Health and Civic Engagement, Proceedings of the Copenhagen Symposium, 11–18 (Richard Desjardins & Tom Schuller eds., 2006); Jane Junn, *The Political Costs of Unequal Education,* in Symposium on the Economic and Social Costs of Inadequate Education (2005). Available at http://devweb. tc.columbia.edu/manager/symposium/Files/73_junn_paper.ed.pdf.

11. Thomas S. Dee, *Are There Civic Returns to Education?* 88 J. Pub. Econ. 1697 (2004); Norman H. Nie, Jane Junn, and Kenneth Stehlik-Barry, Education and Democratic Citizenship in America (1996).

12. P. Kenney & T. Rice, *Voter Turnout in Presidential Primaries: A Cross-Sectional Examination.* 7 Pol. Behav. 101 (1985).

13. Junn, *supra* note 193, at 2.

14. David McCullough, John Adams, 364 (2001).

15. ALEXIS DE TOCQUEVILLE, DEMOCRACY IN AMERICA, 329 (Vintage 1961).

16. S.D. CONST. art. VIII, § 1 (emphasis added). See also, for example, MINN. CONST. art. VIII, § 2, originally enacted in 1857: "The stability of a republican form of government depending upon the intelligence of the people, it is the duty of the legislature to establish a general and uniform system of public schools."

17. Bonner ex rel. Bonner v. Daniels 885 N.E.2d 673, 691 (Ind. App. 2008) (quoting statement of delegate Bryant of Warren County, 2 REPORT OF THE DEBATES AND PROCEEDINGS OF THE CONVENTION FOR THE REVISION OF THE CONSTITUTION OF THE STATE OF INDIANA 1850, at 1890–91).

18. See, for example, ROGERS M. SMITH, CIVIC IDEALS: CONFLICTING VISIONS OF CITIZENSHIP IN U.S. HISTORY (1997) (discussing systematic exclusion of women, minorities, and working class from exercise of the franchise); Thiel v. Southern Pacific County, 328 U.S. 217, 222 (1946) (discussing systematic exclusion from jury list of those who work for a daily wage.); Taylor v. Louisiana, 419 U.S. 522, 538 (1975) (discussing systematic exclusion of women from jury duty).

19. MICHAEL SCHUDSON, THE GOOD CITIZEN: A HISTORY OF AMERICAN CIVIC LIFE, 8 (1998).

20. Rodriguez v. San Antonio Indep. Sch. Dist., 411 U.S. 1, 36. See discussion of Rodriguez, chapter 2.

21. A Separation of Powers Dialogue, infra, appendix at 114.

22. Burt Neuborne, Toward Procedural Parity in Constitutional Litigation, 22 WM. & MARY L. REV. 725, 732 (1981).

23. MATHEW H. BOSWORTH, COURTS AS CATALYSTS: STATE SUPREME COURTS AND PUBLIC SCHOOL FINANCE EQUITY, 99 (2001).

24. Judith S. Kaye, Contributions of State Constitutional Law to the Third Century of American Federalism, 13 VT. L. REV. 49, 56 (1988).

25. Adam Liptak, Rendering Justice, with One Eye on Re-election, NEW YORK TIMES, May 25, 2008, at A1.

26. Burt Neuborne, Forward: State Constitutions and the Evolution of Positive Rights, 20 RUTGERS L.J. 881, 900 (1989). See also Douglas S. Reed, Popular Constitutionalism: Toward a Theory of State Constitutional Meanings, 30 RUTGERS L. REV. 871 (1999) (arguing that the meanings of state constitutions are generated through an exchange between popular mobilization and judicial interpretation, especially in states in which the initiative mechanism exists).

27. A Separation of Powers Dialogue, infra, appendix at 110.

28. Id. at 114–15.

29. Nebraska Coalition for Educational Equity and Adequacy v. Heineman, 731 N.W.2d 164, 183 (Neb. 2007). This case is discussed in chapter 2.

30. John Dayton & Anne Dupre, School Funding Litigation: Who's Winning the War? 57 VAND L. REV. 2351, 2409 (2004).

31. Komesar's comparative institutional analysis further develops an approach to law, economics, and public choice theory that initially had been articulated by

Ronald Coase, *The Problem of Social Cost*, 3 J.L. & Econ. 1 (1960). This methodology has also been adapted and applied in a range of other contexts. See, for example, Matthew Stephenson, *Legislative Allocation of Delegated Power: Uncertainty, Risk and the Choice Between Agencies and Courts*, 119 Harv. L. Rev. 1035 (2006) (utilizing comparative institutional analysis to guide legislative decisions on delegating primary interpretive authority to the judiciary or administrative agencies); Edwin L. Rubin, *The New Legal Process: The Synthesis of Discourse and the Microanalysis of Institutions*, 109 Harv. L. Rev. 1393 (1996) (calling for a synthesis of process, law and economics, and critical legal theories into a "new realm of comparative legal analysis that explores institutional capacities under particular circumstances"); William W. Buzbee, *Sprawl's Dynamics: A Comparative Institutional Analysis Critique*, 35 Wake Forest L. Rev. 509 (2000) (applying theory to issue of urban sprawl); William N. Eskridge, Jr., *Politics without Romance: Implications of Public Choice Theory for Statutory Interpretation*, 74 Va. L. Rev. 275, 275–76 (1988) (exploring courts' comparative institutional advantages in fairly considering all views and formulating balanced public policy from a "public choice" perspective); Kenneth A. Shepsle & Barry R. Weingast, *Political Solutions to Market Problems*, 78 Am. Pol. Sci. Rev. 417–34 (1984) (utilizing comparative institutional analysis to question whether intervention of political institutions can improve upon market performance).

32. Neil K. Komesar, Imperfect Alternatives: Choosing Institutions in Law, Economics and Public Policy, 149 (1994). Adrian Vermeule uses the phrase "the nirvana fallacy" to describe "a pseudo-institutional analysis that compares a worst-case picture of one institution to a best case picture of another." Adrian Vermeule, Judging under Uncertainty: An Institutional Theory of Legal Interpretation 17 (2006). His comparative institutional analysis, however, downplays the role of the courts, so much so that he candidly asserts that under his conceptual framework, the U.S. Supreme Court should not have struck down racial segregation in schools in *Brown v. Board of Education*. *Id.* at 231.

33. Komesan, Imperfect Alternatives, Supra, Note 32 at 3. Komesar elaborates on his comparative analytic approach in Law's Limits: The Rule of Law and the Supply and Demand of Rights (Cambridge University Press, 2001); *Taking Institutions Seriously: Introduction to a Strategy for Constitutional Analysis*, 51 Chi. L. Rev 366 (1984); and *A Job for the Judges: The Judiciary and the Constitution in a Massive and Complex Society*, 86 Mich. L. Rev. 657, 698 (1988).

34. NCLB's conflicting theories of action and failure to ensure truly challenging standards, appropriate assessment instruments, truly qualified teachers, and other critical resources necessary to reach its stated goals are discussed in detail in Michael A. Rebell & Jessica R. Wolff, Moving Every Child Ahead: From NCLB Hype To Meaningful Educational Opportunity (2008).

35. *A Separation of Powers Dialogue, infra,* appendix at 113

36. Aileen Kavanagh, *Participation and Judicial Review: A Reply to Jeremy Waldron*, 22 LAW & PHIL. 451, 466–67 (2003).

37. See discussion in chapter 1.

38. "Severe biases in other institutions, in particular the political process, are sometimes avoided or reduced in the adjudicative process. This comparative advantage should tell judges that they should employ the limited resources of the adjudicative process . . . when the balance of bias, competence and scale favors that substitution." KOMESAR, IMPERFECT ALTERNATIVES, *supra* note 32, at 150.

39. See, for example, Thomas Corcoran & Nathan Scovronick, *More Than Equal: New Jersey's Quality Education Act*, in STRATEGIES FOR SCHOOL EQUITY: CREATING PRODUCTIVE SCHOOLS IN A JUST SOCIETY 55 (Marilyn Gittell ed., 1998) (discussing how the legislature in New Jersey is "always too divided to take on [education] issues . . . [.]"); Clayton P. Gillette, *Reconstructing Local Control of School Finance: A Cautionary Note*, 25 CAP. U. L. REV 36, 43 (1996) ("[I]f the representatives from wealthier school districts can form a majority without the inclusion of representatives from poorer school districts, the latter will be unable to logroll for their agenda."); Michael Heise, *Schoolhouses, Courthouses, and Statehouses: Constitutional Structure, Education Finance, and the Separation of Powers Doctrine*, 33 LAND & WATER LAW REV. 281 (1998) 305–306 ("[T]he very fact that state legislatures are comprised of locally elected officials to some degree works against the development of a coherent, comprehensive solution to a statewide problem that some legislators are likely to acknowledge, even if only privately.").

40. Neil F. Theobold & Larence O. Picus, *Living with Equal Amounts of Less: Experiences of States with Primarily State-Funded School Systems*, 17 J. EDUC. FIN. 4, 5 (1991). See also James G. Ward, *Conflict and Consensus in the Historical Process: The Intellectual Foundations of the School Finance Reform Movement*, 14 J. EDUC. FIN. 1–22 (1988).

41. JOHN H. ELY, DEMOCRACY AND DISTRUST (1980).

42. *Id.* at 102.

43. Jeremy Rabkin, *Office for Civil Rights*, in THE POLITICS OF REGULATION 304, 338 (James Q. Wilson ed., 1980). For detailed discussions of the interplay of courts, Congress, and the administrative agencies in establishing and implementing a variety of civil rights laws, see RICHARD K. SCOTCH, FROM GOOD WILL TO CIVIL RIGHTS: TRANSFORMING FEDERAL DISABILITY POLICY (1984); PAUL BERNSTEIN, DISCRIMINATION, JOBS AND POLITICS: THE STRUGGLE FOR EQUAL EMPLOYMENT OPPORTUNITY IN THE UNITED STATES SINCE THE NEW DEAL (1985); and ROBERT A. KATZMANN, INSTITUTIONAL DISABILITY: THE SAGA OF TRANSPORTATION POLICY FOR THE DISABLED (1986).

44. Mills v. Board of Education, 348 F.Supp. 866 (D.C. 1972); Pennsylvania Association of Retarded Children v. Commonwealth, 343 F.Supp. 279 (E.D.Pa. 1972).

45. Individuals with Disabilities Act ("IDEA"), 20 U.S.C. §§ 1400–1462 (2004).

46. Bert J. Combs, *Creative Constitutional Law: The Kentucky School Reform Law,* 28 HARV. J. ON LEGIS. 367, 384 (1991).

47. See ALEXANDER BICKEL, THE LEAST DANGEROUS BRANCH (1962). See also Shirley S. Abrahamson & Robert L. Hughes, *Shall We Dance? Steps for Legislators and Judges in Statutory Interpretation,* 75 MINN. L. REV. 1045 (1991) (discussing "colloquy" between state courts and state legislatures on statutory issues).

48. George D. Brown, *Binding Advisory Opinions: A Federal Court's Perspective on State Court School Finance Decisions,* 35 B.C. L. REV. 543, 566–67 (1994). See also Peter H. Schuck, *Public Law Litigation and Social Reform,* 102 YALE L.J. 1763, 1771–72 (1993) (discussing "dialogic" nature of "interactions between courts, legislatures, agencies and other social processes").

49. See, for example, Paul D. Kahn, *State Constitutionalism and the Problems of Fairness,* 30 VAL. U.L. REV. 459, 465, 468 (1996) ("When the political will is there, courts have proven useful in mobilizing a response to the problem. They do not usually stand against the political branches, but along side them in a common endeavor.").

50. Our comparative institutional findings are summarized in MICHAEL A. REBELL & ARTHUR R. BLOCK, EQUALITY AND EDUCATION: FEDERAL CIVIL RIGHTS ENFORCEMENT IN THE NEW YORK CITY SCHOOL SYSTEM, 190–91 (1985).

51. In regard to interest group representation, our research also demonstrated that legislatures can best digest and reflect input from all of the interests that are sufficiently well organized to exert political pressure, while courts effectively consider input from all those interests that are sufficiently well organized to seek and obtain formal legal representation. There is limited input from affected interests in the administrative process, which tends to discourage active participation by such groups. We also found that representation of minority group interests is most effective in the judicial arena.

52. KOMESAR, IMPERFECT ALTERNATIVES, *supra* note 32. In regard to fact finding, Komesar also noted that "[t]he tradeoff is between a political process that integrates far more information but with a more significant risk of bias and an adjudicative process that suppresses information but decreases distortions in its presentation." *Id.* at 141–42.

53. *Id.* at 128.

54. *Id.* at 125.

55. Susan Perkins Weston & Robert F. Sexton, *Substantial and Yet Not Sufficient: Kentucky's Effort to Build Proficiency for Each and Every Child,* CAMPAIGN FOR EDUCATIONAL EQUITY SYMPOSIUM: EQUAL EDUCATIONAL OPPORTUNITY: WHAT NOW? 19 (2007). Available at http://devweb.tc.columbia.edu/manager/symposium/Files/108_KentuckyCaseStudy_Final.pdf. Weston & Sex-

ton further point out that implementation also often requires "conscious tactical choices" and "choosing what to give priority." *Id.*

Chapter Five

1. JOHN RAWLS, A THEORY OF JUSTICE, 230–31 (1971).

2. Roosevelt Elementary School Dist. No. 66 v. Bishop, 877 P.2d 806, 823 (Ariz. 1994) (Feldman, C.J., concurring).

3. MATHEW H. BOSWORTH: STATE SUPREME COURTS AND PUBLIC SCHOOL FINANCE EQUITY, 97–101 (2001).

4. See, for example, James E. Ryan, *Standards, Testing and School Finance Litigation*, 86 TEX. L. REV. 1223 (2008). Ryan presumes that judicial adoption of legislative standards is a defining expectation in these cases and then claims to have refuted the conventional wisdom when he shows that in most of these cases this has not happened. This view of the role of legislative and regulatory standards in sound basic education cases then leads him to assume that to the extent that standards do significantly drive these cases, the applicable standards will be narrowly construed, defined in practice by limited standardized testing categories and subject to perverse incentives to water down their content. In fact, as discussed in the text, the supervening constitutional imperative to develop educational systems that will prepare students to be capable citizens and competitive workers avoids most of the problems he anticipates.

5. Benjamin Michael Superfine has described the interplay between courts and legislatures in similar terms:

> Thus far, standards-based reform and accountability policies have emerged in the context of school finance litigation in three major ways. First, legislatures have established such policies in order to ensure that students receive constitutionally adequate educations. Second, some courts have used standards and assessments aligned to these standards to define and measure adequacy. Third, some courts have construed these policies as tools that can help states provide students with opportunities to receive adequate education.

BENJAMIN MICHAEL SUPERFINE, THE COURTS AND STANDARDS-BASED REFORM 163 (2008).

6. The various state supreme courts have also tended to engage in a productive dialogue among themselves, by citing, endorsing, and adapting constitutional concepts of adequacy that were developed in sister states. For a discussion of the "consensus" definition of adequate education that appears to have

emerged from this nationwide judicial dialogue, see MICHAEL A. REBELL & JESSICA R. WOLFF, MOVING EVERY CHILD AHEAD: FROM NCLB HYPE TO MEANINGFUL EDUCATIONAL OPPORTUNITY, 70–71 (2008).

7. Claremont Sch. Dist. v. Governor, 703 A.2d at 1357. The New Hampshire Court also focused on the functional distinctions between the roles of the legislature and the executive branch, since it insisted that "in the first instance, it is the legislature's obligation, not that of individual members of the board of education, to establish educational standards that comply with constitutional requirements." *Id.*

8. 790 S.W.2d at 212.

9. Susan Perkins Weston & Robert F. Sexton, *Substantial and Yet Not Sufficient: Kentucky's Effort to Build Proficiency for Each and Every Child,* in CAMPAIGN FOR EDUCATIONAL EQUITY SYMPOSIUM: EQUAL EDUCATIONAL OPPORTUNITY: WHAT NOW? 3–4 (2007). Available at http://devweb.tc.columbia.edu/manager/symposium/Files/108_KentuckyCaseStudy_Final.pdf.

10. The *Rose* standards have essentially been adopted by the courts in Alabama (Opinion of the Justices, 624 So.2d 107, 107–8 (Ala. 1993)); Massachusetts (McDuffy v. Sec'y, 615 N.E.2d 516, 554 (Mass. 1993)), New Hampshire, (Claremont Sch. Dist. v. Governor, 635 A.2d 1375, 1378 (N.H. 1993)); North Carolina (Leandro v. State, 488 S.E.2d 249, 255 (N.C. 1997)); and South Carolina, (Abbeville County Sch. Dist. v. State, 515 S.E.2d 535 (S.C. 1999)).

11. Lake View, 91 S.W.3d 472, at 488 ("Many of the 'Rose standards,' as we will call them, were adopted by our General Assembly with Act 1108 and Act 1307 in 1997, as has already been set forth in this opinion."). See also N.H. RSA 193-E (2007) (adopting essence of *Rose* standards).

12. Columbia Falls Elementary School District No. 6 v. State, 109 P.3d 257, 312 (Mont. 2005).

13. *Id.* at 263. The Montana court's decision explicitly belies Ryan's expectation that "courts will inevitably rely on test scores to determine if schools are providing an adequate education." Ryan, *supra* note 4, at 1225. See also, Hoke County Sch. Bd v. State, 599 S.E. 2d 365, 384 (N.C. 2004) ("[W]e reject the State's contention that the trial court used test scores as the "exclusive measure" of a sound basic education.).

14. Columbia Falls, 109 P.3d 257 at 263.

15. Mont. Code Ann. § 20-9-309 (2005).

16. Seattle School District No. 1 v. State, 585 P.2d 71, 94–95 (1978).

17. *Id.* at 95–96.

18. Basic Education Act of 1977, Wash. Rev. Code § 28A.150.210 (1977) (amended 1993) In fact, the legislature in Washington responded to the initial directive of the trial court and was already in compliance by the time the case reached the Supreme Court. The Washington legislature is currently in the process of rethinking "what exactly is a basic education in the 21st century? How do

we know whether the state is meeting its constitutional obligation to fund it . . . "
Joint Task Force on Basic Education Finance, Final Report to the Washington
State Legislature (January 14, 2009).

19. Leandro v. State, 488 S.E.2d 249, 259 (N.C. 1997).

20. Tico A. Almeida, *Refocusing School Finance Litigation on At-Risk Children: Leandro v. State of North Carolina,* 22 YALE L. & POL'Y REV. 525, 545
(2004). The trial judge to whom the case was remanded agreed: "Judge Manning
described the standards program as instrumental in his task of gauging constitutional adequacy, commenting that, 'The ABCs are a great tool, and without it, I
couldn't have done it. I would have had to have said [to the State], you've got to
have an accountability system, because we can't measure your results from what
you tell us.'" *Id.*

21. Hoke County Board of Education v. State, 599 S.E.2d 365, 382 (N.C.
2004). In Kansas, a trial court similarly articulated broad constitutional standards, which were then codified in specific, operational form by the legislature,
and the Supreme Court then enforced those operational standards in a follow-up
decision. Specifically, in Mock v. State, no. 91-CV 1009 (Kan. Dist. Ct., October
14, 1991), the trial judge developed ten goals for preparing learners to live, learn,
and work in a global society that became the basis for settling the litigation and
were codified in KSA 72-6439. This legislation was subsequently upheld as meeting constitutional requirements by the Kansas Supreme Court in Unified Sch.
Dist. No. 229 v. State, 885 P.2d 1170, 1186 (Kan. 1994). The ten goals were subsequently repealed by the legislature, but, nevertheless, in a later case, the Supreme Court again stated that "we need look no further than the legislature's
own definition of suitable education [as set forth in the state's school accreditation and student performance standards] to determine that the standard is not
being met under the current financing formula." Montoy v. State, 120 P.3d 306,
309 (Kan. 2005) (*per curiam*).

22. CFE I, 655 N.E.2d 661, 666 (N.Y. 1995).

23. CFE v. State, 719 N.Y.S. 2d 475, 485 (2001); see also Michael A. Rebell,
Education Adequacy, Democracy and the Courts, in ACHIEVING HIGH EDUCATIONAL STANDARDS FOR ALL 244–47 (Christopher Edley, Timothy Ready, &
Catherine Snow eds., 1992) (describing detailed trial testimony on the Regents
standards and its impact on court's decision).

24. CFE v. State, 719 N.Y.S. 2d at 483.

25. *Id.* at 484.

26. CFE v. State, 801 N.E.2d 326 (N.Y. 2003).

27. A similar result was reached by the Alaska trial court, which held

this court does not find it necessary or appropriate to adopt the State's existing content
and performance standards as a constitutional definition of educational adequacy . . .
it is sufficient that the State has demonstrated that it adopted a comprehensive set of

content and performance standards through an extensive collaborative process, and the resultant standards define an education that meets or exceeds the "constitutional floor" of an adequate education. Moore v. State of Alaska, no. 3AN-04-0756 (Super. Ct. Alaska, 3rd Jud'l Dist., June 21, 2007) at 175. Available at http://www.schoolfunding .info/states/ak/Moore_trialcourt_6-07.pdf

28. James Ryan has argued in *Standards, Testing and School Finance Litigation, supra* note 4, at 1247, that "[i]f funding is linked to standards and tests, states will have an incentive to decrease funding requirements by lowering standards and making tests easier to pass." New York's experience to date has belied this expectation. In response to the Court of Appeals order in *CFE II*, the governor appointed a commission to hold hearings and recommend a remedial response. The first item on the commission's agenda was reconsidering the Regents Learning Standards. After conducting a series of statewide hearings, at which strong opposition to such a course of action was expressed, the commission dropped that topic, and no governor or legislator has subsequently broached the subject. The political reality appears to be that no political leader wants to be associated with the notion of lowering academic standards at a time when excellence and equity are being widely touted as being the nation's prime educational policy. "Perverse incentives" in the No Child Left Behind Act do cause some states to lower their definition of "proficiency" for federal reporting purposes, but some of these states at the same time retain a more demanding definition of proficiency for internal state standards reform purposes. See Rebell & Wolff, *supra* note 6, at 114, 125.

29. Idaho Schools for Equal Educational Opportunity v. State (ISEEO III), 976 P.2d 913, 919 (Idaho 1998).

30. In West Virginia, the trial court developed exacting constitutional requirements and a 356-page master plan for implementing the general concepts for a "thorough and efficient education" that had been articulated by the West Virginia Supreme Court in Pauley v. Kelley, 255 S.E.2d 859 (W.Va. 1979). After the State Board of Education failed to implement these operational guidelines of the master plan, the West Virginia Supreme Court, indicating that the state board of education should develop its own operational standards, declined to establish a timetable for enforcing the trial court's plan. See Pauley v. Bailey, 324 S.E.2d 128, 132–33 (W.Va. 1984).

31. New Hampshire has been a rare exception to this pattern. The New Hampshire legislature still had not complied with the court's direction to develop a set of adequacy standards almost a decade after the court's initial directive. Londonderry Sch. Dist. v. State, 907 A.2d 988, 989 (N.H. 2006). In 2008, the legislature finally responded to the definitional issue. Plaintiffs in the *Londonderry* case did not challenge the adequacy definition, but they alleged that accountability and funding provisions of the new law are still inadequate. See

Londonderry Sch. Dist. v. State, 2008 WL 4570474 (N.H. October 15, 2008) (declaring pending case moot and holding that plaintiffs must initiate a new action in order to challenge the new legislation).

32. Superfine, *supra* note 5, at 162.

33. CFE II, 801 N.E.2d at 334 n.4.

34. PETER SCHRAG, FINAL TEST: THE BATTLE FOR ADEQUACY IN AMERICA'S SCHOOLS, 246 (2003).

35. For an overview of these methodologies, and of the courts' role in ensuring the integrity of the studies, see Michael A. Rebell, *Professional Rigor, Public Engagement and Judicial Review: A Proposal for Enhancing the Validity of Education Adequacy Studies,* 109 TCHRS C. REC. 1303 (2007). Eric Hanushek takes the extreme position that since none of the existing cost study methodologies can precisely define the minimum expenditure that is necessary to achieve a specified outcome standard, they all should be abandoned. Eric A. Hanushek, *Science Violated: Spending Projections and the 'Costing Out' of an Adequate Education* 257, in COURTING FAILURE: HOW SCHOOL FINANCE LAWSUITS EXPLOIT JUDGES' GOOD INTENTIONS AND HARM OUR CHILDREN, 340 (Eric A. Hanushek ed., 2006); and Eric A. Hanushek, *Pseudo-Science and a Sound Basic Education,* EDUC. NEXT 5 (2005). The "scientific" precision that Hanushek seeks is, however, an illusion, because no type of economic analysis can establish a definitive causal connection between a precise funding amount and a specific educational outcome since the educational process inherently involves an array of judgmental and environmental factors. Hanushek himself does not offer any alternative "scientific" methodology that would be superior to the existing approaches. See also WILLIAM DUNCOMBE, RESPONDING TO THE CHARGE OF ALCHEMY: STRATEGIES FOR EVALUATING THE RELIABILITY AND VALIDITY OF COSTING-OUT RESEARCH (Paper Presented at the O'Leary Symposium, "Funding of Public Schools: The Economic and Social Value of Adequate Funding," Chicago, February 17, 2006), 4: "To argue as Hanushek does that there is no role for technical analysis in the costing out process is akin to arguing that there is no role for technical analysis in forecasting state revenues, because forecasts by different methods and organizations can vary significantly."

36. State v. Campbell County Sch. Dist., 19 P.3d 518, 549 (Wyo. 2001).

37. CFE II, 801 N.E.2d at 348.

38. Campbell Co. Sch. Dist. v. State, Civ. No. 129059 (Wyo. Dist. Ct., 1997), slip op. at 2.

39. State v. Campbell County Sch. Dist., 19 P.3d 518 (Wyo. 2001); Legislative Service Office, School Finance Synopsis 5 (1999).

40. DeRolph v. State, 712 N.E. 2d 125, 194 (Ohio Ct. of Com. Pl., 1999), aff'd, 728 N.E.2d 993 (Ohio 2000).

41. West Orange Cove v. Neeley. no. GV-100528 (Travis County Dist. Ct. 2004), 57–58.

42. Rebell, *supra* note 35, at 1348.

43. LEGISLATIVE COUNCIL ON THE OREGON QUALITY EDUCATION MODEL, THE OREGON QUALITY EDUCATION MODEL: RELATING FUNDING AND PERFORMANCE (1999); OREGON QUALITY EDUCATION COMMISSION, QUALITY EDUCATION MODEL, FINAL REPORT (2004). Although the governor and the legislature created the QEM, they apparently have not adhered to the results that emerged from the QEM process. For example, a recent QEM Commission's report concluded that the legislature would need to appropriate $7.1 billion for the 2005–2007 biennium to meet the K-12 quality goals established by law, but the budget approved for that period was just under $5.3 billion, a $1.8 billion shortfall. *Pendleton School District 16R v. State of Oregon,* no. 0603-02980. First Amended Complaint (Circuit Court, County of Multnomah 2006), sections 5–6. See also Pendleton Sch. Dist. v. State, 200 P.3d (Or. 2009) (holding that state failed to adequately fund public education but declining to mandate full funding).

44. Hanushek's criticism of current costing-out methodologies is based in large part on the premise that these analyses do not consider more efficient practices that might significantly reduce costs. But, "the Hanushek criticism is too strong. While it is reasonable to call for the use of best practices in estimating the costs of an adequate education, it seems unreasonable to calculate the required level of resources based on an assumption that there will be dramatic gains in the efficiency with which those resources will be used." Helen F. Ladd, *Reflections on Equity, Adequacy and Weighted Student Funding,* 3 EDUC. FIN. & POL'Y 402, 414 (2008).

45. See, for example, Abbott v. Burke, Dkt. no. M-969, opinion. Recommendations to the Supreme Court (Super. Ct. N.J., March 24, 2009) (discussing and approving the state's "intricate and prolonged" cost analysis and formula development process).

46. CFE III, 861 N.E.2d at 57. Chief Judge Kaye, dissenting, stated that it was the court's obligation to scrutinize the allegations of improprieties in the use of the study; she proceeded to do so and concluded that the weightings used by the state and their application of a "cost effectiveness filter" were improper. *Id.* at 67. Judge Rosenblatt, concurring, hoped that the legislature would "avail themselves of the valuable work performed by the distinguished panel of referees" and indicated that he did not believe that the minimum amount approved by the majority was "necessarily the proper budgetary amount to provide New York City schools" and that he hoped that the Governor-elect would "continue in a direction above the minimum." He joined the majority because the "state budget plan had already calculated the amount in a way that, as a matter of law, was not arbitrary or irrational." *Id.* at 61. Since the court's order called for a determination of the "actual cost" of providing a sound basic education, it is not clear that the traditional "arbitrary or irrational" standard was appropriate in this context.

47. Report and Recommendations of the Judicial Referees. CFE v. State of

New York. Index 111070/93 (Supreme Court of New York County, 2004), 39 ("We recommend, on a going-forward basis, the simultaneous use of complementary costing-out studies, on a cycle to be repeated every four years."). See also, for example, State v. Campbell County Sch. Dist., 19 P.3d 518, 549 (Wyo. 2001) ("[T]he model and statute must be adjusted for inflation/deflation every two years at a minimum . . . "). Abbott v. Burke, —A.2d—, 2009 WL1578814 (N.J. May 28, 2009) calling for a review and update of resources and costs every three years.

48. JOHN YINGER, HELPING CHILDREN LEFT BEHIND: STATE AID AND THE PURSUIT OF EDUCATIONAL EQUITY 46 (2004).

49. George D. Brown, *Binding Advisory Opinions: A Federal Court's Perspective on State Court School Finance Decisions,* 35 B.C. L. REV. 543, 566 (1994). See also, Colin S. Diver, *The Judge as Political Powerbroker: Superintending Structural Change in Public Institutions,* 65 VA. L. REV. 43, 92 (1979) (The courts' role "is to stir the governmental entities to action to make sure that issues are addressed and choices made, not to make those choices itself.").

50. CFE II, 86 N.E.2d at 348. See also Leandro, 488 S.E.2d 249, 258 (N.C. 1997) (holding that "the General Assembly . . . has the duty of providing the children of every school district with access to a sound basic education . . . [and] has inherent power to do those things reasonably related to meeting that constitutionally prescribed duty."); Lake View Sch. Dist. No. 25 v. Huckabee, 91 S.W.3d 472, 484 (Ark. 2002) (noting that "all departments of state government [are] responsible for providing a general, suitable, and efficient system of public education to the children of this state.").

51. 960 P.2d 634 (Ariz. 1998).

52. *Id.* at 1146. The legislature responded by enacting a complex Students FIRST (Fair and Immediate Resources for Students Today) Act, which the courts ultimately upheld so long as it ensured through state funding that all school districts would be able to comply with the minimum adequacy standards for capital facilities that the Act had established. Roosevelt Elem. Sch. Dist. No. 66 v. State, 74 P.3d 258 (Ariz. Ct. App. 2003), motion for review denied, 2004 Ariz. LEXIS 8 (2004).

53. E. Levy, *Gunfight at the K-12 Corral: Legislative vs Judicial Power in the Kansas School Finance Litigation,* 54 U. KAN. L. REV. 1021 (2006).

54. 16 V.S.A. §§ 4025, 4026. If the money in the education fund were to be used for any purpose other than education, the statewide property tax would become null and void. § 4025(d).

55. Christa Kumka, *Experts: Education Fund Stable Despite State Budget Woes,* RUTLAND HERALD, December 1, 2008. The article stated that even though sales tax revenues were declining, and Vermont officials called the weakening state economy "grim," education finance experts said that the education fund was so healthy that they expected education allocations to be maintained and

that residential tax rates might even be reduced slightly for next year. One official noted, "While the Legislature is faced with cutting the state's Transportation and General Fund budgets, there is no reason why it (the education fund) should be affected."

56. Some, but certainly not all, public officials seem to recognize the constitutional preeminence of educational services in times of recession. For example, Tennessee governor Phil Bredesen was committed to maintaining K-12 educational services, even at a time that he was cutting the state budget for other departments by 20 percent. Erik Schelzig, *Bredesen Predicts Budget Shortfall,* MEMPHIS COMMERCIAL APPEAL, December 12, 2008.

57. William E. Thro, *A New Approach to State Constitutional Analysis in School Finance,* 14 J.L. & POL'Y 525 (1998).

58. CFE II, 801 N.E.2d at 369 (Read, J., dissenting).

59. 648 F.2d 989 (5th Cir. 1981).

60. *Id.* at 1009–10. Cf. Green v. County Sch. Bd, 391 U.S. 430, 439 (1968) (requiring desegregation plans that "promise[] realistically to work and promise realistically to work *now.*"). The *Castaneda* framework has been adopted by federal courts throughout the country in other cases involving the implementation of language remediation programs. See, for example, Keyes v. School Dist. No. 1, Denver, 576 F. Supp 1503 (D.C. Colo., 1983); Gomez v. Ill State Board of Ed. 811 F.2d 1030 (7th Cir. 1987); Teresa P. V. Berkeley Unified Sch. Dist. 724 F.Supp. 698 (N.D. Cal. 1989); Valeria G. v. Wilson, 12 F.Supp. 2d 1007 (N.D. Cal. 1998); Flores v. Arizona, 516 F.3d 1140, 1239 (9th Cir. 2008), petition for cert. granted, 129 S.Ct. 893 (January 9, 2009); U.S. v. Texas, 572 F.Supp. 2d 726 (E.D. Tex. 2008).

61. Thus the presidential veto power granted "legislative" authority to the chief executive; the Senate's ratification of presidential appointments and treaties and Congress's power to impeach the president and try high government officers granted "executive" and "judicial" authority to the legislature. For a more detailed discussion of "blending," see Malcolm P. Sharp, *The Classical American Doctrine of "the Separation of Powers,"* 2 CHI. L. REV. 385, 427 (1935); Edward Levi, *Some Aspects of the Separation of Powers,* 76 COLUM. L. REV. 371, 372–75 (fear of legislative, not judicial power, was framers' prime concern).

62. THE FEDERALIST PAPERS; ALEXANDER HAMILTON, JAMES MADISON, JOHN JAY 302–3 (Cliniton Rossiter ed., 1961). See also THOMAS JEFFERSON, NOTES ON THE STATE OF VIRGINIA 195 (1787) ("The concentrating of these in the same hands is precisely the definition of despotic government.").

63. James S. Liebman & Charles F. Sabel, *A Public Laboratory Dewey Barely Imagined: The Emerging Model of School Governance and Legal Reform,* 28 N.Y.U. REV. L & SOC. CHANGE 183, 184 (2003) (describing the "experimentalist" model and its application in the implementation of the remedial decrees in the Texas and Kentucky sound basic education litigations).

64. See Justice Greaney's detailed description of the steps he would have

taken to ensure compliance if the majority of the Massachusetts Supreme Judicial Court had retained jurisdiction of the *Hancock* cases. *A Separation of Powers Dialogue, infra* appendix, at 118–19. Cf. DOUGLAS S. REED, ON EQUAL TERMS: THE CONSTITUTIONAL POLITICS OF EDUCATIONAL OPPORTUNITY, 171 (2001) (recommending that courts issue a "policy blueprint" that would sketch out a "vision of what a constitutional program of educational financing would look like." The danger of courts becoming overly involved in programmatic details was illustrated in Ohio, where the state supreme court attempted at one point to direct the legislature to adopt a specific remedy, only to later learn that the math and some of the factual assumptions on which it had relied in crafting its solution were erroneous. Subsequently, and partially as a result of this embarrassing situation, the court abruptly terminated its jurisdiction, even as it acknowledged that constitutional compliance had not been achieved. See Larry J. Obhof, *DeRolph v. State and Ohio's Long Road to an Adequate Education,* 2005 B.Y.U. EDUC. & L.J. 83, 133–37 (2005).

65. *A Separation of Powers Dialogue, infra* appendix, at 120. Representative Elliott expressed the same view from a legislator's perspective. She said,

> The court was very careful not to prescribe to us exactly what to do. What they'd say was, "Here is what's wrong. We're not going try to tell you just how to fix it, but fix it." I look at that like what I did when I was teaching, and I handed a student back a paper. I would say, "Here are some issues that you have; maybe you need to take a look at coherency or stream of consciousness or whatever." I didn't say, "You have to do it exactly like this." And that student expected me to look at it again and say whether or not he or she had remedied what I had pointed out." *Id.* at 116.

66. Hoke County Sch. Bd. v. State, 599 S.E.2d 365, 393 (N.C. 2004).

67. Jenkins v. Leininger, 659 N.E.2d 1366 (Ill. App. 1 Dist., 1995); Crawford v. Davy, Dkt. no. C-137-06 (Super. Ct., Chancery Div., Mercer Co., N.J. 2006).

68. Abbott v. Burke, 575 A.2d 359 (N.J. 1990).

69. Abbott v. Burke, 693 A.2d 417 (N.J. 1997). Even in ordering this review, the court was highly sensitive to the distinct functional roles of the court and the executive department, as discussed in this chapter:

> The determination of appropriate remedial relief in the critical area of the special needs of at-risk children and the programs necessary to meet those needs is both fact-sensitive and complex; it is a problem squarely within the special expertise of educators. A court alone cannot, and should not, assume the responsibility for independently making the critical educational findings and determinations that will be the basis for such relief. We can, however, provide necessary procedures and identify the parties who best may devise the educational, programmatic, and fiscal measures to be incorporated in such remedial relief. *Id.* at 444

70. Abbott v. Burke, 710 A.2d 450, 473 (N.J. 1998).

71. Lake View Sch. Dist. 25 v. Huckabee, 189 S.W.3d 1 (Ark. 2003); Tucker v. Lake View Sch. Dist. No. 25, 917 S.W.2d 530 (Ark. 1996).

72. 189 S.W.3d at 15.

73. "Top-down" implementation of extensive reforms is particularly difficult in regard to education because schools are "loosely coupled" organizations in which local principals and individual classroom teachers have enormous discretion, which is difficult for state bureaucrats to regulate. See JAMES Q. WILSON, BUREAUCRACY: WHAT GOVERNMENT AGENCIES DO AND WHY THEY DO IT (1989). For discussions of the difficulties of implementing standards-based reform in this loosely coupled schooling environment, see JAMES SPILLANE, STANDARDS DEVIATION: HOW SCHOOLS MISUNDERSTAND EDUCATION POLICY (2004), and SUSAN H. FURHMAN, ED., FROM THE CAPITOL TO THE CLASSROOM: STANDARDS-BASED REFORM IN THE STATES (2001).

74. Superfine, *supra* note 5, at 175.

75. 189 S.W.3d at 10–11. Similarly, the Kentucky Supreme Court explicitly reversed the lower court's ruling "with respect to the requirement that the General Assembly, or any of the defendants in the trial court, further report to the trial court." Rose v. Council for Better Educ., 790 S.W.2d 186, 214–15 (Ky. 1989).

76. Lake View Sch. Dist. No. 25 v. Huckabee, 189 S.W.3d 1 (Ark. 2004). See also McDuffy v. Secretary, 615 N.E. 2d 516, 555–56 (Mass. 1993) ("We shall presume at this time that the Commonwealth will fulfill its responsibility with respect to defining the specifics and the appropriate means to provide the constitutionally-required education.").

77. Claremont School District v. Governor, 794 A.2d 744, 754. (N.H. 2002).

78. *Id.*

79. Abbott v. Burke, 710 A.2d 450 (N.J. 1998).

80. See, for example, Abbott v. Burke 748 A.2d 82 (N.J. 2000) (requiring the state education department to adopt substantive guidance for preschool programs and clarifying the requirement that community care providers must use certified preschool teachers); Abbott v. Burke 751 A. 2d 1032 (N.J. 2000) (requiring the state to fully fund the construction of any new classrooms needed to correct capacity deficiencies).

81. Moore v. State, no. 3AN-04-9756Cl (Super. Ct., Alaska, February 4, 2009).

82. CFE II, 801 N.E.2d at 348.

83. Report and Recommendations of the Judicial Referees, supra note 47, at 47–48 ("The parties have agreed on several enhancements to the current system of accountability that we believe are appropriate.").

84. CFE III, 861 N.E.2d at 58 ("[I]n fashioning specific remedies for consti-

tutional violations, we must avoid intrusion on the primary domain of another branch of government.").

85. See N.Y. Educ. Law § 211-d.

86. See, for example, Koret Task Force on K-12 Education, *Funding for Performance, in* COURTING FAILURE, *supra* note 35, at 340 (accusing courts of "almost always turn[ing] to calls for increased spending on schools" without providing strong accountability systems); Frederick M. Hess, *Adequacy Judgments and School Reform, in* SCHOOL MONEY TRIALS: THE LEGAL PURSUIT OF EDUCATIONAL ADEQUACY 159 (Martin R. West & Paul E. Peterson eds., 2007) (arguing that court interventions lead to ineffective "accommodative reforms" instead of needed "disruptive reforms.").

87. See, for example, Alfred A. Lindseth, "The Legal Backdrop to Adequacy," *in* COURTING FAILURE, supra, note 35, at 34 (criticizing the fact that courts "act as superlegislatures on matters affecting k-12 education. . . . For many years and even decades . . .); and ROSS SANDLER & DAVID SCHOENBROD, DEMOCRACY BY DECREE: WHAT HAPPENS WHEN COURTS RUN GOVERNMENT 218–19 (2003) (calling for "automatic term limits" for court decrees).

88. 822 N.E. 2d 1134 (Mass. 2005).

89. *Id.* at 1147.

90. Hancock, 822 N.E.2d at 1140.

91. *Id.* at 1148.

92. *Id.* at 1158 (Marshall, C.J., concurring with plurality opinion).

93. *Id.* at 1169.

94. *Id.* at 1170. Developments since 2005 appear to have borne out Justice Greaney's expectations. The results of the 2007 Massachusetts Comprehensive Assessment System (MCAS) examinations show continuing dismal results for most minority students: while 39 percent of white students and 43 percent of Asian students scored "proficient" or better on the 2007 administration of the science exam, these figures fall to 8 percent for African American students and 7 percent for Hispanic students. Also, while 52 percent of white eighth grade students and 65 percent of Asian eighth grade students achieved "proficient" or above on the 2007 MCAS math examination, less than 20 percent of both Hispanic students and African American students earned this distinction. In addition, on the grade 10 MCAS English Language Arts examination, at least 75 percent of both white and Asian students scored "proficient" or better, while 42 percent of Hispanic students and 47 percent of African American students earned this distinction. Paul Reville, *The Massachusetts Case: A Personal Account,* CAMPAIGN FOR EDUCATIONAL EQUITY SYMPOSIUM: EQUAL EDUCATIONAL OPPORTUNITY: WHAT NOW? (2007). Available at http://devweb.tc.columbia.edu/manager/symposium/Files/110_Massachusetts%20Case%20Study.pdf. at 4.

95. Board of Education v. Dowell, 498 U.S. 237, 249–50 (1991).

96. Justice Greaney also agreed with the trial judge that a cost study should be ordered because

> Actual spending levels strongly suggest, however, that the formula now relied on by the department to reflect the minimum amount each district needs to provide an adequate education to its students does not reflect the true cost of successful education in the Commonwealth, at least in the focus districts . . . a realistic assessment of the costs of effectively implementing an educational plan in such districts reasonably could, and should, contemplate other factors that affect student performance such as poverty, teenage pregnancy, nutrition, family issues, drugs, violence, language deficiencies and the need for remedial teaching and tutoring. It also should include a cost assessment of measures necessary to improve the administrative ability of the districts successfully to implement the educational plan. Hancock, 822 N.E.2d at 1169–70.

97. The trial judge had found, among other things, that "in the three years since the department developed the school accountability system, it has been able to conduct school panel reviews in only twelve to fourteen schools each year, although the annual pool of schools demonstrating 'low' or 'critically low' performance is in the hundreds." *Id.* at 1149.

98. Young v. Williams, Case Nos. 03-CI-00055 and 03-CI-01152 (Ky., February 13, 2007).

99. The progress made by Kentucky's students in the past eighteen years is not, however, self-evidently satisfactory. For example, in fourth grade math, the state was four points below the national average on the National Assessment of Education Progress test in 1990 and was still four points below in 2007, although on eighth grade math its average score rose from five points below the national average to one point below. See Weston & Sexton, *supra* note 9, at 12–13.

100. Reville, *supra* note 94. See also Rebell & Wolff, *supra* note 6, at chapter 4.

101. For a detailed discussion of these issues, see DANIEL M. KORETZ, MEASURING UP: WHAT EDUCATIONAL TESTING REALLY TELLS US (2008). See also, discussion, *supra* in chapter 3.

102. See Debra Satz, *Equality, Adequacy and Educational Policy,* 3 EDUC. FIN. & POL'Y 424 (2008) (arguing that education adequacy must be judged not in terms of achievement scores but in terms of achievement of civic equality); Diana Pullin, *Ensuring An Adquate Education: Opportunity to Learn, Law and Social Science,* 27 B.C. THIRD WORLD L. J. 83, 108 (2007) (noting that in *McDuffy,* the Massachusetts Supreme Judicial Court emphasized the constitutional duty to produce educated citizens but that in *Hancock,* the court focused only on MCAS examination scores).

103. These five categories of knowledge and skills, which directly relate to the citizenship and workplace preparation concepts that many of the state courts

have identified as being the prime expected outcomes of a sound basic education, are among the eight outcomes of education that both historical sources and contemporary polls have agreed should be the outcome goals of American education, according to Richard Rothstein, Rebecca Jacobsen, & Tamara Wilder, GRADING EDUCATION: GETTING ACCOUNTABILITY RIGHT, 14 (2008). The other three categories, appreciation of arts and literature, physical health, and emotional health, are self-fulfillment goals that some, but not most, of the courts that have articulated sound basic education outcomes have included in their definitions.

104. See *id.*, chapter 8, for a discussion of particular tests, sampling techniques, and other tools for assessing these broad skills.

105. 20 U.S.C. § 6301 et seq. (2001). The implications of Congress's adoption of an impossible goal as a legal mandate are discussed in detail in Rebell & Wolff, *supra* note 6.

106. Amit R. Paley, *"No Child" Target Is Called out of Reach*, WASHINGTON POST, March 14, 2001, at A01.

107. Columbia Falls Elementary Sch. Dist. No. 6 v. State, No. BDV-2002-528 (1st Jud. Dist. Ct., Lewis & Clark Co., May 5, 2008). The New Hampshire Supreme Court ignored these judicial economy concerns in its recent decision in Londonderry Sch. Dist. v. State, 958 A.2d 930 (N.H. 2008). There the court terminated jurisdiction of the latest in a long series of challenges to the state's compliance with the court's original 1995 finding that the state education finance system is unconstitutional by holding that the particular statute that the plaintiffs had attacked in their 2005 complaint had now been replaced; although plaintiffs maintained that the revised funding system is still unconstitutional, the court held that they would need to file a new action to litigate these issues.

108. Ryan, *supra* note 4, at 1260.

109. *A Separation of Powers Dialogue, infra* appendix, at 117.

110. McDuffy v. Sec'y of the Exec. Office of Educ., 615 N.E.2d 516, 556 (Mass. 1993).

111. Arkansas provides further evidence that although technically a court may maintain oversight for a lengthy time period, actual invocation of judicial authority is likely to be infrequent. Once the Arkansas Supreme Court demonstrated its resolve to ensure constitutional compliance by appointing the Masters, the legislature promptly enacted constitutionally acceptable legislation even before the Masters' report was issued or the court had acted on it. See discussion in chapter 3, *supra.*

112. Judicial oversight under the successful remedies model would have been much more modest that the elaborate plan of action that Justice Greaney apparently had in mind. Justice Greaney's plan of action for how he would have proceeded if the Court had maintained jurisdiction in *Hancock* is set forth in detail in *Separation of Powers Dialogue, infra* appendix, at 118–20.

Chapter Six

1. It is worth noting here that legislative and executive reform initiatives rarely are subjected to any similar "reality check." Legislators can take credit for bold stances that they and the policy-conscious public know will never actually materialize. A prime case in point is the mandate under the No Child Left Behind Act that 100 percent of the students in the United States must be proficient in challenging state standards by 2014. Since Congress has restricted judicial review of this law by denying would be litigants any "private right of action," see Newark Parents Association v. Newark Public Schools, 547 F.3d 199 (3rd Cir. 2008), the courts are unable to call them to account for this political grandstanding. These points are discussed in more detail in MICHAEL A. REBELL & JESSICA R. WOLFF, MOVING EVERY CHILD AHEAD: FROM NCLB HYPE TO MEANINGFUL EDUCATIONAL OPPORTUNITY (2008).

2. MATTHEW H. BOSWORTH, COURTS AS CATALYSTS: STATE SUPREME COURTS AND PUBLIC SCHOOL FINANCE EQUITY, 213 (2001).

3. Campaign for Fiscal Equity, Inc. v. State ("CFE III"), 861 N.E.2d 50 (N.Y. 2006).

4. De Rolph v. State, 780 N.E.2d 529, 536 (2002). (*"De Rolph IV"*)

5. State *ex rel.* State v. Lewis, 789 N.E.2d 195 (Ohio 2003). In this case, the *DeRolph* plaintiffs asked the trial court judge to convene a conference to address the state's compliance with *DeRolph IV*. The plaintiffs also requested that the state be ordered to prepare a report setting forth proposals to comply with the *DeRolph* decisions. The state immediately sought a writ of prohibition from the Ohio Supreme Court to prevent Judge Lewis and the common pleas court from exercising further jurisdiction in *DeRolph*. In the cited case, the Ohio Supreme Court ordered Judge Lewis to stop any proceedings in his court aimed at enforcing *DeRolph IV*.

6. GERALD ROSENBERG, THE HOLLOW HOPE: CAN COURTS BRING ABOUT SOCIAL CHANGE, 3 (1991).

7. See also, for example, RICHARD J. KLARMAN, FROM JIM CROW TO CIVIL RIGHTS: THE SUPREME COURT AND THE STRUGGLE FOR RACIAL EQUALITY (2004).

8. Stephen Halpern argues that litigation focused on the funding termination threat of Title VI of the 1964 Civil Rights Act distorted priorities and distracted efforts and attention from *Brown*'s core concern, that is, the need to overcome the impact of poverty and provide significant educational opportunities to black students. STEPHEN C. HALPERN, ON THE LIMITS OF THE LAW: THE IRONIC LEGACY OF TITLE VI OF THE 1964 CIVIL RIGHTS ACT (1995). Halpern ignored, however, the role of the state court adequacy litigations in highlighting this need and mandating remedies to meet it. He also overlooked the point that, without judicial intervention, the federal executive and legislative branches are not likely to muster the political will to take significant action in this regard.

9. MICHAEL W. McCANN, RIGHTS AT WORK: PAY EQUITY REFORM AND THE POLITICS OF LEGAL MOBILIZATION (1994). See also STUART A. SCHEINGOLD, THE POLITICS OF RIGHTS: LAWYERS, PUBLIC POLICY AND POLITICAL CHANGE, 98–107 (1974) (discussing the relationship between legal rights and progressive social movements).

10. Kevin J. McMahon & Michael Paris, *The Politics of Rights Revisited: Rosenberg, McCann and the New Institutionalism,* in LEVERAGING THE LAW: US-ING THE COURTS TO ADVANCE SOCIAL REFORM (David A. Schultz ed., 1998).

11. DOUGLAS S. REED, ON EQUAL TERMS: THE CONSTITUTIONAL POLITICS OF EDUCATIONAL OPPORTUNITY, 16 (2001).

12. Peter Schuck, *Book Review: Public Law Litigation and Social Reform* 102 YALE L.J. 1763, 1771–72 (1991). See also Neal Devins, *Review Essay: Judicial Matters,* 80 CAL. L. REV 1027, 1030 (stating that Rosenberg gives "short shrift . . . to the essential role that courts do play in 'constitutional dialogues' with elected government"); Sheingold, *supra* note 9, at 36–37 ("The judges' function is to call the other branches to constitutional account—to engage them in a continuing colloquy having to do with the fundamental goals and methods of American politics."); Barry Friedman, *Dialogue and Judicial Review,* 91 MICH. L. REV. 577, 668–70 (1993) (The courts' role in the dialogue over the meaning of the Constitution is highly interactive. . . . Courts *synthesize* society's views on constitutional meaning . . . Courts also *focus* debate . . . Similarly, court decisions may act as a *catalyst,* causing society to debate issues that might not otherwise have stood at the top of the agenda).

13. ROSENBERG, THE HOLLOW HOPE, *supra* note 6, at 35.

14. BOSWORTH, COURTS AS CATALYSTS, *supra,* note 2, at 156, 128.

15. *A Separation of Powers Dialogue, infra* appendix, at 116.

16. Bosworth, *supra* note 14, at 198.

17. *Id.* at 154–55.

18. DOUGLAS S. REED, ON EQUAL TERMS, *supra* note 11, at 46. Reed also points out that "despite intense and vociferous fights, no state has amended its state constitution to allow for greater inequalities or inadequacies in the wake of a state supreme court decision or stripped the state judiciary of its jurisdiction over school financing." *Id.* The only clear instance of a sound basic education decision leading to adoption of a constitutional amendment occurred in Florida, where the state Supreme Court's refusal to consider an adequacy claim on justiciability grounds (see discussion in chapter 2) led to a strong counterreaction and a 71 percent favorable vote to amend the state constitution to guarantee all children in the state a high-quality education. See Jon Mills & Timothy Mclendon, *Setting a New Standard for Public Education: Revision 6 Increases the Duty of the State to Make Adequate Provision for Florida Schools,* 52 FLA. L. REV. 329, 367 (2000).

Reed also notes that "[s]urprisingly . . . State supreme court justices are rarely punished by voters for their stances on school financing case." *Id.* (Ohio may be the exception that proves the rule in this regard. *See* discussion in chapter 3, note 8.)

19. See, for example, *Majority of Voters Indicate They Will Vote for Candidates Who Make Education a Top Priority; Report to Reveal Mixed Support for No Child Left Behind,* EDUC. WEEK, April 1, 2004, available at http://www .publiceducation. org/doc/2004_Poll_Press_Release.doc (interpreting the results from Public Education Network/Education Week Poll 2004 and stating that "[a] majority of voters (59 percent) say they are willing to pay higher taxes to improve public education."); Lowell C. Rose & Alec M. Gallup, *38th Annual Phi Delta Kappa/Gallup Poll of the Public's Attitudes Toward the Public Schools,* 88 PHI DELTA KAPPAN 41, 47 (2006), available at http://www.pdkintl.org/kappan/ k0609pol.htm (finding that 66 percent of Americans responded affirmatively to the question, "Would you be willing to pay more taxes for funding preschool programs for children from low-income or poverty-level households?"); *Americans Willing to Pay for Improving Schools,* NPR ONLINE (1999), available at http://www.npr.org/programs/specials/poll/education/education.front.html (interpreting the data from the 1999 National Public Radio poll and stating that "[t]hree out of four Americans [most of whom do not currently have children in the schools] say they would be willing to have their taxes raised by at least $200 a year to pay for specific measures to improve community public schools."); DOUGLAS S. REED, ON EQUAL TERMS, *supra* note 11, chapter 6 (finding that public opinion strongly supports equalization of education finance, except when countervailing issues of local control come to the fore).

20. The growing gap between haves and have-nots in America is illustrated by the fact that from 1973 to 2000, the average real income of the bottom 90 percent of American taxpayers declined by 7 percent, while the income of the top 1 percent rose by 148 percent. Heather Boushey & Christian E. Weller, *What the Numbers Tell Us,* in INEQUALITY MATTERS: THE GROWING ECONOMIC DIVIDE IN AMERICA AND ITS POISONOUS CONSEQUENCES, 27, 31 (James Lardner & David A. Smith eds., 2005). Another ominous reflection of these trends is the fact that whereas in 1965 a corporate CEO's income was twenty-six times the average wage, in 2003 it was 185 times the average wage. LAWRENCE MISHEL ET AL., THE STATE OF WORKING AMERICA, 7 (2004/2005).

21. William H. Clune, *New Answers to Hard Questions Posed by Rodriguez: Ending the Separation of School Finance and Educational Policy by Bridging the Gap between Wrong and Remedy,* 24 CONN. L. REV. 721, 731 (1992).

22. E. Levy, *Gunfight at the K-12 Corral: Legislative vs Judicial Power in the Kansas School Finance Litigation,* 54 U. KAN. L. REV. 1021 (2006) (footnotes omitted).

23. See, for example, N.Y. Judiciary Law §§ 753, 773; Tamia Perry, *In the Interest of Justice: The Impact of Court-Ordered Reform on the City of New York,*

42 N.Y. L. Sch. L. Rev. 1239, 1247 (1998) (discussing how daily fines, which eventually totaled over $6 million, were imposed on New York City officials for failing to obey court orders to house the homeless appropriately in McCain v. Dinkins, 639 N.E.2d 1132 (N.Y. 1994)).

24. In May 1976, the New Jersey Supreme Court enjoined "every public officer" from "expending any funds for the support of any free public school" after July 1, 1976, but stated that this injunction would "not become effective if timely legislative action is taken." Robinson v. Cahill, 358 A.2d 457, 459 (N.J. 1976). One week after the injunction took effect, the legislature passed and the governor signed the law needed to fund the new education finance system. Robinson v. Cahill, 360 A.2d 400 (N.J. 1976). In Texas in 1988, the state district court declared the education finance system unconstitutional and enjoined the state from expending funds under the unconstitutional system, effective in September 1989. The Texas Supreme Court affirmed the decision but modified the trial court's judgment to stay the effect of its injunction until May 1990. Edgewood Indep. Sch. Dist. v. Kirby, 777 S.W.2d 391, 397–99 (Tex. 1989). This ruling led to subsequent enactments by the legislature, further guidance by the Supreme Court, and eventually a constitutional funding system. See Edgewood Indep. Sch. Dist. v. Meno, 917 S.W.2d 717, 750 (Tex. 1995). In Arizona, the courts set a deadline for the state to adopt a constitutionally acceptable school capital finance system and stated that if the state failed to do so, the court would prohibit the state from distributing money to school districts, effectively shutting down the schools, Hull v. Albrecht, 960 P.2d 634, 640 (Ariz. 1998). The legislature complied a month later.

25. See, for example, Aaron Jay Saiger, *The Last Wave: The Rise of the Contingent School District,* 84 N.C. L. Rev 857, 892 (2006) ("legislatures are structurally dominated by suburban interests that fundamentally oppose both redirecting funds from richer to poorer districts and capping the ability of the rich to finance their own schools."); Marilyn Gittell, *The Politics of Equity in Urban School Reform,* in Bringing Equity Back: Research for a New Era in American Educational Policy, 16 (Janice Petrovich & Amy Stuart Wells eds., 2005) (discussing the impact of suburbanization on the politics of equity); Michael Mintrom, *Why Efforts to Equalize School Funding Have Failed: Towards a Positive Theory,* 46 Pol. Res. Q. 847–62 (1993) (arguing that equalization efforts will generally be opposed or undermined by various local actors).

26. Jeffrey Metzler, *Inequitable Equilibrium: School Finance in the United States,* 36 Ind. L. Rev. 561, 564 (2003).

27. In Washington, although the legislature responded to the state Supreme Court's order with a series of thoroughgoing equalization reforms in the late 1970s and early 1980s, by the 1990s, inequities in the state's treatment of Seattle, the plaintiff district, were greater than ever. See Diane W. Cipollone, *Defining a "Basic Education": Equity and Adequacy in the State of Washington* (1998), avail-

able at http://www.schoolfunding.info/resource_center/research/WASHINGTON .PDF; see also League of Education Voters, A Brief History of School Finance in Washington (2005) (gap between rich and poor is "almost back to where we started"). The situation in Kansas is discussed in Levy, *supra* note 22.

28. Jeffrey Metzler, *Inequitable Equilibrium, supra* note 26, at 564.

29. Owen M. Fiss, *Forward: The Forms of Justice,* 93 Harv. L. Rev. 1, 2 (1979).

30. Alexander M. Bickel, The Least Dangerous Branch, 25–26 (2d ed. 1986). See also Michael S. Moore, *Law as a Functional Kind, in* Natural Law Theory, 188, 230 (Robert George ed. 1992) ("[J]udges are better positioned for . . . moral insight than are legislatures because judges have moral thought experiments presented to them everyday with the kind of detail and concrete personal involvement needed for moral insight.").

31. *A Separation of Powers Dialogue, infra* appendix, at 121.

32. Brown v. Board of Education of Topeka, 347 U.S. 483, 494, n.10 (1954).

33. *Id.* at 495.

34. Brown v. Board of Education of Topeka (II), 349 U.S. 294, 301 (1954).

35. Green v. County School Board of New Kent County, 391 U.S. 430, 438–39 (1968) (emphasis added).

36. Howard J. Kalodner & James Fishman, Limits of Justice, 7 (1978). See also Michael A. Rebell & Robert L. Hughes, *Efficacy and Engagement: The Remedies Problem Posed by Sheff v. O'Neill—And a Proposed Solution,* 29 Conn L. Rev. 1115, 1154–56 (discussing extensive use of biracial citizens committees in desegregation cases to help develop viable desegregation plans and to foster public communication and support for desegregation).

37. See, for example, American Institute of Public Opinion, *Gallup Opinion Index, Report no. 127* (February 1976), at 9. See also A. Wade Smith, *White Attitudes Toward School Desegregation 1954–80,* 25 Pac. Soc. Rev. 3 (1982) (reporting a significant increase in racial tolerance from 1954 to 1980); Howard Schuman, Charlotte Steeh, & Lawrence Bobo, Racial attitudes in America: Trends in Interpretation (1985) (finding significant evidence of increased commitment to racial equality among Americans).

38. Parents Involved in Community Schools v. Seattle Sch. Dist. 127 S. Ct. 2738 (2007).

39. See, for example, Gary Orfield & Susan E. Eaton, Dismantling Desegregation: The Quiet Reversal of Brown v. Board of Education (1996).

40. Susan Perkins Weston & Robert F. Sexton, *Substantial and Yet Not Sufficient: Kentucky's Effort to Build Proficiency for Each and Every Child,* Campaign for Educational Equity Symposium: Equal Educational Opportunity: What Now? 16 (2007). Available at http://devweb.tc.columbia.edu/ manager/symposium/Files/108_KentuckyCaseStudy_Final.pdf. Despite the continuing strong public support for education reform in Kentucky, the lack of con-

tinuing court oversight has hobbled attempts to maintain consistent funding levels in times of recession. See discussion in chapter 5, at notes 98 and 99.

41. Michael N. Danielson & Jennifer Hochschild, *Changing Urban Education: Lessons, Cautions Prospects*, 277, 290, in CHANGING URBAN EDUCATION (Clarence Stone ed., 1998).

42. Weston & Sexton, *supra* note 40, at 20. For detailed discussions of the role that the Prichard Committee has played, see ROBERT F. SEXTON, MOBILIZING CITIZENS FOR BETTER SCHOOLS (2004), and Molly A. Hunter, *All Eyes Forward: Public Engagement and Educational Reform in Kentucky*, 28 J.L. & EDUC. 485 (1999).

43. Weston & Sexton, *supra* note 40, at 21.

44. For a detailed discussion of the Citizens for Fair School Funding's public engagement campaign, see Cipollone, *Defining a "Basic Education," supra* note 27.

45. For a discussion of the Arizona Summit, see Molly A. Hunter, *Building on Judicial Intervention: The Redesign of School Facilities Funding in Arizona*, 34 J.L. & EDUC. 173, 182–84 (2005); the plaintiffs' political efforts are described by Timothy M. Hogan, *Arizona School Finance: A Primer on Strategy and Enforcement*, 83 NEB. L. REV. 869 (2005).

46. Additional information about the development and implementation of the CFE public engagement process can be found in Michael A. Rebell, *Adequacy Litigations: A New Path to Equity?* in BRINGING EQUITY BACK, *supra* note 25; Amanda R. Broun & Wendy Puriefoy, *Public Engagement in School Reform: Building Public Responsibility for Public Education*, 4 STAN. J. CIV. RTS & CIV. LIBERTIES 217 (2008); Maurice R. Dyson, *A Covenant Broken: The Crisis of Educational Remedy for New York City's Failing Schools*, 44 How. L.J. 107 (2000); Kent K. Anker, *Differences and Dialogue: School Finance in New York State*, 24 N.Y.U. REV. L. & SOC. CHANGE 345 (1998).

47. The proposed definition was formally presented by Tom Sobol, the former state commissioner of education, who had agreed to be an expert witness for the plaintiffs; three other plaintiff witnesses also endorsed the definition. Dr. Sobol strongly supports public engagement, and he personally participated in a number of the forums.

48. The ultimate position paper that was issued on the remedial issues did not include a voucher proposal because there was little statewide support for the concept at the discussions. Most upstate participants found little relevance in the voucher idea because, as one participant put it, "If I don't like the quality of education my kid is receiving at the local school, I'll just move to a neighboring district and get what I want."

49. *A School Funding Remedy After All?* WESTCHESTER JOURNAL NEWS, January 11, 1998, at A16. The fact that diverse constituencies from around the state participated in formulating many of the major positions that were adopted by the

trial court meant that when the trial court's decision was issued in 2001, and the final Court of Appeals' decision was issued in 2003, they received broad state-wide support from education stakeholders and newspapers and other media throughout the state (see, for example, *Judge Orders Reform: Victory for School Equity,* SYRACUSE POST-STANDARD, January 11, 2001, at A8; *Changing School Funding Won't Solve Whole Problem,* BINGHAMTON PRESS AND SUN-BULLETIN, January 11, 2001, at 6, *Fix the School Aid Formula,* WESTCHESTER JOURNAL NEWS, July 14, 2003, at 6b; *Schools Here May Gain from N.Y. City Ruling,* BUF-FALO NEWS, June 27, 2003, at C1, C4.

50. There was, in fact, a cordial relationship between the commission and the task force and a sharing of data and ideas between the two entities.

51. Campaign for Fiscal Equity v. State, 2005 WL 5643844 (N.Y. Sup. Ct., Co., February 14, 2005).

52. CFE III, 861 N.E.2d 50 (N.Y. 2006).

53. The Contract for Excellence provisions require New York City and other districts receiving large funding increases to submit a plan detailing how the money will be spent to the state commissioner of education. The CFE funds must be spent in one or more of six priority areas (teacher quality, smaller class sizes, additional time on task, English language learning programming, full-day kindergarten or prekindergarten services, and middle and high school restruc-turing); up to 15 percent of the funds may also be used for "experimental pro-grams" approved by the commissioner. Each district's plan must also be vetted at public hearings before being submitted to the commissioner. See N.Y. Educ. Law § 211-d.

54. CFE's statewide public engagement campaign and advocacy for its posi-tions in the legislature have also been substantially aided in recent years by the Alliance for Quality Education, a group formed by a number of unions, civic or-ganizations, and foundations to promote the implementation of effective reme-dies for the CFE litigation.

55. Recent events in Ohio also illustrate the important interplay among judi-cial rulings, politics, and public engagement. Despite the serious judicial setback that plaintiffs experienced in Ohio in 2002 when the state supreme court ter-minated jurisdiction of the sound basic education litigation (see note 5, *supra*), the main plaintiff group, the Ohio Coalition for Equity and Adequacy in Fund-ing, working with a number of other parent and education advocacy groups, has persevered for the past seven years in promoting a variety of public engagement activities to keep the issue of fair education funding at the top of the political agenda. Their efforts have begun to pay off, as Ted Strickland, the state's newly elected governor has announced an extensive long-range plan for radically ex-panding educational opportunities, increasing the state's share of educational expenditures, and simplifying the state funding formula. See Mary Ann Zehr,

Despite Ohio's Tough Economy, Governor Has Plan for Schools, EDUC. WEEK, February 4, 2009.

56. *A Separation of Powers Dialogue, infra* appendix, at 123.

57. John DiStaso, *ABC Sent to Supreme Court. Claremont Amendments On Hold. Constitutionality at Heart of ABC Questions. High Court Open to Public's ABC Comments,* UNION LEADER (Manchester, N.H.), May 22, 1998, at A1.

58. Andru H. Volinsky, *New Hampshire's Education-Funding Litigation: Claremont School District v. Governor,* 83 U. NEB L. REV. 836, 852 (2005). Open access of this sort can be especially important in cases in which school districts or teachers unions are the plaintiffs in a sound basic education case and the parent and student perspective on issues like the need for monitoring and accountability may not otherwise be satisfactorily considered.

59. See Molly A. Hunter, *All Eyes Forward, supra* note 42, at 495.

60. David A. Paterson, who had been elected lieutenant governor, assumed the office when Eliot Spitzer resigned early in 2008. Paterson, who had been a staunch supporter of CFE during the litigation, maintained the state's basic commitment to the CFE remedy during the second year of the phase-in

61. Daryl J. Levinson, *Rights Essentialism and Remedial Equilibrium,* 99 COLUM. L. REV. 857, 914 (1999).

62. Goodwin Liu, *Rethinking Constitutional Welfare Rights,* 61 STAN.L. REV 203, 228 (2008). The state courts' engagement with state legislatures and executive branches in developing standards and cost analysis techniques is a prime example of how "superstatutes" [like standards based reform] establish a new normative or institutional framework for state policy that over time becomes deeply embedded in the constitutional culture of the society. See, William N. Eskridge, Jr. & John Ferejohn,, *Super-Statutes,* 50 DUKE L. J. 1215 (2001).

63. Matthew G. Springer & James W. Guthrie, *The Politicization of the School Finance Legal Process,* in SCHOOL MONEY TRIALS: THE LEGAL PURSUIT OF EDUCATIONAL ADEQUACY, 102, 121 (Martin R. West & Paul E. Peterson eds., 2007).

64. Reynolds v. Sims, 377 U.S. 533, 566 (1964).

Appendix

1. Chief Justice Marshall, joined by two other justices stated, "The education clause 'impose[s] an enforceable duty on the magistrates and Legislatures of this Commonwealth to provide education in the public schools for the children there enrolled, whether they be rich or poor and without regard to the fiscal capacity of the community or district in which such children live." *McDuffy v. Secretary,* 615 N.E.2d 516 (Mass. 1993). It remains "the responsibility of the Com-

monwealth to take such steps as may be required in each instance effectively to devise a plan and sources of funds sufficient to meet the constitutional mandate.' *Id.* I do not suggest that the goals of education reform adopted since *McDuffy* have been fully achieved. Clearly they have not. Nothing I say today would insulate the Commonwealth from a successful challenge under the education clause in different circumstances."

2. Eliot Spitzer, then governor of New York, had served as attorney general for eight of the twelve years that his predecessor, Governor George Pataki, was in office. In New York, as in West Virginia, the attorney general is elected and is not appointed by the governor. Spitzer, who was a Democrat, represented Pataki, the Republican governor, in the *CFE* litigation.

3. Grutter v. Bollinger, 539 U.S. 306, 343 (2003): "It has been 25 years since Justice Powell first approved the use of race to further an interest in student body diversity in the context of public higher education. Since that time, the number of minority applicants with high grades and test scores has indeed increased. . . . We expect that 25 years from now, the use of racial preferences will no longer be necessary to further the interest approved today."

4. See Rose v. Council for Better Education, 790 S.W.2d 186, 212 (Ky. 1989).

Index